Global Justice

Ethics, Human Rights and Global Political Thought

Series Editors: Sebastiano Maffettone and Aakash Singh Rathore, Centre for Ethics and Global Politics, Luiss University, Rome

Whereas the interrelation of ethics and political thought has been recognized since the dawn of political reflection, over the last sixty years — roughly since the United Nations' Universal Declaration of Human Rights — we have witnessed a particularly turbulent process of dilating, indeed globalizing, of the coverage and application of that interrelation. At the very instant the decolonized globe consolidated the universality of the sovereign nation-state, that sovereignty — and the political thought that grounded it — was eroded and outstripped, not, as in eras past, by imperial conquest and instruments of war, but rather by instruments of peace (charters, declarations, treaties, conventions), and instruments of commerce and communication (multinational enterprises, international media, global aviation and transport, internet technologies).

Has political theory kept pace with global political realities? Can ethical reflection illuminate the murky challenges of real global politics?

This Routledge book series Ethics, Human Rights and Global Political Thought addresses these crucial questions by bringing together outstanding monographs and anthologies that deal with the intersection of normative theorizing and political realities with a global focus. The volumes in the series discuss key aspects of the contemporary chiasmus of the local and the global, cultural norms and normative demands, social movements and global justice, folkways and human rights, poverty and sustainability, rural realities and the cosmopolitan hyperreal. Treating diverse topics by means of interdisciplinary techniques — including ethics and applied philosophy, political theory, international relations and human rights theories, international political economy, and theories of globalization, including postcolonial studies — all of the books in the series will illuminate the nature of the global impact of local or regional phenomena, and vice versa.

The series aims to meet the research needs of all those interested in in-depth, expert research on the most urgent normative dilemmas raised by globalization. Presenting up-to-date research, it is an easily accessible, practical yet scholarly source of information for researchers, policy makers and practitioners. It uniquely provides perspectives from all the major social science disciplines and covers all the world regions. The series will prove of great relevance to researchers, educators and students, as well as to politicians, policy makers and government officials.

Also in the Series

Wronging Rights? Philosophical Challenges for Human Rights
Editors: Aakash Singh Rathore and Alex Cistelecan
978-0-415-61529-7

Conflict Society and Peacebuilding: Comparative Perspectives
Editors: Raffaele Marchetti and Nathalie Tocci
978-0-415-68563-4

Global Justice

Critical Perspectives

EDITORS

Sebastiano Maffettone
Aakash Singh Rathore

Routledge
Taylor & Francis Group
LONDON NEW YORK NEW DELHI

First published 2012 in India
by Routledge
912 Tolstoy House, 15–17 Tolstoy Marg, Connaught Place, New Delhi 110 001

Simultaneously published in the UK
by Routledge
2 Park Square, Milton Park, Abingdon, Oxfordshire OX14 4RN

First issued in paperback 2015

Routledge is an imprint of the Taylor & Francis Group, an informa business

Typeset by
Star Compugraphics Private Limited
5, CSC, Near City Apartments
Vasundhara Enclave
Delhi 110 096

British Library Cataloguing-in-Publication Data
A catalogue record of this book is available from the British Library

ISBN 13: 978-1-138-66256-8 (pbk)
ISBN 13: 978-0-415-53505-2 (hbk)

Contents

Acknowledgements

The editors are grateful to the following for their kind permission to reprint these articles in the present volume:

Philosophy and Public Affairs for Peter Singer's 'Famine, Affluence, and Morality' (1972, vol. 1, no. 1, pp. 229–43) and Thomas Nagel's 'The Problem of Global Justice' (2005, vol. 33, no. 2, pp. 113–47).

Ioanna Kuçuradi and Thomas Pogge for his '"Assisting" the Global Poor', originally published in the *Proceedings of the Twenty-First World Congress of Philosophy,* vol. 13: *Philosophy Facing World Problems* (Ankara: Philosophical Society of Turkey, 2007).

Amartya Sen and the American Bar Association for his 'Global Justice', originally prepared for the World Justice Forum (Vienna, 2–5 July 2008).

Introduction

The Rawlsian Provenance of the Global Justice Debate

Sebastiano Maffettone and Aakash Singh Rathore

The Aim(s) of This Volume

The global justice debate has been raging for forty years, and yet an introduction to it still remains urgently required — why? Simple: because it remains necessary to include more (global) voices into this (global) debate of global reach and significance. For, not merely the terms and conditions but, more profoundly, the ontological, epistemological and axiological grounds of the international relations of persons, states and institutions are being determined, debated and negotiated, and yet so very few people are active in it. With this dilemma in mind, this book aspires to contribute to the global justice debate in primarily two, closely related ways. First, in Part I, it seeks to introduce the main contours of the debate by means of reproducing three of the most fundamental and influential essays that have been composed on the topic, thereby providing more people the background necessary to enter and take part in this debate in a meaningful way. Second, in Part II, the volume aspires to make a decisive critical intervention into the main stream of the debate by means of, in the first place, exposing the 'participation deficit' hitherto present in the debate, which we — following Amartya Sen's coinage — refer to as its 'parochialism', and, in the second place, taking our own steps to 'deparochialize' the debate, in a series of lively essays newly composed for this volume.

A Sketch of Part I: Introducing the Debate

The first three chapters, along with the writings of John Rawls in general — about which more later — are key, pioneering cornerstones in the development of the global justice debate. This debate was inaugurated in the early 1970s primarily through Peter Singer's path-breaking paper, 'Famine, Affluence and Morality' (Chapter One). Singer was inspired by the Bangladeshi famine to launch a line of work that posits and systematically defends the demand for affluent persons of developed nations to donate income to charitable causes beyond their borders. From the original essay composed in 1971, through its restatement in 1979 in his book *Practical Ethics*, up to his recent 2009 book *The Life You Can Save*, Singer has consistently maintained as a moral obligation that 'if it is in our power to prevent something bad from happening, without thereby sacrificing anything of comparable moral importance, we ought, morally, to do it' (this volume, p. 17). Putting aside the question of whether Singer is correct about this claim, we are nevertheless forced to ask if moral obligations are inevitably the content and concern of justice. Thomas Nagel, in his hugely influential essay appearing herein as Chapter Two, suggests not.

For Nagel, forcing out one prominent interpretation of Rawlsian thought, justice, strictly speaking, is not reducible to moral obligation, but has an entirely different genealogy and sphere of operation. Justice, strictly speaking, arises only subsequent to institutions or the established basic structure of a regime. While morality may (or may not) stretch out beyond borders and make demands upon us irrespective of distance, justice — above all, demands of distributive justice — at the global level would require a global basic structure, which does not at present exist. Global justice, therefore, according to this Hobbesian reading of Rawls, is oxymoronic, a 'chimera', if Rawls's theory of justice is correct.

But is global justice a chimera from the Rawlsian perspective? Thomas Pogge (Chapter Three) circumvents much of the problem of global justice put forth by Nagel by taking a slight corrective departure away from Rawls, and certainly from the Hobbesian reading of Rawls. Pogge's essay is a third contemporary classic, a cornerstone of the debate relied upon by many champions of global justice, and is essential reading. Pogge in a certain way radicalizes Singer's demand, insofar as Singer merely demanded a duty to act, whereas Pogge demands that same duty simultaneously with a duty *not* to act, that is, to refrain from harm. According to Pogge, the present system of international and transnational relations is rigged, with richer and more powerful nations systemically benefitting at the concrete expense of the global poor and vulnerable. Pogge maintains that his mentor, John Rawls, was insufficiently aware of the actual dynamics of this system, and thus some of his premises need to be recalibrated accordingly. At any rate, global justice, in Pogge's view, should not be at odds with the fundamental Rawlsian orientation as Nagel seems to suggest, although Pogge does not go quite as far as to suggest — as does Sebastiano Maffettone in the final chapter of this book — that it is in fact its logical culmination.

The final chapter of Part I, newly commissioned for this volume, is not yet a classic as are the first three, but it does feature an element of the global justice debate that serves to round out this introduction to it. That is, it implicitly brings into dialogue the Rawlsian (Nagel) and utilitarian (Singer) approaches to global justice, which allows us to comprehend at once both the nature and the scope of the current debate in its present, mature form. In particular, the chapter argues that a typical charge against utilitarianism, the demandingness of its requisites, applies also to Rawlsian justice, and that, for this reason, current attempts to dispel this objection have failed. There can be no doubt that, despite the strong utilitarian contribution running alongside it, the global justice debate has long been dominated by the political philosophy of John Rawls.

John Rawls and Global Justice

Issues central to global justice are considered sporadically in Rawls's main works from 1950 to 1993. As Nagel (Chapter Two) highlights, these works are limited to justice within a 'basic structure', the borders of which coincide largely with those of the nation-state. Many commentators (such as Pogge in Chapter Three) consider this to be a serious limitation, particularly in a time in which globalization has become a central issue. Yet, even in *A Theory of Justice* (henceforth *TJ*; see Rawls 1999b), there are references to the possibility of extending the basic model of justice to the international realm by means of what Rawls called 'the law of nations'. He developed his most systematic treatment of global justice in the book *The Law of Peoples* (henceforth *LoP*; Rawls 1999a), which he completed during the academic year 1997–98.[1]

[1] The manuscript itself was, however, never subjected to a full revision due to the stroke that disabled Rawls in 1998.

The Law of Peoples raises questions regarding its relation to Rawls's earlier thought. It also raises questions regarding the inherent difficulties of developing an ethical–political theory of international relations such as that offered in the book. Regarding questions of the first kind, Rawls himself insists on the continuity of his thought in the introduction to *LoP*, when he writes, 'Both TJ and PL [*Political Liberalism*] try to say how a liberal society might be possible. LoP hopes to say how a world Society of liberal and decent Peoples might be possible' (Rawls 1999a: 6). Rawls also emphasizes that the conception of justice employed in *LoP* is the political conception first presented in *PL* (Rawls 1996) rather than the thicker one employed in *TJ*. This continuity raises a problem of its own. For the theoretical model that Rawls employs — both in *TJ* and in *PL* — was first developed in his treatment of domestic politics in a pluralistic society, before being transferred to issues that extended beyond the national context.

From a socio-economic perspective, the main issue raised by extending the national model to the international context concerns the possibility of defending a normative requirement of relative socio-economic equality between peoples. In *LoP*, Rawls removes the three pillars of the egalitarianism of *TJ*: the fair value of the basic liberties, the fair equality of opportunity and the difference principle (Pogge 1994). Clearly, he does this because there is no global basic structure comparable to the national one. It is not surprising that many critics, including many sympathetic to Rawls's theory at the national level, have been perplexed by this lack of egalitarian liberalism at the international level.

Of course, it must be said that the issues treated in *LoP* are intrinsically controversial and that they present difficulties for any view of international relations. Even political realism, the dominant theory of international relations in the 20th century from Morgenthau to Kissinger, faced its fair share of problems in recent decades, particularly from the 1970s onwards. In particular, it had to adapt to a new world in which two of its basic theoretical pillars had been much weakened, namely, national sovereignty and the traditional identification between people and state. At the same time, the traditional opponent of realism, the natural law tradition originating in Christian philosophers such as Vitoria, Suarez, Grotius, and Pufendorf and extending to contemporary liberal cosmopolitanism, has significant problems in applying its conception of universal justice to the concrete problems of the world.

Rawls himself thinks that cosmopolitanism's ultimate concern is for the wellbeing of individuals and not — as he thinks it should be — for the justice of societies (Rawls 1999a: 119). When elaborating his central notion of a 'realistic utopia' in *LoP*, Rawls seeks to avoid the most obvious weaknesses of both political realism and the abstract utopianism involved in certain cosmopolitan views. In this respect, the use of the term 'peoples' is itself significant. As mentioned, Rawls prefers it to alternatives such as 'states' or 'individuals'. Rawls defines the 'law of peoples' as 'a particular political conception of right and justice that applies to the principles and norms of international law and practice' (*ibid.*: 3). The fundamental idea is that there is a 'Society of Peoples' constituted by those peoples that respect some principles of justice in their relations with each other. The notion of justice implicit in the behaviour of these peoples is based on the social contract. It must nonetheless be sensitive to a particularity of the international context, namely, that each people has its own autonomous government and cultural tradition.

A particularly significant issue treated by Rawls in the section of *LoP* concerned with non-ideal theory regards the relationships between peoples that are members of the Society of Peoples and 'burdened societies'. By 'burdened societies', Rawls means societies lacking in 'the political and cultural traditions, the human capital and know-how, and, often, the material and technical resources needed to be well-ordered' (Rawls 1999a: 106). Such societies, while not participating in the Society of Peoples, differ from outlaw states such as Nazi Germany insofar as they are economically underdeveloped and do not necessarily have expansionist aspirations. With regard to these burdened societies, well-ordered societies have a general duty to assist them to satisfy the conditions necessary for entrance into the Society of Peoples. This duty is expressed by Article 8 of the international contract that binds members of the Society of Peoples, which reads as follows: 'Peoples have a duty to assist other peoples living under unfavorable conditions that prevent their having a just or decent political and social regime' (*ibid.*: 37).

How exactly a 'people' is to respect this principle is not specified in *LoP*. Rawls does not think that it is a matter of applying principles of distributive justice to burdened societies. Instead, he thinks this duty includes applying a principle analogous to that which, with respect to national politics, Rawls calls the principle of 'just savings'. The principle of just savings is presented in *TJ* as a kind of saving that present generations undertake in the interests of future generations. This claim has provoked controversy because the principle of just savings requires less than the second principle of justice. The lack of the difference principle in *LoP* has been amply discussed by critical Rawlsians such as Thomas Pogge and Charles Beitz and is seen as a problem in Rawls's position. Indeed, the theory presented in *LoP*, for many interpreters of Rawls, lacks not only a principle analogous to the difference principle, but any theory of distributive justice whatsoever. The most common criticism, made by Pogge in Chapter Three, for instance, is that the ethical double standard regarding the national and global levels that Rawls's theory involves cannot be justified philosophically. In other words, Rawls's theory would tolerate socio-economic injustices at the global level that would not be tolerated within a single nation. Pogge claims, therefore, that there is a kind of inconsistency between Rawls's position in *TJ* and that presented in *LoP*.

Let us try to understand why Rawls limits the responsibility of assistance in a way that might appear inconsistent with his general view of distributive justice. First, from *TJ* onwards, Rawls assumes that distributive justice concerns a basic structure, treated as corresponding approximately to the fundamental institutions of the nation-state (see Thomas Nagel's forceful presentation of this assumption in Chapter Two of this volume). In this limited sphere, one may presume that global interdependence is negligible. Second, Rawls makes a claim regarding international economics, according to which the causes of a nation's poverty are substantially endogenous. They consist of the limited capacities of local elites, and particularly of a society's political culture. Rawls thus tends to exclude both the direct responsibility of first-world citizens for economic conditions in burdened societies and the possibility of improving these conditions by the investment of economic resources. Third, Rawls invokes comparative fairness. If, of two peoples that begin from approximately the same socio-economic level, such as Korea and Sudan in the early 1970s, only one works to improve its situation, it would not be fair to redistribute the benefits that it obtains. On the basis of these claims, Rawls attributes responsibility for the unfavourable economic situation of a burdened society to the inhabitants of those societies. It is precisely for this reason that, on the broadly Kantian assumption that duties cannot exist without corresponding responsibilities, Rawls limits the duty of assistance.

Post-Rawlsian critics such as Thomas Pogge and Charles Beitz reply by emphasizing how, in today's world, global socio-economic interdependence has increased considerably. This is particularly true for burdened societies, the objects of the duty of assistance, which are frequently obliged to accept the normative authority of international economic institutions such as the World Trade Organization, the World Bank and the International Monetary Fund. For these critics, such fundamental changes in the global economy require Rawls to expand the basic structure to the international level.

As Pogge's critique is available in Chapter Three of this volume, here we shall focus on Charles Beitz, who criticizes *LoP* by means of a distinction between two general approaches to the question of global justice. He calls the first approach 'social liberalism', and attributes it to Rawls, while he calls the second 'cosmopolitan liberalism', and attributes it to himself and other critics of Rawls (Beitz 2000: 677). According to Beitz, for 'social liberals', international society serves only to ensure the basic conditions under which individual nations can cultivate, internally, the wellbeing of their citizens. For 'cosmopolitan liberals', on the other hand, the social world comprises not nations but persons. On these grounds, Beitz criticizes Rawls's social liberal claims in various ways, including Rawls's claims regarding distributive justice and the related duty of assistance. Unlike the principles of justice presented in *TJ*, the duty of assistance has a clear limit beyond which it does not hold. On Beitz's reading of Rawls, duties of justice are limited to the point at which the burdened society 'can support just institutions and a decent life for its people'. Beyond this point, Rawls expresses no further concern for distributive justice (*ibid.*: 688). Beitz considers such a limit to be arbitrary and unsatisfactory, for three reasons. First, he maintains that Rawls could not justify his claim that the economic situation of burdened societies is caused exclusively by endogenous conditions. Second, Beitz doubts that Rawls could justify his claim regarding comparative fairness: that it is wrong to redistribute economic wealth irrespective of states' different behaviours. Third, and most importantly, Beitz maintains that the true reason for Rawls's failure to discuss global distributive justice lies in his treatment of the national and international realms as two distinct things, as if the economic differences between nations were irrelevant to the dignity of people and the stability of the international system.

While Pogge's and Beitz's criticisms are not mistaken in themselves, perhaps they misunderstand the general framework of distributive justice that Rawls adopts. Thomas Nagel and Samuel Freeman have offered interesting replies to this effect. For Nagel (Chapter Two of this volume), as discussed earlier, Rawls is right to follow Hobbes in holding that the full standards of justice do not apply beyond the state. According to Freeman, Rawls's aim in *LoP* is not to provide a theory of global distributive justice, but instead to furnish the basic theoretical principles of foreign policy for a liberal state (Freeman 2006). If we accept this premise, then Rawls holds that the current lack of a basic structure at the international level means that the legal grounds for cooperation, which would justify a theory of distributive justice, are lacking. In short, distributive justice, including the difference principle, rests upon an institutional order that has established itself over time and not merely upon economic interdependence. It is this concentration upon and centrality of the institutional order that takes us to a new set of developments in the global justice debate.

A Sketch of Part II: Deparochializing the Debate

Amartya Sen, who like many other contributors to this volume holds John Rawls as a dear friend and mentor, has finally made a decisive break with the Rawlsian tradition of political theorizing, with specific reference to its institutionalism and the problem of global justice. As he argues in Chapter Five, the Rawlsian approach — which he refers to as 'transcendental institutionalism' — has ultimately ended up in a cul-de-sac with respect to the pressing demands of global justice, which Nagel (Chapter Two) has shown convincingly to be no more than a 'chimera' in light of the Rawlsian requirement of an institutional order, or global basic structure. Sen, therefore, opts for an approach he refers to as 'comparative', which concentrates on procedures to eradicate palpable global injustice rather than fixating on its (im)possibilities.

As admirable as Sen's motivation may be, his alternative position may be as beset with complications as the Rawlsian one he aims to overcome. In an article in the *Indian Journal of Human Development* dedicated to Sen's recent work, Sebastiano Maffettone, co-editor of this volume, exposes the high risk of paternalism present in Sen's person-centred approach to justice, which Sen had proposed as a corrective to Rawls's institution-centred approach. Interestingly, Maffettone concludes by proposing a synthetic framework accommodating both of these orientations through a differential grounded by the 'urgency' of the situation (Maffettone 2011). This synthetic or reconciliatory approach is not unlike the technique deployed by Maffettone in Chapter Eight of the present volume, as discussed further later in this introduction.

However, it is not actually Sen's technical critique of Rawls that interests us at this point quite so much as some of his motivations behind it. Specifically, in his new writings on the global justice debate (Chapter Five), Sen importantly inaugurates the project of deparochializing it. Sen does not get much further in this project than striving toward it somewhat in terms of both form (introducing a non-Western vocabulary by speaking of *nyaya* and *niti*[2]) and content (contrasting the urgency of the unjust scenario *in situ* with the comfort of the ideal theorist). However, it is now possible for others to pick up the torch where he left off. As mentioned earlier, the present volume aspires in some little respect to aid in that effort in a general way.

In Chapter Six, Neera Chandhoke reviews the parochial nature of the global justice debate in a lively and provocative paper newly written for this volume (as are all the remaining chapters of Part II). Chandhoke examines an entirely neglected element of the notion of redistribution at the global level, which is the *effect* that this may be understood to have with respect to the agency of the recipients of the beneficence. Agency is, of course, a concept absolutely central to debates in moral philosophy. However, the agency of those suffering under an unjust global order has hitherto been a blind spot among the limited participants of the global justice debate, who concentrate exclusively on their own agency (e.g., reparations), or on that of the local elites (e.g., just savings, corruption).

Co-editor Aakash Singh Rathore continues along the path of deparochialization in Chapter Seven, bringing more radical postcolonial elements into the debate. According to Rathore, the global justice debate in its current predominant manifestation is not merely parochial (i.e., a monological, mainly Anglo-American exercise), it is also romantic (i.e., academic

---

[2] See the essay by Amartya Sen, Chapter Five, this volume, p. 123, for a fuller discussion of these terms.

and privileged/elitist, out of touch with ground realities, and yet self-satisfied and glib). While Amartya Sen's recent writings, such as his paper in Chapter Five of the present volume and his book *The Idea of Justice*, serve to provide a valuable framework for deparochializing the debate, Rathore argues that Sen does not go far enough. A foray into the quandary of Dalit Marxism — a case where global justice and social justice may be antagonistic rather than complementary — reveals that, though not parochial, Sen's conception of (global) justice nevertheless remains rather romantic.

In the final chapter, Sebastiano Maffettone cautions us about hastily pursuing the postcolonial line of argumentation in the global justice debate and with respect to other crucial issues in the theory of international relations, where postcolonial critique relies upon postmodernist thought. Though fully sympathetic both to the need for deparochializing the global justice debate in particular, as well as to the broader postcolonial complaints within international relations (IR) more generally, Maffettone argues that the liaison of postcolonialism with postmodernism is manifestly a dangerous one for realizing these goals. In a reconciliatory gesture, Maffettone presents a technique for reading the liberal political theory of John Rawls in a manner that functions inclusively toward postcolonial concerns, and vice versa, where liberal rather than postmodern thought supports and follows through with postcolonial critique. Thus, Chapter Eight brings this volume full circle, out from the work of John Rawls, along several breaks away from it, finally reconciling with it in an inventive — and now rather less parochial — way.

It is, naturally, up to the reader herself to decide which of these approaches to the global justice debate she finds most convincing. The book offers many such approaches: from the utilitarian one available in Chapters One (Singer) and Four (Pellegrino); to the Hobbesian–Rawlsian line against global justice in Chapter Two (Nagel); to the ambivalent attitudes toward the global justice debate articulated in Chapters Six (Chandhoke) and Seven (Rathore); or the post-Rawlsian pro–global justice alternatives presented in Chapters Three (un-Rawlsian Pogge), Five (anti-Rawlsian Sen) and Eight (neo-Rawlsian Maffettone). Or, indeed, perhaps the reader will find none of these approaches satisfactory and push out a novel one independently. That would be a good result too, as it would prove that our task of introducing and deparochializing the global justice debate would have been meaningfully achieved.

References

Beitz, Charles. 2000. 'Rawls's *The Law of Peoples*', *Ethics* 110(4): 669–96.

Freeman, Samuel. 2006. '*The Law of Peoples*: Social Cooperation, Human Rights, and Distributive Justice', *Social Philosophy and Policy* 23(1): 29–68.

Maffettone, Sebastiano. 2011. 'Sen's *Idea of Justice* versus Rawls' *Theory of Justice*', *Indian Journal of Human Development* 5(1).

Pogge, Thomas. 1994. 'An Egalitarian Law of Peoples', *Philosophy and Public Affairs* 23(3): 195–224.

Rawls, John. 1996. *Political Liberalism*, Columbia University Press, New York.

———. 1999a. *The Law of Peoples*, Harvard University Press, Cambridge, MA.

———. 1999b. *Theory of Justice*, Harvard University Press, Cambridge, MA (rev. edn).

Part I

INTRODUCING THE DEBATE

1

Famine, Affluence and Morality

Peter Singer

As I write this, in November 1971, people are dying in East Bengal from lack of food, shelter and medical care. The suffering and death that are occurring there now are not inevitable, not unavoidable in any fatalistic sense of the term. Constant poverty, a cyclone and a civil war have turned at least nine million people into destitute refugees; nevertheless, it is not beyond the capacity of the richer nations to give enough assistance to reduce any further suffering to very small proportions. The decisions and actions of human beings can prevent this kind of suffering. Unfortunately, human beings have not made the necessary decisions. At the individual level, people have, with very few exceptions, not responded to the situation in any significant way. Generally speaking, people have not given large sums to relief funds; they have not written to their parliamentary representatives demanding increased government assistance; they have not demonstrated in the streets, held symbolic fasts or done anything else directed toward providing the refugees with the means to satisfy their essential needs. At the government level, no government has given the sort of massive aid that would enable the refugees to survive for more than a few days. Britain, for instance, has given rather more than most countries. It has, to date, given £14,750,000. For comparative purposes, Britain's share of the non-recoverable development costs of the Anglo-French Concorde project is already in excess of £275,000,000, and on present estimates will reach £440,000,000. The implication is that the British government values a supersonic transport more than thirty times as highly as it values the lives of the nine million refugees. Australia is another country which, on a per capita basis, is well up in the 'aid to Bengal' table. Australia's aid, however, amounts to less than one-twelfth of the cost of Sydney's new opera house. The total amount given, from all sources, now stands at about £65,000,000. The estimated cost of keeping the refugees alive for one year is £464,000,000. Most of the refugees have now been in the camps for more than six months. The World Bank has said that India needs a minimum of £300,000,000 in assistance from other countries before the end of the year. It seems obvious that assistance on this scale will not be forthcoming. India will be forced to choose between letting the refugees starve or diverting funds from her own development programme, which will mean that more of her own people will starve in the future.[1]

These are the essential facts about the present situation in Bengal. So far as it concerns us here, there is nothing unique about this situation except its magnitude. The Bengal emergency is just the latest and most acute of a series of major emergencies in various parts of the world, arising both from natural and from manmade causes. There are also many parts of the world in which people die from malnutrition and lack of food independent of any special emergency. I take Bengal as my example only because it is the present concern, and because the size of the problem has ensured that it has been given adequate publicity. Neither individuals nor governments can claim to be unaware of what is happening there.

What are the moral implications of a situation like this? In what follows, I shall argue that the way people in relatively affluent countries react to a situation like that in Bengal cannot be justified; indeed, the whole way we look at moral issues — our moral conceptual scheme — needs to be altered, and, with it, the way of life that has come to be taken for granted in our society.

In arguing for this conclusion I will not, of course, claim to be morally neutral. I shall, however, try to argue for the moral position that I take, so that anyone who accepts certain assumptions, to be made explicit, will, I hope, accept my conclusion.

I begin with the assumption that suffering and death from lack of food, shelter and medical care are bad. I think most people will agree about this, although one may reach the same view by different routes. I shall not argue for this view. People can hold all sorts of eccentric positions, and

---

[1] There was also a third possibility: that India would go to war to enable the refugees to return to their lands. Since I wrote this paper, India has taken this way out. The situation is no longer that described above, but this does not affect my argument, as the next paragraph indicates.

perhaps from some of them it would not follow that death by starvation is in itself bad. It is difficult, perhaps impossible, to refute such positions, and so for brevity I will henceforth take this assumption as accepted. Those who disagree need read no further.

My next point is this: if it is in our power to prevent something bad from happening, without thereby sacrificing anything of comparable moral importance, we ought, morally, to do it. By 'without sacrificing anything of comparable moral importance' I mean without causing anything else comparably bad to happen, or doing something that is wrong in itself, or failing to promote some moral good, comparable in significance to the bad thing that we can prevent. This principle seems almost as uncontroversial as the last one. It requires us only to prevent what is bad, and to promote what is good, and it requires this of us only when we can do it without sacrificing anything that is, from the moral point of view, comparably important. I could even, as far as the application of my argument to the Bengal emergency is concerned, qualify the point so as to make it: if it is in our power to prevent something very bad from happening, without thereby sacrificing anything morally significant, we ought, morally, to do it. An application of this principle would be as follows: if I am walking past a shallow pond and see a child drowning in it, I ought to wade in and pull the child out. This will mean getting my clothes muddy, but this is insignificant, while the death of the child would presumably be a very bad thing.

The uncontroversial appearance of the principle just stated is deceptive. If it were acted upon, even in its qualified form, our lives, our society and our world would be fundamentally changed. For the principle takes, firstly, no account of proximity or distance. It makes no moral difference whether the person I can help is a neighbour's child ten yards from me or a Bengali whose name I shall never know, ten thousand miles away. Secondly, the principle makes no distinction between cases in which I am the only person who could possibly do anything and cases in which I am just one among millions in the same position.

I do not think I need to say much in defence of the refusal to take proximity and distance into account. The fact that a person is physically near to us, so that we have personal contact with him, may make it more likely that we shall assist him, but this does not show that we ought to help him rather than another who happens to be further away. If we accept any principle of impartiality, universalizability, equality, or whatever, we cannot discriminate against someone merely because he is far away from us (or we are far away from him). Admittedly, it is possible that we are in a better position to judge what needs to be done to help a person near to us than one far away, and perhaps also to provide the assistance we judge to be necessary. If this were the case, it would be a reason for helping those near to us first. This may once have been a justification for being more concerned with the poor in one's town than with famine victims in India. Unfortunately for those who like to keep their moral responsibilities limited, instant communication and swift transportation have changed the situation. From the moral point of view, the development of the world into a 'global village' has made an important, though still unrecognized, difference to our moral situation. Expert observers and supervisors, sent out by famine relief organizations or permanently stationed in famine-prone areas, can direct our aid to a refugee in Bengal almost as effectively as we could get it to someone in our own block. There would seem, therefore, to be no possible justification for discriminating on geographical grounds.

There may be a greater need to defend the second implication of my principle — that the fact that there are millions of other people in the same position, in respect of the Bengali refugees, as I am, does not make the situation significantly different from a situation in which I am the only person who can prevent something very bad from occurring. Again, of course, I admit that there is a psychological difference between the cases; one feels less guilty about doing nothing if one can point to others, similarly placed, who have also done nothing. Yet this can make no real difference to our moral obligations.[2] Should I consider that I am less obliged to pull the drowning child out of the pond if on looking around I see other people, no further away than I am, who have also noticed the child

[2] In view of the special sense philosophers often give to the term, I should say that I use 'obligation' simply as the abstract noun derived from 'ought', so that 'I have an obligation to' means no more, and no less, than 'I ought to.' This usage is in accordance with the definition of 'ought' given by the *Shorter Oxford English Dictionary*: 'the general verb to express duty or obligation'. I do not think any issue of substance hangs on the way the term is used; sentences in which I use 'obligation' could all be rewritten, although somewhat clumsily, as sentences in which a clause containing 'ought' replaces the term 'obligation'.

but are doing nothing? One has only to ask this question to see the absurdity of the view that numbers lessen obligation. It is a view that is an ideal excuse for inactivity; unfortunately most of the major evils — poverty, overpopulation, pollution — are problems in which everyone is almost equally involved.

The view that numbers do make a difference can be made plausible if stated in this way: if everyone in circumstances like mine gave £5 to the Bengal Relief Fund, there would be enough to provide food, shelter and medical care for the refugees; there is no reason why I should give more than anyone else in the same circumstances as I am; therefore I have no obligation to give more than £5. Each premise in this argument is true, and the argument looks sound. It may convince us, unless we notice that it is based on a hypothetical premise, although the conclusion is not stated hypothetically. The argument would be sound if the conclusion were: if everyone in circumstances like mine were to give £5, I would have no obligation to give more than £5. If the conclusion were so stated, however, it would be obvious that the argument has no bearing on a situation in which it is not the case that everyone else gives £5. This, of course, is the actual situation. It is more or less certain that not everyone in circumstances like mine will give £5. So there will not be enough to provide the needed food, shelter and medical care. Therefore by giving more than £5 I will prevent more suffering than I would if I gave just £5.

It might be thought that this argument has an absurd consequence. Since the situation appears to be that very few people are likely to give substantial amounts, it follows that I and everyone else in similar circumstances ought to give as much as possible, that is, at least up to the point at which by giving more one would begin to cause serious suffering for oneself and one's dependents — perhaps even beyond this point to the point of marginal utility, at which by giving more one would cause oneself and one's dependents as much suffering as one would prevent in Bengal. If everyone does this, however, there will be more than can be used for the benefit of the refugees, and some of the sacrifice will have been unnecessary. Thus, if everyone does what he ought to do, the result will not be as good as it would be if everyone did a little less than he ought to do, or if only some do all that they ought to do.

The paradox here arises only if we assume that the actions in question — sending money to the relief funds — are performed more or less simultaneously, and are also unexpected. For if it is to be expected that everyone is going to contribute something, then clearly each is not obliged to give as much as he would have been obliged to had others not been giving too. And if everyone is not acting more or less simultaneously, then those giving later will know how much more is needed, and will have no obligation to give more than is necessary to reach this amount. To say this is not to deny the principle that people in the same circumstances have the same obligations, but to point out that the fact that others have given, or may be expected to give, is a relevant circumstance: those giving after it has become known that many others are giving and those giving before are not in the same circumstances. So the seemingly absurd consequence of the principle I have put forward can occur only if people are in error about the actual circumstances — that is, if they think they are giving when others are not, but in fact they are giving when others are. The result of everyone doing what he really ought to do cannot be worse than the result of everyone doing less than he ought to do, although the result of everyone doing what he reasonably believes he ought to do could be.

If my argument so far has been sound, neither our distance from a preventable evil nor the number of other people who, in respect of that evil, are in the same situation as we are, lessens our obligation to mitigate or prevent that evil. I shall therefore take as established the principle I asserted earlier. As I have already said, I need to assert it only in its qualified form: if it is in our power to prevent something very bad from happening, without thereby sacrificing anything else morally significant, we ought, morally, to do it.

The outcome of this argument is that our traditional moral categories are upset. The traditional distinction between duty and charity cannot be drawn, or at least, not in the place we normally draw it. Giving money to the Bengal Relief Fund is regarded as an act of charity in our society. The bodies which collect money are known as 'charities'. These organizations see themselves in this way — if you send them a cheque, you will be thanked for your 'generosity'. Because giving money is regarded as an act of charity, it is not thought that there is anything wrong with not giving. The charitable man may be praised, but the man who is not charitable is not condemned. People do not feel in any way ashamed or guilty about spending money on new clothes or a new car instead of giving it to famine relief. (Indeed, the alternative does not occur to them.) This way of looking at the matter cannot be justified. When we buy new clothes not to keep ourselves warm but to look 'well-dressed' we are not providing for any important need. We would not be sacrificing anything significant if we were to continue to wear our old clothes, and give the money to famine relief. By doing so, we would be preventing another person from starving. It follows from what I have said earlier that we ought to give money away, rather than spend it on clothes which we do not need to keep us warm. To do so is not charitable, or generous. Nor is it the kind of act which philosophers and theologians have called 'supererogatory' — an act which it would be good to do, but not wrong not to do. On the contrary, we ought to give the money away, and it is wrong not to do so.

I am not maintaining that there are no acts which are charitable, or that there are no acts which it would be good to do but not wrong not to do. It may be possible to redraw the distinction between duty and charity in some other place. All I am arguing here is that the present way of drawing the distinction, which makes it an act of charity for a man living at the level of affluence which most people in the 'developed nations' enjoy to give money to save someone else from starvation, cannot be supported. It is beyond the scope of my argument to consider whether the distinction should be redrawn or abolished altogether. There would be many other possible ways of drawing the distinction — for instance, one might decide that it is good to make other people as happy as possible, but not wrong not to do so.

Despite the limited nature of the revision in our moral conceptual scheme which I am proposing, the revision would, given the extent of both affluence and famine in the world today, have radical implications. These implications may lead to further objections, distinct from those I have already considered. I shall discuss two of these.

One objection to the position I have taken might be simply that it is too drastic a revision of our moral scheme. People do not ordinarily judge in the way I have suggested they should. Most people reserve their moral condemnation for those who violate some moral norm, such as the norm against taking another person's property. They do not condemn those who indulge in luxury instead of giving to famine relief. But given that I did not set out to present a morally neutral description of the way people make moral judgements, the way people do in fact judge has nothing to do with the validity of my conclusion. My conclusion follows from the principle which I advanced earlier, and unless that principle is rejected, or the arguments are shown to be unsound, I think the conclusion must stand, however strange it appears. It might, nevertheless, be interesting to consider why our society, and most other societies, do judge differently from the way I have suggested they should. In a well-known article, J. O. Urmson suggests that the imperatives of duty, which tell us what we must do, as distinct from what it would be good to do but not wrong not to do, function so as to prohibit behaviour that is intolerable if men are to live together in society (Urmson 1958; Sidgwick 1907).

This may explain the origin and continued existence of the present division between acts of duty and acts of charity. Moral attitudes are shaped by the needs of society, and no doubt society needs people who will observe the rules that make social existence tolerable. From the point of view of a particular society, it is essential to prevent violations of norms against killing, stealing and so on. It is quite inessential, however, to help people outside one's own society.

If this is an explanation of our common distinction between duty and supererogation, however, it is not a justification of it. The moral point of view requires us to look beyond the interests of our own society. Previously, as I have already mentioned, this may hardly have been feasible, but it is quite feasible now. From the moral point of view, the prevention of the starvation of millions of people outside our society must be considered at least as pressing as the upholding of property norms within our society.

It has been argued by some writers, among them Sidgwick and Urmson, that we need to have a basic moral code which is not too far beyond the capacities of the ordinary man, for otherwise there will be a general breakdown of compliance with the moral code. Crudely stated, this argument suggests that if we tell people that they ought to refrain from murder and give everything they do not really need to famine relief, they will do neither, whereas if we tell them that they ought to refrain from murder and that it is good to give to famine relief but not wrong not to do so, they will at least refrain from murder. The issue here is: where should we draw the line between conduct that is required and conduct that is good although not required, so as to get the best possible result?

This would seem to be an empirical question, although a very difficult one. One objection to the Sidgwick–Urmson line of argument is that it takes insufficient account of the effect that moral standards can have on the decisions we make. Given a society in which a wealthy man who gives 5 per cent of his income to famine relief is regarded as most generous, it is not surprising that a proposal that we all ought to give away half our incomes will be thought to be absurdly unrealistic. In a society which held that no man should have more than enough while others have less than they need, such a proposal might seem narrow-minded. What it is possible for a man to do and what he is likely to do are both, I think, very greatly influenced by what people around him are doing and expecting him to do. In any case, the possibility that by spreading the idea that we ought to be doing very much more than we are to relieve famine we shall bring about a general breakdown of moral behaviour seems remote. If the stakes are an end to widespread starvation, it is worth the risk. Finally, it should be emphasized that these considerations are relevant only to the issue of what we should require from others, and not to what we ourselves ought to do.

The second objection to my attack on the present distinction between duty and charity is one which has from time to time been made against utilitarianism. It follows from some forms of utilitarian theory that we all ought, morally, to be working full time to increase the balance of happiness over misery. The position I have taken here would not lead to this conclusion in all circumstances, for if there were no bad occurrences that we could prevent without sacrificing something of comparable moral importance, my argument would have no application. Given the present conditions in many parts of the world, however, it does follow from my argument that we ought, morally, to be working full time to relieve great suffering of the sort that occurs as a result of famine or other disasters. Of course, mitigating circumstances can be adduced — for instance, that if we wear ourselves out through overwork, we shall be less effective than we would otherwise have been. Nevertheless, when all considerations of this sort have been taken into account, the conclusion remains: we ought to be preventing as much suffering as we can without sacrificing something else of comparable moral importance. This conclusion is one which we may be reluctant to face. I cannot see, though, why it should be regarded as a criticism of the position for which I have argued, rather than a criticism of our ordinary standards of behaviour. Since most people are self-interested to some degree, very few of us are likely to do everything that we ought to do. It would, however, hardly be honest to take this as evidence that it is not the case that we ought to do it.

It may still be thought that my conclusions are so wildly out of line with what everyone else thinks and has always thought that there must be something wrong with the argument somewhere. In order to show that my conclusions, while certainly contrary to contemporary Western moral standards, would not have seemed so extraordinary at other times and in other places, I would like to quote a passage from a writer not normally thought of as a way-out radical, Thomas Aquinas.

> Now, according to the natural order instituted by divine providence, material goods are provided for the satisfaction of human needs. Therefore the division and appropriation of property, which proceeds from human law, must not hinder the satisfaction of man's necessity from such goods. Equally, whatever a man has in superabundance is owed, of natural right, to the poor for their sustenance. So Ambrosius says, and it is also to be found in the Decretum Gratiani: 'The bread which you withhold belongs to the hungry; the clothing you shut away, to the naked; and the money you bury in the earth is the redemption and freedom of the penniless.' (Aquinas 1948)

I now want to consider a number of points, more practical than philosophical, which are relevant to the application of the moral conclusion we have reached. These points challenge not the idea that we ought to be doing all we can to prevent starvation, but the idea that giving away a great deal of money is the best means to this end.

It is sometimes said that overseas aid should be a government responsibility, and that therefore one ought not to give to privately run charities. Giving privately, it is said, allows the government and the non-contributing members of society to escape their responsibilities.

This argument seems to assume that the more people there are who give to privately organized famine relief funds, the less likely it is that the government will take over full responsibility for such aid. This assumption is unsupported, and does not strike me as at all plausible. The opposite view — that if no one gives voluntarily, a government will assume that its citizens are uninterested in famine relief and would not wish to be forced into giving aid — seems more plausible. In any case, unless there were a definite probability that by refusing to give one would be helping to bring about massive government assistance, people who do refuse to make voluntary contributions are refusing to prevent a certain amount of suffering without being able to point to any tangible beneficial consequence of their refusal. So the onus of showing how their refusal will bring about government action is on those who refuse to give.

I do not, of course, want to dispute the contention that governments of affluent nations should be giving many times the amount of genuine, no-strings-attached aid that they are giving now. I agree, too, that giving privately is not enough, and that we ought to be campaigning actively for entirely new standards for both public and private contributions to famine relief. Indeed, I would sympathize with someone who thought that campaigning was more important than giving oneself, although I doubt whether preaching what one does not practice would be very effective. Unfortunately, for many people the idea that 'it's the government's responsibility' is a reason for not giving which does not appear to entail any political action either.

Another, more serious reason for not giving to famine relief funds is that until there is effective population control, relieving famine merely postpones starvation. If we save the Bengal refugees now, others, perhaps the children of these refugees, will face starvation in a few years' time. In support of this, one may cite the now well-known facts about the population explosion and the relatively limited scope for expanded production.

This point, like the previous one, is an argument against relieving suffering that is happening now, because of a belief about what might happen in the future; it is unlike the previous point in that very good evidence can be adduced in support of this belief about the future. I will not go into the evidence here. I accept that the earth cannot support indefinitely a population rising at the present rate. This certainly poses a problem for anyone who thinks it important to prevent famine. Again, however, one could accept the argument without drawing the conclusion that it absolves one from any obligation to do anything to prevent famine. The conclusion that should be drawn is that the best means of preventing famine, in the long run, is population control. It would then follow from the position reached earlier that one ought to be doing all one can to promote population control (unless one held that all forms of population control were wrong in themselves, or would have significantly bad consequences). Since there are organizations working specifically for population control, one would then support them rather than more orthodox methods of preventing famine.

A third point raised by the conclusion reached earlier relates to the question of just how much we all ought to be giving away. One possibility, which has already been mentioned, is that we ought to give until we reach the level of marginal utility — that is, the level at which, by giving more, I would cause as much suffering to myself or my dependents as I would relieve by my gift. This would mean, of course, that one would reduce oneself to very near the material circumstances of a Bengali refugee. It will be recalled that earlier I put forward both a strong and a moderate version of the principle of preventing bad occurrences. The strong version, which required us to prevent bad things from happening unless in doing so we would be sacrificing something of comparable moral significance, does seem to require reducing ourselves to the level of marginal utility. I should also say that the strong version seems to me to be the correct one. I proposed the more moderate version — that we should prevent bad occurrences unless, to do so, we had to sacrifice something morally significant — only in order to show that, even on this surely undeniable principle, a great change in our way of life is required. On the more moderate principle, it may not follow that we ought to reduce ourselves to the level of marginal utility, for one might hold that to reduce oneself and one's family to this level is to cause something significantly bad to happen. Whether this is so I shall not discuss, since, as I have said, I can see no good reason for holding the moderate version of the principle rather than the strong version. Even if we accepted the principle only in its moderate form, however, it should be clear that we would have to give away enough to ensure that the consumer society, dependent as it is on people spending on trivia rather than giving to famine relief, would slow down and perhaps disappear entirely. There are several reasons why this would be desirable in itself. The value and necessity of economic growth are now being questioned not only by conservationists, but by economists as well (Galbraith 1967; Mishan 1967). There is no doubt, too, that the consumer society has had a distorting effect on the goals and purposes of its members. Yet looking at the matter purely from the point of view of overseas aid, there must be a limit to the extent to which we should deliberately slow down our economy; for it might be the case that if we gave away, say, 40 per cent of our Gross National Product, we would slow down the economy so much that in absolute terms we would be giving less than if we gave 25 per cent of the much larger GNP that we would have if we limited our contribution to this smaller percentage.

I mention this only as an indication of the sort of factor that one would have to take into account in working out an ideal. Since Western societies generally consider 1 per cent of the GNP an acceptable level for overseas aid, the matter is entirely academic. Nor does it affect the question of how much an individual should give in a society in which very few are giving substantial amounts.

It is sometimes said, though less often now than it used to be, that philosophers have no special role to play in public affairs, since most public issues depend primarily on an assessment of facts. On questions of fact, it is said, philosophers as such have no special expertise, and so it has been possible to engage in philosophy without committing oneself to any position on major public issues. No doubt there are some issues of social policy and foreign policy about which it can truly be said that a really expert assessment of the facts is required before taking sides or acting, but the issue of famine is surely not one of these. The facts about the existence of suffering are beyond dispute. Nor, I think, is it disputed that we can do something about it, either through orthodox methods of famine relief or through population control or both. This is therefore an issue on which philosophers are competent to take a position. The issue is one which faces everyone who has more money than he needs to support himself and his dependents, or who is in a position to take some sort of political action. These categories must include practically every teacher and student of philosophy in the universities of the Western world. If philosophy is to deal with matters that are relevant to both teachers and students, this is an issue that philosophers should discuss.

Discussion, though, is not enough. What is the point of relating philosophy to public (and personal) affairs if we do not take our conclusions seriously? In this instance, taking our conclusion seriously means acting upon it. The philosopher will not find it any easier than anyone else to alter his attitudes and way of life to the extent that, if I am right, is involved in doing everything that we ought to be doing. At the very least, though, one can make a start. The philosopher who does so will have to sacrifice some of the benefits of the consumer society, but he can find compensation in the satisfaction of a way of life in which theory and practice, if not yet in harmony, are at least coming together.

Postscript

The crisis in Bangladesh that spurred me to write the above article is now of historical interest only, but the world food crisis is, if anything, still more serious. The huge grain reserves that were then held by the United States have vanished. Increased oil prices have made both fertilizer and energy more expensive in developing countries, and have made it difficult for them to produce more food. At the same time, their population has continued to grow. Fortunately, as I write now, there is no major famine anywhere in the world; but poor people are still starving in several countries, and malnutrition remains very widespread. The need for assistance is, therefore, just as great as when I first wrote, and we can be sure that without it there will, again, be major famines.

The contrast between poverty and affluence that I wrote about is also as great as it was then. True, the affluent nations have experienced a recession, and are perhaps not as prosperous as they were in 1971. But the poorer nations have suffered as least as much from the recession, in reduced government aid (because if governments decide to reduce expenditure, they regard foreign aid as one of the expendable items, ahead of, for instance, defence or public construction projects) and in increased prices for goods and materials they need to buy. In any case, compared with the difference between the affluent nations and the poor nations, the whole recession was trifling; the poorest in the affluent nations remained incomparably better off than the poorest in the poor nations.

So the case for aid, on both a personal and a governmental level, remains as great now as it was in 1971, and I would not wish to change the basic argument that I put forward then.

There are, however, some matters of emphasis that I might put differently if I were to rewrite the article, and the most important of these concerns the population problem. I still think that, as I wrote then, the view that famine relief merely postpones starvation unless something is done to check population growth is not an argument against aid, it is only an argument against the type of aid that should be given. Those who hold this view have the same obligation to give to prevent starvation as those who do not; the difference is that they regard assisting population control schemes as a more effective way of preventing starvation in the long run. I would now, however, have given greater space to the discussion of the population problem; for I now think that there is a serious case for saying that if a country refuses to take any steps to slow the rate of its population growth, we should not give it aid. This is, of course, a very drastic step to take, and the choice it represents is a horrible choice to have to make; but if, after a dispassionate analysis of all the available information, we come to the conclusion that without population control we will not, in the long run, be able to prevent famine or other catastrophes, then it may be more humane in the long run to aid those countries that are prepared to take strong measures to reduce population growth, and to use our aid policy as a means of pressuring other countries to take similar steps.

It may be objected that such a policy involves an attempt to coerce a sovereign nation. But since we are not under an obligation to give aid unless that aid is likely to be effective in reducing starvation or malnutrition, we are not under an obligation to give aid to countries that make no effort to reduce a rate of population growth that will lead to catastrophe. Since we do not force any nation to accept our aid, simply making it clear that we will not give aid where it is not going to be effective cannot properly be regarded as a form of coercion.

I should also make it clear that the kind of aid that will slow population growth is not just assistance with the setting up of facilities for dispensing contraceptives and performing sterilizations. It is also necessary to create the conditions under which people do not wish to have so many children. This will involve, among other things, providing greater economic security for people, particularly in their old age, so that they do not need the security of a large family to provide for them. Thus, the requirements of aid designed to reduce population growth and aid designed to eliminate starvation are by no means separate; they overlap, and the latter will often be a means to the former. The obligation of the affluent is, I believe, to do both. Fortunately, there are now many people in the foreign aid field, including those in the private agencies, who are aware of this.

One other matter that I should now put forward slightly differently is that my argument does, of course, apply to assistance with development, particularly agricultural development, as well as to direct famine relief. Indeed, I think the former is usually the better long-term investment. Although this was my view when I wrote the article, the fact that I started from a famine situation, where the need was for immediate food, has led some readers to suppose that the argument is only about giving food and not about other types of aid. This is quite mistaken, and my view is that the aid should be of whatever type is most effective.

On a more philosophical level, there has been some discussion of the original article which has been helpful in clarifying the issues and pointing to the areas in which more work on the argument is needed. In particular, as John Arthur has shown in 'Rights and the Duty to Bring Aid' (1977), something more needs to be said about the notion of 'moral significance'. The problem is that to give an account of this notion involves nothing less than a full-fledged ethical theory; and while I am myself inclined toward a utilitarian view, it was my aim in writing 'Famine, Affluence and Morality' to produce an argument which would appeal not only to utilitarians, but also to anyone who accepted the initial premises of the argument, which seemed to me likely to have a very wide acceptance. So I tried to get around the need to produce a complete ethical theory by allowing my readers to fill in their own version — within limits — of what is morally significant, and then see what the moral consequences are. This tactic works reasonably well with those who are prepared to agree that such matters as being fashionably dressed are not really of moral significance; but Arthur is right to say that people could take the opposite view without being obviously irrational. Hence, I do not accept Arthur's claim that the weak principle implies little or no duty of benevolence, for it will imply a significant duty of benevolence for those who admit, as I think most non-philosophers and even off-guard philosophers will admit, that they spend considerable sums on items that by their own standards are of no moral significance. But I do agree that the weak principle is nonetheless too weak, because it makes it too easy for the duty of benevolence to be avoided.

On the other hand, I think the strong principle will stand, whether the notion of moral significance is developed along utilitarian lines, or once again left to the individual reader's own sincere judgement. In either case, I would argue against Arthur's view that we are morally entitled to give greater weight to our own interests and purposes simply because they are our own. This view seems to me contrary to the idea, now widely shared by moral philosophers, that some element of impartiality or universalizability is inherent in the very notion of a moral judgement.[3] Granted, in normal circumstances, it may be better for everyone if we recognize that each of us will be primarily responsible for running our own lives and only secondarily responsible for others. This, however, is not a moral ultimate, but a secondary principle that derives from consideration of how a society may best order its affairs, given the limits of altruism in human beings. Such secondary principles are, I think, swept aside by the extreme evil of people starving to death.

References

Aquinas, Thomas. 1948. *Selected Political Writings* (ed. A. P. d'Entrèves), Blackwell, Oxford.

Arthur, John. 1977. 'Rights and the Duty to Bring Aid', in Will Aiken and Hugh LaFolette (eds), *World Hunger and Morality*, Prentice Hall, Englewood Cliffs, NJ, 37–49.

Galbraith, John Kenneth. 1967. *The New Industrial State*, Houghton Mifflin, Boston.

Hare, R. M. 1972. 'Rules of War and Moral Reasoning', *Philosophy and Public Affairs* 1(2): 166–81.

Mishan, E. J. 1967. *The Costs of Economic Growth*, Praeger, New York.

Sidgwick, Henry. 1907. *The Methods of Ethics*, Dover Press, London (7th edn).

Urmson, J. O. 1958. 'Saints and Heroes', in Abraham I. Melden (ed.), *Essays in Moral Philosophy*, University of Washington Press, Seattle, 198–216.

[3] For a discussion of the different formulations of this idea, and an indication of the extent to which they are in agreement, see Hare (1972).

2

'Assisting' the Global Poor

Thomas W. Pogge

We citizens of the affluent countries tend to discuss our obligations toward the distant needy mainly in terms of donations and transfers, assistance and redistribution: how much of our wealth, if any, should we give away to the hungry abroad? Using one prominent theorist to exemplify this way of conceiving the problem, I show how it is a serious error — and a very costly one for the global poor.

The Thesis of the Purely Domestic Causation of Poverty (PDPT) in Rawls

In his book *The Law of Peoples*, John Rawls adds an eighth law to his previous account: 'Peoples have a duty to assist other peoples living under unfavorable conditions that prevent their having a just or decent political and social regime' (Rawls 1999: 37; *cf.* Rawls 1993: 55). The addition is meant to show that Rawls's proposal can give a plausible account of global economic justice, albeit a less egalitarian one than his cosmopolitan critics have been urging upon him (Rawls 1999: 115–19; Beitz 1979; Pogge 1994). This newly added duty is, however, more than Rawls's account can justify and less than what is needed to do justice to the problem of world poverty.

It is doubtful that the new amendment would be adopted in Rawls's international original position, which represents liberal and decent peoples only. Each such representative is rational (Rawls 1999: 32, 63, 69) and seeking an international order that enables his or her own people to be stably organized according to its own conception of justice or decency (*ibid.*: 29, 33, 34–35, 40, 63–67, 69, 115, 120). Such representatives may well agree to assist one another in times of need. But why is it rational for them to commit to assisting poor peoples that never had a liberal or decent institutional order?

This challenge highlights how Rawls's international original position is too strongly focused on safeguarding the well-orderedness of liberal and decent societies and therefore triply implausible: first, peoples neither liberal nor decent are not represented in the international original position, and the interests of their members are thereby discounted completely. Second, because (liberal and decent) *peoples* count equally, the interests of their individual members (in the viability and stability of their domestic order) are represented unequally to the detriment of those who belong to more populous peoples.[1] Third, other important interests of members of liberal or decent peoples are not represented — for example, their interest in their socio-economic position relative to that of other societies (Pogge 1994: 208–9).

Though more demanding than what his international original position can justify, Rawls's duty of assistance is not demanding enough. This duty stipulates only an *absolute* target: no people should be prevented by poverty from organizing itself as a liberal or decent society. Rawls opposes any *relative* target: above the absolute threshold, international inequalities are unconstrained and hence a matter of moral indifference.

Rawls suggests why he opposes any relative target: once a people has attained the modest economic capacities necessary to sustain a liberal or decent institutional order, it is morally free to decide whether to make further net savings. If it does not, then its per capita income may fall further and further behind that of other peoples who save and invest more. It has a right to make this decision. But it also must then accept responsibility for the consequences. It cannot plausibly complain later about the evolved discrepancy in affluence — let alone demand a share of the much greater incomes other societies have become able to generate (Rawls 1999: 106–7, 117–18).

One might adduce against this argument that the effects of crucial decisions made for a society are often borne by persons who had no role in this decision — by later generations, or by persons at the bottom of

[1] Rawls recognizes this problem, in general terms at least, and is concerned to defend his use of an original position 'that is fair to peoples and not to individual persons' (Rawls 1999: 17n9).

a 'decent hierarchical society' (*cf.* Rawls 1999: 59). Both parts of Rawls's second principle of domestic justice forbid social institutions that impose the burdens (above some absolute threshold) of costly decisions made for a family upon members of this family alone. Decent societies, as Rawls describes them, may well be committed to similar domestic burden sharing. So it is unclear why liberal and decent societies should be categorically opposed to any analogous scheme of *international* burden sharing, even to a scheme that demands little from the wealthier societies and is adjusted according to the actual impact of perverse incentives and moral hazards (Pogge 1989: 252–53).

A further point is that the global institutional context in which national decisions are made co-determines their effects. Consider two ways in which the global order can be structured. It can be structured so that the rules of the world economy reflect the bargaining power of the various states, effectively preventing the smaller and poorer societies from achieving the solid rates of economic growth that are easily available to the bigger and richer ones. Or this order can be structured so that it, regardless of the distribution of power, maintains fair and open markets that actually make it easier for poorer than for richer countries to achieve high rates of economic growth. Without any burden sharing, the latter design would clearly engender much less hardship and inequality than the former would. The choice of global order then co-determines what the effects of poor national decisions are. Even rejecting any and all international burden sharing, Rawls could still have expressed a preference over these contrasting institutional designs. The contrast suggests that he should have complemented his duty of assistance after all, perhaps by a duty to help structure the global order so as to minimize personal poverty and international inequality.

Rawls does not see this point, I think, because he believes that the causes of severe poverty lie within the poor countries themselves. He stresses repeatedly that this is true of the world as it is:

> the causes of the wealth of a people and the forms it takes lie in their political culture and in the religious, philosophical, and moral traditions that support the basic structure of their political and social institutions, as well as in the industriousness and cooperative talents of its members, all supported by their political virtues. . . . the political culture of a burdened

> society is all-important. . . . Crucial also is the country's population policy. (Rawls 1999: 108)

When societies fail to thrive, 'the problem is commonly the nature of the public political culture and the religious and philosophical traditions that underlie its institutions. The great social evils in poorer societies are likely to be oppressive government and corrupt elites' (*ibid.*: 77).

These passages suggest that poverty is due to domestic factors, not to foreign influences. This empirical view about poverty leads rather directly to the important moral error to be exposed: to the false idea that the problem of world poverty concerns us citizens of the rich countries mainly as potential helpers. I will therefore examine in detail the empirical view of the domestic causation of severe poverty, showing why it is false and also why it is so widely held in the developed world.

Reasons against the PDPT

It is well to recall that existing peoples have arrived at their present levels of social, economic and cultural development through an historical process that was pervaded by enslavement, colonialism, even genocide. Though these monumental crimes are now in the past, they have left a legacy of great inequalities which would be unacceptable even if peoples were now masters of their own development. Even if the peoples of Africa had had, in recent decades, a real opportunity to achieve similar rates of economic growth as the developed countries, achieving such growth could not have helped them reduce their initial 30:1 disadvantage in per capita income. Even if, starting in 1960, African annual growth in per capita income had been a full percentage point above ours each and every year, the ratio would still be 20:1 today and would not be fully erased until early in the 24th century.[2] It is unclear then whether we may simply take for granted the existing inequality as if it had come about through choices freely made within each people. By seeing the problem of poverty merely in terms of assistance, we overlook that our enormous economic advantage is deeply tainted by how it accumulated over the course of *one* historical process that has devastated the societies and cultures of four continents.

---

[2] In fact, this ratio has increased to 40:1, showing that average annual growth in per capita income was 0.7 per cent *less* in Africa than in the developed world.

But let us leave aside the continuing legacies of historical injustice and focus on the empirical view that at least in the postcolonial era, which brought impressive growth in global per capita income, the causes of the *persistence* of severe poverty, and hence the key to its eradication, lie within the poor countries themselves. Many find this view compelling in light of the great variation in how the former colonies have evolved over the last forty years. Some of them have done quite well in economic growth and poverty reduction while others exhibit worsening poverty and declining per capita incomes. Isn't it obvious that such strongly divergent national trajectories must be due to differing *domestic* causal factors in the countries concerned? And isn't it clear, then, that the persistence of severe poverty has local causes?

This reasoning connects three thoughts: there are great international variations in the evolution of severe poverty. These variations must be caused by local (country-specific) factors. These factors, together, fully explain the overall evolution of severe poverty worldwide. To see the fallacy, consider this parallel: there are great variations in the performance of my students. These variations must be caused by local (student-specific) factors. These factors, together, fully explain the overall performance of my class.

Clearly, the parallel reasoning results in a falsehood: the overall performance of my class also crucially depends on the quality of my teaching and on various other 'global' factors as well. This shows that the second step is invalid. To see this more precisely, one must appreciate that there are two distinct questions about the evolution of severe poverty. One question concerns observed *variations* in national trajectories. In the answer to this question, local factors must play a central role. Yet, however full and correct, this answer may not suffice to answer the second question, which concerns the *overall* evolution of poverty worldwide: even if student-specific factors fully explain observed variations in the performance of my students, the quality of my teaching may still play a major role in explaining why they did not on the whole do much better or worse than they actually did. Likewise, even if country-specific factors fully explain the observed variations in the economic performance of the poor countries, global factors may still play a major role in explaining why they did not on the whole do much better or worse than they did in fact.

This is not merely a theoretical possibility. There is considerable international economic interaction regulated by an elaborate system of treaties and conventions about trade, investments, loans, patents, copyrights, trademarks, double taxation, labour standards, environmental protection, use of seabed resources, and much else. In many ways, such rules can be shaped to be more or less favourable to various affected parties such as, for instance, the poor or the rich societies. Had these rules been shaped to be more favourable to the poor societies, much of the great poverty in them today would have been avoided.

Let me support this point with a quote from the *Economist* which — being strongly supportive of WTO globalization and having vilified, on its cover and in its editorial pages, the protesters of Seattle, Washington and Genoa as enemies of the poor[3] — is surely not biased in my favour:

> Rich countries cut their tariffs by less in the Uruguay Round than poor ones did. Since then, they have found new ways to close their markets, notably by imposing anti-dumping duties on imports they deem 'unfairly cheap.' Rich countries are particularly protectionist in many of the sectors where developing countries are best able to compete, such as agriculture, textiles, and clothing. As a result, according to a new study by Thomas Hertel, of Purdue University, and Will Martin, of the World Bank, rich countries' average tariffs on manufacturing imports from poor countries are four times higher than those on imports from other rich countries. This imposes a big burden on poor countries. The United Nations Conference on Trade and Development (UNCTAD) estimates that they could export $700 billion more a year by 2005 if rich countries did more to open their markets. Poor countries are also hobbled by a lack of know-how. Many had little understanding of what they signed up to in the Uruguay Round. That ignorance is now costing them dear. Michael Finger of the World Bank and Philip Schuler of the University of Maryland estimate that implementing commitments to improve trade procedures and establish technical and intellectual-property standards can cost more than a year's development budget for the poorest countries. Moreover, in those areas where poor countries could benefit from world trade rules, they are often unable to do so. . . . Of the WTO's 134 members, 29 do not even have

[3] See, for instance, the *Economist* cover of 11 December 1999, showing an Indian child in rags with the heading 'The Real Losers of Seattle'. *Cf.* also its editorial in the same issue (*ibid.*: 15), its flimsy 'The Case for Globalisation', *Economist*, 23 September 2000, 19–20 and 85–87, and the lead editorial, 'A Question of Justice?' *Economist*, 11 March 2004.

missions at its headquarters in Geneva. Many more can barely afford to bring cases to the WTO.[4]

Such effects of the going WTO rules show that the causes of the persistence of severe poverty do not, *pace* Rawls, lie solely in the poor countries themselves. The global economic order also plays an important role. It is not surprising that this order is shaped to reflect the interests of the rich countries and their citizens and corporations. In the world as it is, the 15.6 per cent of humankind living in the 'high-income economies' have 81 per cent of global income while the other 84.4 per cent of humankind share the remaining 19 per cent (World Bank 2003: 235). It is of great importance for these other countries to be allowed access to the markets of the high-income economies, where per capita incomes are 23 times higher on average. This fact gives our governments greatly superior bargaining power. If our officials serve us well in intergovernmental negotiations about the ground rules of the world economy, they use this superior bargaining power, and their advantages in information and expertise, to shape each facet of the global order to our benefit, allowing us to capture the lion's share of the gains from economic interaction. In this way, large inequalities, once accumulated, have a tendency to intensify — and this is happening, quite dramatically, on the global plane: 'The income gap between the fifth of the world's people living in the richest countries and the fifth in the poorest was 74 to 1 in 1997, up from 60 to 1 in 1990 and 30 to 1 in 1960' (UNDP 1999: 3).

If the global economic order plays a major role in the persistence of severe poverty worldwide and if our governments, acting in our name, are prominently involved in shaping and upholding this order, then the deprivation of the distant needy may well engage not merely positive duties to assist but also more stringent negative duties not to harm. Yet, this obvious thought is strangely absent from the debates about our relation

[4] *Economist*, 25 September 1999, 89. The three cited studies are: Thomas W. Hertel and Will Martin, 'Would Developing Countries Gain from Inclusion of Manufactures in the WTO Negotiations?' www.gtap.agecon.purdue.edu/resources/download/42.pdf, 1999; UNCTAD (United Nations Conference on Trade and Development), *Trade and Development Report 1999*, UN Publications, New York, 1999; and J. Michael Finger and Philip Schuler, 'Implementation of Uruguay Round Commitments: The Development Challenge', World Bank Research Working Paper 2215, www.itd.org/wb/finger.doc, 1999.

to the distant needy. Even those who have most forcefully presented the eradication of severe poverty as an important moral task for us are content to portray us as mere bystanders. Thus, Peter Singer argues that we should donate most of our income to save lives in the poor countries. He makes his case by telling the story of a healthy young professor who, walking by a shallow pond, sees a small child in it about to drown. Surely, Singer says, the professor has a duty to save the child, even at the cost of dirtying his clothes. And similarly, he argues, we have a duty to send money to poverty relief organizations that can, for each few dollars they receive, save one more child from a painful hunger death. It is, in one way, a virtue of Singer's argument that it reaches even those who subscribe to the Purely Domestic Poverty Thesis (PDPT), the view that the persistence of severe poverty is due solely to domestic causes. But by catering to this empirical view, Singer also reinforces the common moral judgement that the citizens and governments of the affluent societies, whom he is addressing, are as innocent in regard to the persistence of severe poverty abroad as the professor is in regard to the child's predicament.[5]

An Explanation for Why the PDPT Is So Widely Accepted

Having argued that the PDPT, though widely held in the developed countries, is nonetheless quite far from the truth, I should be able to give some reasons for its popularity. I can see four main such reasons. The first is that belief in this thesis is rather comfortable for people in the developed world. Most of us know at least vaguely of the horrendous conditions among the global poor. We confront poverty statistics such as these: out of a total of 6 billion human beings, some 2.8 billion live below \$2/day, and nearly 1.2 billion of them live below the \$1/day international poverty line (World Bank 2000/2001: 23; Chen and Ravallion 2001: 290). Seven hundred ninety-nine million are undernourished, 1 billion lack access to safe water, 2.4 billion lack access to basic sanitation, and 876 million adults are illiterate (UNDP 2003: 87, 9, 6). More than 880 million lack access to basic health services (UNDP 1999: 22). Approximately

[5] Singer may not regard this reinforcement as regrettable. As a utilitarian, he believes that the stringency of our duty to combat world poverty is unaffected by whether the PDPT is true or false.

1 billion have no adequate shelter and 2 billion no electricity (UNDP 1998: 49). 'Two out of five children in the developing world are stunted, one in three is underweight and one in ten is wasted' (FAO 1999: 11). The International Labour Organization reports that 250 million children between 5 and 14 do wage work outside their household — often under harsh or cruel conditions: as soldiers, prostitutes or domestic servants, or in agriculture, construction, textile, or carpet production. And the World Health Organization attributes roughly one-third of all human deaths, some 50,000 daily, to poverty-related causes, easily preventable through better nutrition, safe drinking water, vaccines, cheap re-hydration packs, and antibiotics. Severe deprivations on such a scale would be considerably more disturbing to us were we to see them as due, in part, to a global institutional order that also sustains our comparatively lavish lifestyles by securing our resources and economic dominance. The PDPT shields us from such discomfort.

A second reason for the popularity of the PDPT in the developed world is awareness of the great differences among developing countries' economic performance. These differences draw our attention to domestic factors and international differences and thus away from global factors. Many ignore the causal role of global factors completely, often falling prey to the fallacy discussed above. Others fall for a different fallacy by concluding from the success of a few developing countries that the existing global economic order is quite hospitable to poverty eradication. This reasoning involves a some–all fallacy: the fact that *some* persons born into poverty in the US become millionaires does not show that *all* such persons can do likewise (Cohen 1988: 262–63). The reason is that the pathways to riches are sparse. They are not rigidly limited, to be sure, but the US clearly cannot achieve the kind of economic growth rates needed for everyone to become a millionaire (keeping fixed the value of the currency and the real income millionaires can now enjoy). The same holds true for developing countries. The Asian tigers (Hong Kong, Taiwan, Singapore, and South Korea), which together constitute well under 2 per cent of the population of the developing world, achieved impressive rates of economic growth and poverty reduction. They did so through a state-sponsored build-up of industries that mass-produce low-tech consumer products. These industries were globally successful by using their considerable labour-cost advantage to beat competitors in the developed countries and by drawing on greater state support and/or a better-educated workforce to beat competitors in other developing countries. Building such industries was hugely profitable for the Asian tigers. But if many other poor countries had adopted this same developmental strategy, competition among them would have rendered it much less profitable. We cannot conclude then that the existing global economic order, though less favourable to the poor countries than it might be, is still favourable enough for all of them to do as well as the Asian tigers have done in fact.

A third reason for the popularity of the PDPT in the developed world is the prevailing research focus among social scientists who, like the rest of us, pay much more attention to the differences among national and regional developmental trajectories than to the overall evolution of poverty and inequality worldwide. Across several academic disciplines, there is a vast literature analyzing the causal roles of the local climate, natural environment, resources, food habits, diseases, history, culture, social institutions, economic policies, leadership personalities, and much else. Advice dispensed by development economists and others is also overwhelmingly focused on the design of national economic institutions and policies. Thus, libertarian economists of the 'freshwater' school (so dubbed because its leading lights have taught in Chicago) argue that a country's best way to expel human misery is economic growth and its best way to achieve economic growth is to foster free enterprise with a minimum in taxes, regulations and red tape. A competing, more left-leaning school of thought, represented by Amartya Sen, contends that poverty persists because poor countries have *too little* government: public schools, hospitals and infrastructure. Sen's favourite poster child is the poor Indian state of Kerala whose socialist government has given priority to fulfilling basic needs and thereby achieved more for that population's health, education and life expectancy than the governments of other, more affluent Indian states. These hot and worthwhile debates about appropriate economic policies and social institutions for the poor countries overshadow the far more important question what causal role the rules of our globalized world economy play in the persistence of severe poverty.

This research focus among social scientists is surely partly due to the first two reasons: they, too, and their readers, are overly impressed by dramatic international differentials in economic performance and feel emotionally more comfortable, and careerwise more confident, with work that traces the persistence of severe poverty back to local causes rather than to global institutions we are involved in upholding. But there is also a good methodological reason for the research bias toward national and local causes: there being only this one world to observe, it is hard to obtain solid evidence about how the overall incidence of poverty would have evolved differently if this or that global factor had been different. By contrast, solid evidence about the effects of national and local factors can be gleaned from many poor countries that differ in their natural environment, history, culture, political and economic system, and government policies.

A fourth reason for the popularity of the PDPT is the prevalence of brutal and corrupt governments and elites in the poor countries. It seems far-fetched, even preposterous, to blame the global economic order for the persistence of severe poverty in countries that are ruled by obvious thugs and crooks. It also seems that whatever benefits global institutional reforms might bring to such countries would be captured by their corrupt elites, bringing little relief to the general population while reinforcing the power of their oppressors. Many among us believe then that we should postpone reforms that would make the global order fairer to the poor countries until they will have put their house in order by making their national political and economic order fairer to the domestic poor.

Important Domestic Factors are Themselves Sustained by Foreign Influences

This last reason, too, is a bad one, because the existing world order is itself a crucial causal factor in the prevalence of corruption and oppression in the poor countries. It was only in 1999, for example, that the developed countries finally agreed to curb their firms' bribery of foreign officials by adopting the OECD Convention on Combating Bribery of Foreign Public Officials in International Business Transactions. Until then, most developed states did not merely legally authorize their firms to bribe foreign officials, but even allowed them to deduct such bribes from their taxable revenues, thereby providing financial inducements and moral support to the practice of bribing politicians and officials in the poor countries. This practice diverts the loyalties of officials in these countries and also makes a great difference to which persons are motivated to scramble for public office in the first place. Developing countries have suffered staggering losses as a result, most clearly in the awarding of public contracts. These losses arise in part from the fact that bribes are priced in: bidders on contracts must raise their price in order to get paid enough to pay the bribes. Additional losses arise as bidders can afford to be non-competitive, knowing that the success of their bid will depend on their bribes more than on the substance of their offer. Even greater losses arise from the fact that officials focused on bribes pay little attention to whether the goods and services they purchase in their country's behalf are of good quality or even needed at all. Much of what developing countries have imported over the decades has been of no use to them — or even harmful, by promoting environmental degradation or violence (bribery is especially pervasive in the arms trade). Preliminary evidence suggests that the new convention is ineffective in curbing bribery by multinational corporations.[6] But even if it were effective, it would be very hard to purge the pervasive culture of corruption that is now deeply entrenched in many developing countries thanks to the extensive bribery they were subjected to during their formative years.

The issue of bribery is part of a larger problem. The political and economic elites of poor countries interact with their domestic inferiors, on the one hand, and with foreign governments and corporations, on the other. These two constituencies differ enormously in wealth and power. The former are by and large poorly educated and heavily preoccupied with the daily struggle to make ends meet. The latter, by contrast, have vastly greater rewards and penalties at their disposal. Politicians with a normal interest in their own political and economic success can thus be expected to cater to the interests of foreign governments and corporations rather than to competing interests of their much poorer compatriots. And this, of course, is what we find: there are plenty of poor-country governments that came to power or stay in power only thanks to foreign support. And there are plenty of poor-country politicians and bureaucrats who, induced or even bribed by foreigners, work against the interests of their people: *for* the development of a tourist-friendly sex industry

[6] 'Plenty of laws exist to ban bribery by companies. But big multinationals continue to sidestep them with ease' — so the current situation is summarized in 'The Short Arm of the Law', *Economist*, 2 March 2002, 63–65, at 63.

(whose forced exploitation of children and women they tolerate and profit from), *for* the importation of unneeded, obsolete or overpriced products at public expense, *for* the permission to import hazardous products, wastes or factories, *against* laws protecting employees or the environment, and so on.

To be sure, there would not be such huge asymmetries in incentives if the poor countries were more democratic, allowing their populations a genuine political role. Why then are most of these countries so far from being genuinely democratic? This question brings further aspects of the current global institutional order into view.

It is a very central feature of this order that any group controlling a preponderance of the means of coercion within a country is internationally recognized as the legitimate government of this country's territory and people — regardless of how this group came to power, of how it exercises power and of the extent to which it is supported or opposed by the population it rules. That such a group exercising effective power receives international recognition means not merely that we engage it in negotiations. It means also that we accept this group's right to act for the people it rules, that we, most significantly, confer upon it the privileges freely to dispose of the country's natural resources (international resource privilege) and freely to borrow in the country's name (international borrowing privilege).

The *resource privilege* we confer upon a group in power is much more than mere acquiescence in its effective control over the natural resources of the country in question. This privilege includes the power to effect legally valid transfers of ownership rights in such resources. Thus a corporation that has purchased resources from the Saudis or Suharto, or from Mobuto or Sani Abacha, has thereby become entitled to be — and actually *is* — recognized anywhere in the world as the legitimate owner of these resources. This is a remarkable feature of our global order. A group that overpowers the guards and takes control of a warehouse may be able to give some of the merchandise to others, accepting money in exchange. But the fence who pays them becomes merely the possessor, not the owner, of the loot. Contrast this with a group that overpowers an elected government and takes control of a country. Such a group, too, can give away some of the country's natural resources, accepting money in exchange. In this case, however, the purchaser acquires not merely possession, but all the rights and liberties of ownership, which are supposed to be — and actually *are* — protected and enforced by all other states' courts and police forces.

The international resource privilege, then, is the legal power to confer globally valid ownership rights in the country's resources.

This international resource privilege has disastrous effects in poor but resource-rich countries, where the resource sector constitutes a large segment of the national economy. Whoever can take power in such a country by whatever means can maintain his rule, even against widespread popular opposition, by buying the arms and soldiers he needs with revenues from the export of natural resources and with funds borrowed against future resource sales. The resource privilege thus gives insiders strong incentives toward the violent acquisition and exercise of political power, thereby causing coup attempts and civil wars. Moreover, it also gives outsiders strong incentives to corrupt the officials of such countries who, no matter how badly they rule, continue to have resources to sell and money to spend.

Nigeria is a case in point. It produces about 2 million barrels of oil per day which, depending on the oil price, fetch some $10–20 billion annually, one quarter to one half of GDP. Whoever controls this revenue stream can afford enough weapons and soldiers to keep himself in power regardless of what the population may think of him. And so long as he succeeds in doing so, his purse will be continuously replenished with new funds with which he can cement his rule and live in opulence. With such a powerful incentive, it cannot be surprising that, during 28 of the past 32 years, Nigeria has been ruled by military strongmen who took power and ruled by force. Nor can it be surprising that even a polished elected president fails to stop gross corruption: Olusegun Obasanjo knows full well that, if he tried to spend the oil revenues solely for the benefit of the Nigerian people, military officers could — thanks to the international resource privilege — quickly restore their customary perks. With such a huge price on his head, even the best-intentioned president could not end the theft of oil revenues and survive in power.

The incentives arising from the international resource privilege help explain what economists have long observed and found puzzling: the significant *negative* correlation between resource wealth (relative to GDP) and economic performance.[7] This explanation is confirmed by a recent

[7] This 'resource curse' is exemplified by many developing countries which, despite great natural wealth, have achieved little economic growth and poverty reduction over the last decades.

regression analysis by two Yale economists, which shows that the causal link from resource wealth to poor economic performance is mediated through reduced chances for democracy (Lam and Wantchekon 1999). Holding the global order fixed as a given background, the authors do not consider how the causal link they analyze itself depends on global rules that grant the resource privilege to any group in power, irrespective of its domestic illegitimacy.

The *borrowing privilege* we confer upon a group in power includes the power to impose internationally valid legal obligations upon the country at large. Any successor government that refuses to honour debts incurred by an ever so corrupt, brutal, undemocratic, unconstitutional, repressive, unpopular predecessor will be severely punished by the banks and governments of other countries. At minimum it will lose its own borrowing privilege by being excluded from the international financial markets. Such refusals are therefore quite rare, as governments, even when newly elected after a dramatic break with the past, are compelled to pay the debts of their ever so awful predecessors.

The international borrowing privilege makes three important contributions to the incidence of oppressive and corrupt elites in the developing world. First, this privilege facilitates borrowing by destructive rulers who can borrow more money and can do so more cheaply than they could do if they alone, rather than the whole country, were obliged to repay. In this way, the borrowing privilege helps such rulers maintain themselves in power even against near-universal popular discontent and opposition. Second, the international borrowing privilege imposes upon democratic successor regimes the often huge debts of their corrupt predecessors. It thereby saps the capacity of such democratic governments to implement structural reforms and other political programmes, thus rendering such governments less successful and less stable than they would otherwise be. (It is small consolation that putschists are sometimes weakened by being held liable for the debts of their democratic predecessors.) Third, the international borrowing privilege strengthens incentives toward coup attempts: whoever succeeds in bringing a preponderance of the means of coercion under his control gets the borrowing privilege as an additional reward.

By discussing several global systemic factors in some detail, I hope to have undermined a view that, encouraged by libertarian and more leftist economists alike, most people in the developed world are all too ready to believe: the persistence of severe poverty is due to causes that are indigenous to the countries in which it occurs and thus unrelated to the affluent societies and their governments. This view is dramatically mistaken. Yes, domestic factors contribute to the persistence of severe poverty in many countries. But these contributions often depend on features of the global institutional order, which sustain some of those factors and exacerbate the impact of others. In these ways, the non-indigenous factors I have discussed play a major causal role in the evolution of severe poverty worldwide. They are crucial for explaining the inability and especially the unwillingness of the poor countries' leaders to pursue more effective strategies of poverty eradication. And they are crucial therefore for explaining why global inequality is increasing so rapidly that substantial global economic growth since the end of the Cold War has not reduced income poverty and malnutrition[8] — *despite* substantial technological progress, *despite* a huge poverty reduction in China, *despite* the post–Cold War 'peace dividend', *despite* a 45 per cent drop in real food prices during 1980–2002, *despite* official development assistance, *despite* the efforts of international humanitarian and development organizations, and *despite* the fact that the poor are continuously decimated by some 18 million premature deaths each year. If we are serious about eradicating severe poverty worldwide, we must understand the causal role of such non-indigenous factors and be willing to consider ways of modifying them or of reducing their impact.

If the PDPT were true, the moral issues the distant needy raise for us might plausibly be considered under the assistance label alone. But since the PDPT is seriously mistaken, this label may be misleading insofar as we may also be *contributing to*, or *profiting from*, social factors that exacerbate severe poverty abroad.

[8] *Cf.* the annual UNDP reports for the number of undernourished, stuck around 800 million. (Remark added in 2011 by the author: the FAO reports that this number has broken above 1 billion in 2009 — for the first time in all of human history. Rising food prices make it likely that this feat will be repeated in 2011.) The incidence of $1/day income poverty is reported to be flat and $2/day income poverty to be up about 10 per cent over the 1987–98 period (World Bank 2000/2001: 23; Chen and Ravallion 2001: 290). Severe flaws in the World Bank's method of calculating these numbers make it likely that the actual extent of severe income poverty is substantially greater. Among these flaws is the use of purchasing power parities based on the prices of all commodities rather than on the prices of basic necessities on which poor households are compelled to concentrate their expenditures. See Pogge (2010: chs 3–4) for a comprehensive critique.

How Can Our Design of the Global Order Be Assessed Morally?

We can still deny that we are so contributing or profiting, even if we acknowledge the PDPT's collapse and accept our shared responsibility for the existing global order. We can say for instance that our imposition of this order benefits the global poor, or at least does not harm them by exacerbating their poverty. While such claims are often made, for the current WTO rules for example, it remains quite unclear what their meaning is supposed to be. Benefit, after all, is a comparative notion which implicitly appeals to some baseline scenario under which the global poor would be even worse off than they are now in the world as it is. What baseline might we adduce to show the global poor that they are benefitting from the present global order?

There are three options. We might invoke a *diachronic* comparison, appealing to the *trend* in the depth or incidence of severe poverty worldwide. But this argument fails for three independent reasons. Its premise is false: severe income poverty and malnutrition are not actually in decline globally.[9] Moreover, its inference is invalid: severe poverty might be declining, in China for instance, *despite* the fact that the global economic order tends to exacerbate such poverty. A diachronic comparison does not permit us to judge this possibility one way or the other and is therefore useless for judging the impact of any specific causal factor. Finally, we must not simply assume that the preceding situation was morally unproblematic. Otherwise we would have to conclude that a man is benefitting his children if he beats them up ever less frequently, or that the US economic order of the early 19th century benefitted the slaves if their enslavement became less brutal during this period.

Our second option is to invoke a *subjunctive* comparison with an *historical* baseline. To judge whether the Israeli occupation reduced illiteracy in the West Bank, we should not ask diachronically whether illiteracy declined, but counterfactually whether illiteracy is lower than it would have been without the occupation. Adopting this idea, we might argue that the existing global order is benefitting the global poor insofar as they are better

---

[9] See note 8.

off than they would be if some preceding set of rules had remained in force. But this argument makes the — here inappropriate — assumption that those preceding rules were neutral, neither harming nor benefitting the global poor. By the same reasoning the military junta under Senior General Than Shwe could be said to be benefitting the Burmese people if merely they are better off than they would now be if the predecessor junta under General Ne Win were still in power.

Our third option is to invoke a *subjunctive* comparison with a *hypothetical* baseline — arguing perhaps that even more people would live and die even more miserably in some fictional state of nature than in this world as we have made it. But this option, too, is unpromising so long as we lack a precise and morally uniquely appropriate specification of that fictional world and a morally uniquely appropriate standard for comparing the two worlds in regard to severe poverty. You may think that these worries are merely academic, that our world is surely vastly better in this regard than any conceivable state of nature. And so it indeed appears from our vantage point. And yet: 'Worldwide 34,000 children under age five die daily from hunger and preventable diseases.'[10] Try to conceive a state of nature that can match this amazing feat of our globalized civilization, not just briefly, but every day for decades on end! (Pogge 2008: 142–45)

None of our three options is suitable for explicating our question — whether the existing world order harms or benefits the global poor — in a way that is both clear and appropriate to the assessment of this order. This failure suggests the inverse strategy: instead of basing our justice assessment of this order on whether it does harm (independently defined), we can make our judgement of whether the imposition of this order does harm turn on an assessment of this order by some harm-independent criterion of justice.

To illustrate the idea, consider the institutional order of the US in its infancy, which greatly disadvantaged women vis-à-vis men. Our judgement of this order as unjust is not based on an historical comparison with how women had fared under British rule. It is not based on a comparison with how women would have fared had British rule continued. And it is

[10] USDA (1999: iii). The US government mentions this fact whilst arguing that the developed countries should *not* follow the FAO proposal to increase development assistance for agriculture by \$6 billion annually, that \$2.6 billion is ample (*ibid.*: Appendix A).

not based on a comparison with how women would fare in some state of nature. (All these comparisons can be more plausibly invoked to justify than to criticize the institutional order under consideration.) Rather, it is because it assigned women a status inferior to men's that we judge this order to have been unjust to women and its imposition therefore a harm done to them.

Many harm-independent criteria might be proposed for assessing the justice of our global order. Such criteria differ in at least three respects. They differ in how they identify the relevant affected parties: as individual persons, households, social groups, nations, or states. They differ in their *absolute* demands — requiring, for instance, that affected parties must enjoy security of self and property or access to basic necessities. And they differ in their *relative* demands — requiring perhaps that basic rights or basic educational or medical opportunities must be equal or that economic inequalities must be constrained in certain ways.

Even if our global order fails to meet compelling absolute or relative requirements, it may still be defended on the grounds that this failure is unavoidable. An assessment of its justice must be sensitive then to information about what alternatives are feasible and about the conditions such feasible alternatives would engender. With regard to alternatives that diverge greatly from the existing global order, it may be impossible to establish such information in a rigorous way. It is quite possible, however, to estimate the impact of the existing global order relative to its nearby institutional alternatives. We saw such estimates in the *Economist* passage quoted above: the developing countries are missing out on some $700 billion annually in export revenues because the developed countries insisted on grandfathering heavy protections of their markets — through tariffs, quotas, anti-dumping duties, export credits, and subsidies to domestic producers.[11] It is quite possible, though unseemly among economists, to

[11] In 2000, the rich countries spent $245 billion on subsidies to their farmers alone (Martin Wolf, 'Broken Promises to the Poor', *Financial Times*, 21 November 2001, 13). In 2002, the US imposed new tariffs against steel imports, with adverse effects in China, Brazil and Russia, and adopted a $173-billion farm bill that increases subsidies to domestic farmers some 70 per cent over current levels and thereby greatly hurts farmers in poor countries. These and many other such examples render somewhat comical the endless polemics for and against free trade and open markets. These debates miss what is happening in the real world: the poor countries are not given access to free trade and

extend this estimate to the number of poverty deaths that would have been avoided by a more symmetrical opening of markets. The number is large, as $700 billion annually is nearly 12 per cent of the gross national incomes of all developing countries, representing 84.4 per cent of humankind (World Bank 2003: 235).

Many features of the existing global order embody similar trade-offs between the interests of the high-income countries and their citizens on the one hand and the global poor on the other. An unconditional resource privilege gives us access to a larger, cheaper and more reliable supply of foreign resources, because we can acquire ownership of them from anyone who happens to exercise effective power without regard to whether the country's population either approves the sale or benefits from the proceeds. Advantageous also to putschists and tyrants in the developing world, broad resource and borrowing privileges are much worse, however, for the global poor than would be narrower such privileges conditional on minimal domestic legitimacy. The existing TRIPs agreement is better for us and worse for the global poor than an alternative that would have required the rich countries to supply funds for shielding the global poor from exorbitant mark-ups on drugs and seeds. The existing Law of the Sea Treaty is better for us and worse for them than an alternative that would have guaranteed the poor countries some share of the value of harvested seabed resources. It is better for us and worse for the global poor that we do not have to pay for the negative externalities we impose on them: for the pollution we have produced over many decades and the resulting effects on their environment and climate, for the rapid depletion of natural resources, for the contribution of our tourists to the AIDS epidemic, and for the violence caused by our demand for drugs and our war on drugs.

The cumulative impact of all these trade-offs upon the global poor is likely to be staggering. In the fourteen years since the end of the Cold War, some 250 million human beings have died prematurely from poverty-related causes, with 18 million more added each year. Had the developed

---

open markets. They cannot take advantage even of the entitlements they do have under the slanted rules of the WTO, because they do not have the resources to bring and win cases against the US or EU. Moreover, a poor country would have far more to lose than to gain from imposing retaliatory countertariffs — as winning such a case would entitle them to do — against the US or EU.

countries shaping the global rules given more weight to the interests of the global poor, the toll in early deaths and deprivations would certainly and foreseeably have been vastly lower at negligible cost to our affluence. It is then very hard to see how we might defend the trade-offs manifested in our global order as compatible with justice. And if this order is unjust, then it follows, without appeal to any historical or state-of-nature baseline, that we are harming the global poor — by imposing on them an unjust global order under which the incidence of severe poverty, malnutrition and premature death is foreseeably much higher than it would be under some feasible alternatives.

To What Extent Must Our Policies Give Weight to the Interests of the Global Poor?

There are three ways of defending the trade-offs that our governments, often in collusion with corrupt and oppressive leaders in the developing world, have imposed. First we might say that it is permissible for us vigorously to promote our own interests in negotiations about how to fine-tune the various rules of the global order, even when doing so conflicts with the interests of the global poor. With our incomes 200 to 300 times larger than theirs and a billion people living on the brink of starvation,[12] this justification of the status quo is rarely voiced in public. To be sure, it is widely thought that our politicians and diplomats ought to represent the interests of their compatriots. But it is also widely thought that this mandate has its limits: even if they are able to do so, our representatives should not impose global rules under which we have unfair advantages that add millions of poverty deaths in the developing world. In the examples I have given, it looks like our politicians and diplomats have done exactly that, in our name.

Our second defence avers that appearances are here deceptive, that the decisions reflected in the existing rules do benefit the global poor as well, at least in the long run. But in some important cases, such a defence strains credulity. It is very hard to deny that world poverty is exacerbated by the special prerogatives the rich countries gave themselves under WTO rules to favour their own firms through tariffs, quotas, anti-dumping duties, export credits, and subsidies. Still, career incentives do produce such

[12] See note 8.

denials which, in the more clear-cut cases of unfair rules, often take a weaker form: instead of claiming that certain prerogatives for the rich countries do not exacerbate poverty, economists merely claim that there are many complicating factors, methodological difficulties and other imponderabilia so that intellectual honesty precludes our drawing any firm conclusions. If all else fails, we can fall back on the weakest claim: yes, the fine-tuning of some important rules was indeed worse for the global poor, but it was an honest mistake. When these rules were designed, development economics was less advanced and the relevant officials could not possibly have known that they were serving our interests at the expense of many additional premature deaths from poverty-related causes.

Boilerplate empirical defences of this kind are easily produced and very well received. And it is quite unlikely that there will ever be a serious inquiry into what our politicians and diplomats and officials in the WTO, IMF and World Bank knew and should have known during their negotiations of international agreements. The possibility that these respectable gentlemen (very few women there) might be hunger's willing executioners, committing a rather large-scale crime against humanity in our name, will never be taken seriously in the developed world. And yet, nagging doubts remain. If our representatives did make honest mistakes to the detriment of the global poor, should we not at least make up for these mistakes through a real effort at reducing the (unexpectedly) large incidence of severe poverty today?

Similar questions are raised by our third defence, which asserts that the global rules we have imposed are not merely good for us, but also good for global efficiency, productivity and economic growth. These rules are Pareto-superior to their alternatives — not in the normal sense (better for some and worse for no one), but in this weaker ('Kaldor–Hicks') sense: the rules are better for some and worse for others but so that the former can, out of their relative gains, fully compensate the latter for their relative losses. I doubt this argument can succeed for the grandfathering clauses in the WTO treaty which still allow us, for many years to come, to favour our firms through tariffs, quotas, anti-dumping duties, export credits, and huge subsidies. But it may well succeed in other cases such as the TRIPs agreement. Still, even when it succeeds, there is the nagging question: given the vast economic inequality between gainers and losers, is the mere *possibility* of compensation sufficient to vindicate our decision?

Or must there not rather be *actual* compensation, so that we may keep only such relative gains as *exceed* their relative losses?

The questions concluding the last two paragraphs indicate more precisely how, with the collapse of the PDPT, conventional discussions of world poverty under the assistance label are misleading. The label is not inaccurate: as affluent people and countries, we surely have positive moral duties to assist persons mired in life-threatening poverty whom we can help at little cost. But the label detracts from weightier, negative duties that also apply to us: we should reduce severe harms we will have caused; and we should not take advantage of injustice at the expense of its victims. These two negative duties apply to us if we (sometimes together with third-world elites) are imposing a global order whose unfairness benefits us while exacerbating severe poverty abroad. We must then at least compensate the global poor. Failing to do this, we would be harming them and profiting from injustice at their expense. And insofar as we do compensate, we are not merely 'assisting' the poor abroad, but reducing the impact of unfair rules that bring us unjust gains at their expense. We are not 'redistributing' from the rich to the poor, but offsetting an unjust institutional redistribution from the poor to the rich — *re*-redistributing, if you like.

Let me illustrate the special weight these two negative duties are generally thought to have: imagine, by the side of a country road, an injured child who must be rushed to the hospital if her leg is to be saved. As a competent bystander who ignores her plight, you are subject to moral criticism for failing to assist. But if you are the driver who injured the child in the first place, then more is morally at stake: by leaving the child's needs unattended, you would greatly increase the harm you will have done her. As we judge such inaction of the driver more harshly than that of the bystander, we should judge our own inaction more harshly, too, if we are involved in upholding unjust rules that contribute to severe poverty we ignore.

Imagine further a society in which an aboriginal minority suffers severe discrimination in education and employment, reducing their wages far below those of their compatriots. As an affluent foreigner, you may think that perhaps you ought to do something to assist these people. But if you are profiting from the discrimination (by employing an aboriginal driver at half the wage other drivers receive, for instance), then more is morally at stake: we judge ourselves more harshly for taking advantage of an injustice by pocketing such gains than for failing to spend other assets we have on supporting the poor. As we do so, we should also judge ourselves more harshly insofar as assets we fail to use toward reducing severe poverty abroad constitute gains we derive from the unfairness of a global order that also contributes to the persistence of this poverty.

Negative duties not to support and not to pocket gains from an unfair institutional order that foreseeably contributes to severe deprivations are not only weightier than the positive duty to help relieve such deprivations. They are also much less sensitive to variations in community and distance. Duties to assist are strongest toward the near and dear and weakest toward foreigners in distant lands. But duties not to harm do not fade in this way. Consider again the driver who hits a child and then leaves her unattended by the side of the road. We do not upgrade our moral assessment of him when we learn that he did this far away from his home to a child with whom he had no communal bond of nationality, language, culture, or religion. If the unfairness of the global order we impose causes poverty to persist in the poor countries, then our moral responsibility for the associated deaths and deprivations is not diminished by diversity of nationality and geographical or cultural distance. It might be so diminished, perhaps, if harming foreigners were necessary to save ourselves from a comparable fate. But in the real world, the global poverty problem — though it involves one-third of all human deaths — is quite small in economic terms: though 2,812 million persons are living below the higher ($2/day) international poverty line, and 43 per cent below it on average, their collective shortfall amounts to only 1.13 per cent of the incomes of the 955 million people in the high-income economies. Clearly, we could eradicate severe poverty — through a reform of the global order or through other initiatives designed to compensate for its effects on the global poor — without 'sacrificing' the fulfilment of our own needs or even mildly serious interests.

It is widely believed in the developed world that we are already spending an inordinate amount on such initiatives. This belief is contradicted by the facts: the high-income countries have reduced their official development assistance (ODA) from 0.33 per cent of their combined GNPs in 1990 to 0.22 per cent, or $52.3 billion, in 2001.[13] Most ODA is allocated for

[13] UNDP (2003: 290), down from aggregate ODA of $53.7 billion in 2000 (UNDP 2002: 202) and $56.4 billion in 1999 (UNDP 2001: 190). The US has led the decline by reducing ODA from 0.21 to 0.11 per cent of GNP in a time of great prosperity

political effect: only 23 per cent goes to the 49 least developed countries;[14] and only $3.7 billion is spent on basic social services — basic education, basic health, population programmes, water supply, and sanitation — far less than the 20 per cent agreed to at the 1995 World Summit for Social Development. This is less than 1 per cent of the developed countries' 'peace dividend' (due to reduced military expenditures after the end of the Cold War) and comes to about $4 per year from each of us citizens of these countries, on average.

When people like us die at a mature age, we can look back on a lifespan in which over a billion human beings, mostly children, have died from poverty-related causes. This massive death toll was and is foreseeable. And it is clear beyond any reasonable doubt that the developed countries could dramatically reduce this continuous death toll and the associated misery at little cost to ourselves. And yet, very few citizens of the developed countries find these facts disturbing. This widespread unconcern can be explained, in large part, by a false view of why severe poverty persists. Most of us subscribe to the view that the causes of the persistence of severe poverty are indigenous to the countries in which it occurs. I am convinced that, with a better understanding of the role global institutional factors play in the persistence of severe poverty, many would take this problem much more seriously — including my esteemed teacher John Rawls.

References

Beitz, C. 1979. *Political Theory and International Relations*, Princeton University Press, Princeton.

Chen, S., and M. Ravallion. 2001. 'How Did the World's Poorest Fare in the 1990s?' *Review of Income and Wealth* 47(3): 283–300.

culminating in enormous budget surpluses. In coming years, ODA is set to increase in the aftermath of September 11 — the figure for 2001 already includes a special $600 million US disbursement toward stabilizing Pakistan's military dictator. (Remark added in 2011 by the author: ODA dispensed by the high-income countries has indeed grown back to 0.3 per cent of their GNP — still far short of the 0.7 per cent repeatedly promised in the 1970s. Of the $20.3 billion the US spent in 2010 on aid in specific developing countries, $2.98 billion went to Afghanistan, $2.35 billion to Iraq, $613 million to Pakistan, $64 million to Bangladesh, and $48 million to India.)

[14] Down from 28 per cent in 1990 (UNDP 2003: 290). India, with more poor people than any other country, receives ODA of $1.70 annually for each of its citizens, while dozens of much richer countries receive between $60 and $260 annually per capita (*ibid.*: 290–94).

Cohen, G. A. 1988. *History, Labour, and Freedom*, Clarendon Press, Oxford.

FAO (Food and Agriculture Organization of the United Nations). 1999. *The State of Food Insecurity in the World*, www.fao.org/news/1999/img/sofi99-e.pdf (accessed 1 January 2011).

Lam, Ricky, and Leonard Wantchekon. 1999. 'Dictatorships as a Political Dutch Disease', Working Paper, 19 January, Economic Growth Centre, Yale University, Centre Discussion Paper 795, www.nyarko.com/wantche1.pdf.

Pogge, T. W. 1989. *Realizing Rawls*, Cornell University Press, Ithaca.

———. 1994. 'An Egalitarian Law of Peoples', *Philosophy and Public Affairs* 23(3): 195–224.

——— (ed.). 2008 [2002]. *World Poverty and Human Rights*, Polity Press, Cambridge.

———. 2010. *Politics as Usual*, Polity Press, Cambridge.

Rawls, John. 1993. 'The Law of Peoples', in Stephen Shute and Susan Hurley (eds), *On Human Rights*, Basic Books, New York, 41–82.

———. 1999. *The Law of Peoples*, Harvard University Press, Cambridge, MA.

UNDP. 1998, 1999, 2001, 2002, 2003. *Human Development Report*, Oxford University Press, New York.

USDA (United States Department of Agriculture). 1999. *U.S. Action Plan on Food Security*, www.fas.usda.gov/icd/summit/usactplan.pdf.

World Bank. 2000/2001, 2003. *World Development Report*, Oxford University Press, New York.

3

The Problem of Global Justice

Thomas Nagel

We do not live in a just world. This may be the least controversial claim one could make in political theory. But it is much less clear what, if anything, justice on a world scale might mean, or what the hope for justice should lead us to want in the domain of international or global institutions, and in the policies of states that are in a position to affect the world order.

By comparison with the perplexing and undeveloped state of this subject, domestic political theory is very well understood, with multiple highly developed theories offering alternative solutions to well-defined problems. By contrast, concepts and theories of global justice are in the early stages of formation, and it is not clear what the main questions are, let alone the main possible answers. I believe that the need for workable ideas about the global or international case presents political theory with its most important current task, and even perhaps with the opportunity to make a practical contribution in the long run, though perhaps only the very long run.

The theoretical and normative questions I want to discuss are closely related to pressing practical questions that we now face about the legitimate path forward in the governance of the world. These are, inevitably, questions about institutions, many of which do not yet exist. However imperfectly, the nation-state is the primary locus of political legitimacy and the pursuit of justice, and it is one of the advantages of domestic political theory that nation-states actually exist. But when we are presented with the need for collective action on a global scale, it is very unclear what, if anything, could play a comparable role.

The concept of justice can be used in evaluating many different things, from the criminal law to the market economy. In a broad sense of the term, the international requirements of justice include standards governing the justification and conduct of war and standards that define the most basic human rights. Some standards of these two kinds have achieved a measure of international recognition over the past half-century. They define certain types of criminal conduct, usually by states, against other states or against individuals or ethnic groups. But this is not the aspect of global justice that I will concentrate on. My concern here is not with war crimes or crimes against humanity but with socio-economic justice, and whether anything can be made of it on a world scale.

I will approach the question by focusing on the application to the world as a whole of two central issues of traditional political theory: the relation between justice and sovereignty, and the scope and limits of equality as a demand of justice. The two issues are related, and both are of crucial importance in determining whether we can even form an intelligible ideal of global justice.

The issue of justice and sovereignty was memorably formulated by Hobbes. He argued that although we can discover true principles of justice by moral reasoning alone, actual justice cannot be achieved except within a sovereign state. Justice as a property of the relations among human beings (and also injustice, for the most part) requires government as an enabling condition. Hobbes drew the obvious consequence for the international arena, where he saw separate sovereigns inevitably facing each other in a state of war, from which both justice and injustice are absent.

The issue of justice and equality is posed with particular clarity by one of the controversies between Rawls and his critics. Rawls argued that the liberal requirements of justice include a strong component of equality among citizens, but that this is a specifically political demand, which applies to the basic structure of a unified nation-state. It does not apply to the personal (non-political) choices of individuals living in such a society, nor does it apply to the relations between one society and another, or between the members of different societies. Egalitarian justice is a requirement on the internal political, economic and social structure of nation-states and cannot be extrapolated to different contexts, which require different standards. This issue is independent of the specific standards of egalitarian justice found in Rawls's theory. Whatever standards of equal rights or equal opportunity apply domestically, the question is whether consistency requires that they also apply globally.

If Hobbes is right, the idea of global justice without a world government is a chimera. If Rawls is right, perhaps there can be something that might be called justice or injustice in the relations between states, but it bears only a distant relation to the evaluation of societies themselves as just or unjust: for the most part, the ideal of a just world for Rawls would have to be the ideal of a world of internally just states.

II

It seems to me very difficult to resist Hobbes's claim about the relation between justice and sovereignty. There is much more to his political theory than this, of course. Among other things, he based political legitimacy and the principles of justice on collective self-interest, rather than on any irreducibly moral premises. And he defended absolute monarchy as the best form of sovereignty. But the relation between justice and sovereignty is a separable question, and Hobbes's position can be defended in connection with theories of justice and moral evaluation very different from his.

What creates the link between justice and sovereignty is something common to a wide range of conceptions of justice: they all depend on the coordinated conduct of large numbers of people, which cannot be achieved without law backed up by a monopoly of force. Hobbes construed the principles of justice, and more broadly the moral law, as a set of rules and practices that would serve everyone's interest if everyone conformed to them. This collective self-interest cannot be realized by the independent motivation of self-interested individuals unless each of them has the assurance that others will conform if he does. That assurance requires the external incentive provided by the sovereign, who sees to it that individual and collective self-interest coincide. At least among sizable populations, it cannot be provided by voluntary conventions supported solely by the mutual recognition of a common interest.

But the same need for assurance is present if one construes the principles of justice differently, and attributes to individuals a non–self-interested motive that leads them to want to live on fair terms of some kind with other people. Even if justice is taken to include not only collective self-interest but also the elimination of morally arbitrary inequalities, or the protection of rights to liberty, the existence of a just order still depends on consistent patterns of conduct and persisting institutions that have a pervasive effect on the shape of people's lives. Separate individuals, however attached to such an ideal, have no motive, or even opportunity, to conform to such patterns or institutions on their own, without the assurance that their conduct will in fact be part of a reliable and effective system.

The only way to provide that assurance is through some form of law, with centralized authority to determine the rules and a centralized monopoly of the power of enforcement. This is needed even in a community most of whose members are attached to a common ideal of justice, both in order to provide terms of coordination and because it doesn't take many defectors to make such a system unravel. The kind of all-encompassing collective practice or institution that is capable of being just in the primary sense can exist only under sovereign government. It is only the operation of such a system that one can judge to be just or unjust.

According to Hobbes, in the absence of the enabling condition of sovereign power, individuals are famously thrown back on their own resources and led by the legitimate motive of self-preservation to a defensive, distrustful posture of war. They hope for the conditions of peace and justice and support their creation whenever it seems safe to do so, but they cannot pursue justice by themselves.

I believe that the situation is structurally not very different for conceptions of justice that are based on much more other-regarding motives. Without the enabling condition of sovereignty to confer stability on just institutions, individuals however morally motivated can only fall back on a pure aspiration for justice that has no practical expression, apart from the willingness to support just institutions should they become possible.

The other-regarding motives that support adherence to just institutions when they exist do not provide clear guidance where the enabling conditions for such institutions do not exist, as seems to be true for the world as a whole. Those motives, even if they make us dissatisfied with our relations to other human beings, are baffled and left without an avenue of expression, except for the expression of moral frustration.

III

Hobbes himself was not disturbed by the appearance of this problem in the international case, since he believed that the essential aim of justice, collective security and self-interest, could be effectively provided for individuals through the sovereignty of separate states. In a famous passage, he says:

> In all times, kings, and persons of sovereign authority, because of their independency, are in continual jealousies, and in the state and posture of gladiators; having their weapons pointing, and their eyes fixed on one another; that is, their forts, garrisons, and guns upon the frontiers of their kingdoms; and continual spies upon their neighbours; which is a posture of war. But because they uphold thereby, the industry of their subjects; there does not follow from it, that misery, which accompanies the liberty of particular men. (Hobbes 1976: 87)

The absence of sovereignty over the globe, in other words, is not a serious obstacle to justice in the relations among the citizens of each sovereign state, and that is what matters.

This position is more problematic for those who do not share Hobbes's belief that the foundation of justice is collective self-interest and that the attachment of any individual to just institutions is based solely on his own good. If Hobbes were right, a person's interest in justice would be served provided he himself lived in a stable society governed in accordance with the rules of peace, security and economic order. But for most of us, the ideal of justice stems from moral motives that cannot be entirely reduced to self-interest.

It includes much more than a condition of legally enforced peace and security among interacting individuals, together with stable property rights and the reliability of contracts. Most modern conceptions of justice impose some limits on the powers of sovereignty — in the name of non-Hobbesian individual rights to liberty — and some condition of fairness or equality in the way the institutions of a just society treat its citizens, not only politically but economically and socially. It is this last element that creates unease over the complete absence of any comparable standards of fairness or equality of opportunity from the practices that govern our relations with individuals in other societies.

The gruesome facts of inequality in the world economy are familiar. Roughly 20 per cent of the world's population live on less than a dollar a day, and more than 45 per cent live on less than two dollars a day, whereas the 15 per cent who live in the high-income economies have an average per capita income of seventy-five dollars a day (Pogge 2002: 97–99; Stiglitz 2002: 25). How are we to respond to such facts?

There is a peculiar problem here for our discussion: the facts are so grim that justice may be a side issue. Whatever view one takes of the applicability or inapplicability of standards of justice to such a situation, it is clearly a disaster from a more broadly humanitarian point of view. I assume there is some minimal concern we owe to fellow human beings threatened with starvation or severe malnutrition and early death from easily preventable diseases, as all these people in dire poverty are. Although there is plenty of room for disagreement about the most effective methods, some form of humane assistance from the well-off to those in extremis is clearly called for quite apart from any demand of justice, if we are not simply ethical egoists. The urgent current issue is what can be done in the world economy to reduce extreme global poverty.

These more basic duties of humanity also present serious problems of what we should do individually and collectively to fulfil them in the absence of global sovereignty, and in spite of the obstacles often presented by malfunctioning state sovereignty. But now I am posing a different question, one that is morally less urgent but philosophically harder. Justice as ordinarily understood requires more than mere humanitarian assistance to those in desperate need, and injustice can exist without anyone being on the verge of starvation.

Humanitarian duties hold in virtue of the absolute rather than the relative level of need of the people we are in a position to help. Justice, by contrast, is concerned with the relations between the conditions of different classes of people, and the causes of inequality between them. My question is about how to respond to world inequality in general from the point of view of justice and injustice rather than humanity alone. The answer to that question will depend crucially on one's moral conception of the relation between the value of justice and the existence of the institutions that sovereign authority makes possible. There are two principal conceptions that I want to consider.

According to the first conception, which is usually called *cosmopolitanism*, the demands of justice derive from an equal concern or a duty of fairness that we owe in principle to all our fellow human beings, and the institutions to which standards of justice can be applied are instruments for the fulfilment of that duty. Such instruments are in fact only selectively available: we may be able to live on just terms only with those others who are fellow members of sufficiently robust and well-ordered sovereign states. But the moral basis for the requirements of justice that should govern those states is universal in scope: it is a concern for the fairness of the terms on which we share the world with anyone (Beitz 1979; Pogge 1989: 240–80; Singer 2002).

If one takes the cosmopolitan view, the existence of separate sovereign states is an unfortunate obstacle, though perhaps for the foreseeable future an insurmountable one, to the establishment or even the pursuit of global justice. But it would be morally inconsistent not to wish, for the world as a whole, a common system of institutions that could attempt to realize the same standards of fairness or equal opportunity that one wants for one's own society. The accident of being born in a poor rather than a rich country is as arbitrary a determinant of one's fate as the accident of being born into a poor rather than a rich family in the same country. In the absence of global sovereignty we may not be able to describe the world order as *un*just, but the absence of justice is a defect all the same.

Cosmopolitan justice could be realized in a federal system, in which the members of individual nation-states had special responsibilities toward one another that they did not have for everyone in the world. But that would be legitimate only against the background of a global system that prevented such special responsibilities from generating injustice on a larger scale. This would be analogous to the requirement that within a state, the institutions of private property, which allow people to pursue their private ends without constantly taking into account the aims of justice, should nevertheless be arranged so that societal injustice is not their indirect consequence.

Unlike cosmopolitanism, the second conception of justice does not have a standard name, but let me call it the *political* conception, since it is exemplified by Rawls's view that justice should be understood as a specifically political value, rather than being derived from a comprehensive moral system, so that it is essentially a virtue — the first virtue — of social institutions.

On the political conception, sovereign states are not merely instruments for realizing the pre-institutional value of justice among human beings. Instead, their existence is precisely what gives the value of justice its application, by putting the fellow citizens of a sovereign state into a relation that they do not have with the rest of humanity, an institutional relation which must then be evaluated by the special standards of fairness and equality that fill out the content of justice.

Another representative of the political conception is Ronald Dworkin, who expresses it this way:

> A political community that exercises dominion over its own citizens, and demands from them allegiance and obedience to its laws, must take up an impartial, objective attitude toward them all, and each of its citizens must vote, and its officials must enact laws and form governmental policies, with that responsibility in mind. Equal concern . . . is the special and indispensable virtue of sovereigns. (Dworkin 2000: 6)

Every state has the boundaries and population it has for all sorts of accidental and historical reasons; but given that it exercises sovereign power over its citizens and in their name, those citizens have a duty of justice toward one another through the legal, social and economic institutions that sovereign power makes possible. This duty is *sui generis,* and is not owed to everyone in the world, nor is it an indirect consequence of any other duty that may be owed to everyone in the world, such as a duty of humanity. Justice is something we owe through our shared institutions only to those with whom we stand in a strong political relation. It is, in the standard terminology, an *associative* obligation.

Furthermore, though the obligations of justice arise as a result of a special relation, there is no obligation to enter into that relation with those to whom we do not yet have it, thereby acquiring those obligations toward them. If we find ourselves in such a relation, then we must accept the obligations, but we do not have to seek them out, and may even try to avoid incurring them, as with other contingent obligations of a more personal kind: one does not have to marry and have children, for example.

If one takes this political view, one will not find the absence of global justice a cause for distress. There is a lot else to be distressed about: world misery, for example, and also the egregious internal injustice of so many of the world's sovereign states. Someone who accepts the political conception of justice may even hold that there is a secondary duty to promote just institutions for societies that do not have them. But the requirements of justice themselves do not, on this view, apply to the world as a whole, unless and until, as a result of historical developments not required by justice, the world comes to be governed by a unified sovereign power.

The political conception of justice therefore arrives, by a different route, at the same conclusion as Hobbes: the full standards of justice, though they can be known by moral reasoning, apply only within the boundaries of a sovereign state, however arbitrary those boundaries may be. Internationally, there may well be standards, but they do not merit the full name of justice.

IV

On either the cosmopolitan or the political view, global justice would require global sovereignty. But there is still a huge difference between the two views in the attitude they take toward this conclusion. On the political view, the absence of global justice need not be a matter of regret; on the cosmopolitan view, it is, and the obstacles to global sovereignty pose a serious moral problem. Let me consider the issue of principle between the two conceptions. While we should keep in mind that different views about the content of justice can be combined with either of these two conceptions of its scope, I will continue to use Rawls to exemplify the political view. But most of what I will say is independent of the main disagreements over the content of domestic justice — political, economic or social.

Rawls's political conception of justice is an example of a more general feature of his approach to moral theory, his rejection of what Liam Murphy calls *monism*. Murphy has introduced this term to designate the idea that 'any plausible overall political/moral view must, at the fundamental level, evaluate the justice of institutions with normative principles that apply also to people's choices.' The opposite view, which Murphy calls dualism, is that 'the two practical problems of institutional design and personal conduct require, at the fundamental level, two different kinds of practical principle' (Murphy 1998: 253–54). (The term 'dualism' is not ideal for the contrast, since, as we shall see, there are more than two levels at which independent moral principles may apply.)

Rawls is famous for insisting that different principles apply to different types of entities: that 'the correct regulative principle for a thing depends on the nature of that thing' (Rawls 1999a: 25). The most noted instance of this is his argument against utilitarianism, which he criticizes for applying to a society of individuals the principles of aggregating and maximizing net benefits minus costs that are appropriate within the life of a single individual, but inappropriate for groups of individuals. 'Utilitarianism', he says, 'does not take seriously the distinction between persons' (*ibid.*: 24).

But the point applies more widely. Rawls's anti-monism is essential to understanding both his domestic theory of a just society and his view of the relation between domestic and international principles, as expressed in *The Law of Peoples*. His two principles of justice are designed to regulate neither the personal conduct of individuals living in a just society, nor the governance of private associations, nor the international relations of societies to one another, but only the basic structure of separate nation-states. It is the nature of sovereign states, he believes, and in particular their comprehensive control over the framework of their citizens' lives, that creates the special demands for justification and the special constraints on ends and means that constitute the requirements of justice.

In Rawls's domestic theory this expresses itself in two ways: first, in the priority of individual liberty, which leaves people free to pursue their own personal ends rather than requiring them to pursue just outcomes privately; and, second, in the application of the difference principle not to the distribution of advantages and disadvantages to individuals, but rather to the probabilistic distribution of ex ante life prospects (which always include a range) to those born into different socio-economic classes. Even if the basic structure supported by law satisfies the difference principle by arranging inequalities to maximize the expectations of the lowest class in this sense, individual choices are not expected to be governed by that principle. Those choices will result in substantial inequalities in actual outcomes among individuals within each socio-economic class, in addition to the inequalities in ex ante life prospects between classes permitted by the difference principle itself.

So Rawls's egalitarianism does not apply either to individual morality or to individual outcomes within the bounds of an egalitarian state. But neither does it apply to the relations between states, nor between the individual members of different states. These are all different cases or types of relation, and the principles that govern them have to be arrived at separately. They cannot be reached by extending to the international case the principles of domestic justice.

Internationally, Rawls finds the main expression of moral constraints not in a relation among individuals but in a limited requirement of mutual respect and equality of status among peoples. This is more constraining than the traditional Hobbesian privileges of sovereignty on the world stage; it is a substantial moral order, far from the state of nature. But the moral units of the order are peoples, not individuals, and the values have to do with the relations among these collective units rather than the relations of individuals across the world.

Just as, within a state, what we owe one another as fellow citizens through our common institutions is very different from what we owe one another as private individuals, so internationally, what we owe to other inhabitants of the globe through our society's respect for the societies of which they are citizens is different both from what we owe to our fellow citizens and from what we as individuals owe to all our fellow human beings. The duties governing the relations among peoples include, according to Rawls, not only non-aggression and fidelity to treaties, but also some developmental assistance to 'peoples living under unfavorable conditions that prevent their having a just or decent political and social regime' (Rawls 1999b: 37). But they do not include any analogue of liberal socio-economic justice.

This limitation is rejected by cosmopolitan critics of Rawls. The issue is the choice of moral units. The monist idea is that the basic constituency for all morality must be individuals, not societies or peoples, and that whatever moral requirements apply either to social institutions or to international relations must ultimately be justified by their effects on individuals — and by a morality that governs the treatment of all individuals by all other individuals.

From this point of view it seems natural to conclude that any such morality must count all individual lives as equally valuable or important, and that in particular it must not allow international boundaries to count at the most basic level in determining how one individual should take into consideration the interests of another. The consequence seems to be that if one wants to avoid moral inconsistency, and is sympathetic to Rawls's theory of justice, one should favour a global difference principle, perhaps backed up by a global original position in which all individuals are represented behind the veil of ignorance.

But whatever we think about the original position, Rawls must resist the charge that moral consistency requires him to take individuals as the moral units in a conception of global justice. To do so would make a huge difference, for it would mean that applying the principles of justice within the bounds of the nation-state was at best a practical stop-gap.

Rawls's anti-monism is in essence a theoretical rejection of such standards for moral consistency. Just as there is no inconsistency in governing interpersonal relations by principles very different from those that govern legal institutions, so there need be no inconsistency in governing the world differently from its political subdivisions. But if what we are looking for is moral, and not just logical, consistency, the differences between the cases must in some way explain why different principles are appropriate.

The way to resist cosmopolitanism fundamentally would be to deny that there is a universal pressure toward equal concern, equal status and equal opportunity. One could admit a universal humanitarian requirement of minimal concern (which, even in the world as it is, would not be terribly onerous, provided all the prosperous countries did their share). But the defence of the political conception of justice would have to hold that beyond the basic humanitarian duties, further requirements of equal treatment depend on a strong condition of associative responsibility, that such responsibility is created by specific and contingent relations such as fellow citizenship, and that there is no general moral requirement to take responsibility for others by getting into those sorts of relations with as many of them as possible.

This would still count as a universal principle, but it would imply a strongly differentiated system of moral obligations. If the conditions of even the poorest societies should come to meet a livable minimum, the political conception might not even see a general humanitarian claim for redistribution. This makes it a very convenient view for those living in rich societies to hold. But that alone doesn't make it false.

V

I find the choice between these two incompatible moral conceptions difficult. The cosmopolitan conception has considerable moral appeal, because it seems highly arbitrary that the average individual born into a poor society should have radically lower life prospects than the average individual born into a rich one, just as arbitrary as the corresponding difference between rich and poor in a rich but unjust society. The cosmopolitan conception points us toward the utopian goal of trying to extend legitimate democratic governance to ever-larger domains in pursuit of more global justice.

But I will not explore that possibility further. Without trying to refute cosmopolitanism I will instead pursue a fuller account of the grounds and content of the political conception. I am going to follow this fork in the path partly because I believe the political conception is accepted by most people in the privileged nations of the world, so that, true or false, it will have a significant role in determining what happens. I also think it is probably correct.

Let me try to spell out the kind of political conception that seems to me plausible. Even though I am sceptical about grounding it in a hypothetical contract of the type Rawls proposes, its debt to the social contract tradition will be obvious.

We can begin by noting that even on the political conception, some conditions of justice do not depend on associative obligations. The protection, under sovereign power, of negative rights like bodily inviolability, freedom of expression and freedom of religion is morally unmysterious. Those rights, if they exist, set universal and pre-political limits to the legitimate use of power, independent of special forms of association. It is wrong for any individual or group to deny such rights to any other individual or group, and we do not give them up as a condition of membership in a political society, even though their precise boundaries and methods of protection through law will have to be determined politically in light of each society's particular circumstances.

Socio-economic justice is different. On the political conception it is fully associative. It depends on positive rights that we do not have against all other persons or groups, rights that arise only because we are joined together with certain others in a political society under strong centralized control. It is only from such a system, and from our fellow members through its institutions, that we can claim a right to democracy, equal citizenship, non-discrimination, equality of opportunity, and the amelioration through public policy of unfairness in the distribution of social and economic goods.

In presenting the intuitive moral case for the particular principles of justice he favours as the embodiment of these ideals, Rawls appeals repeatedly to the importance of eliminating or reducing morally arbitrary sources of inequality in people's life prospects (Rawls 2001). He means inequalities flowing from characteristics of people that they have done nothing to deserve, like their race, their sex, the wealth or poverty of their parents, and their inborn natural endowments. To the extent that such factors, through the operation of a particular social system, generate differences in people's expectations, at birth, of better or worse lives, they present a problem for the justification of that system. In some respects these arbitrary sources of inequality can be eliminated, but Rawls holds that where they remain, some other justification needs to be found for permitting them.

The important point for our purposes is that Rawls believes that this moral presumption against arbitrary inequalities is not a principle of universal application. It might have considerable appeal if recast as a universal principle, to the effect that there is something prima facie objectionable to anyone's having lower life prospects at birth than anyone else just because of a difference between the two of them, such as the wealth of their parents or their nationality, over which neither of them had any control. But this is not the principle Rawls is appealing to. Rather, in his theory the objection to arbitrary inequalities gets a foothold only because of the societal context. What is objectionable is that we should be fellow participants in a collective enterprise of coercively imposed legal and political institutions that generates such arbitrary inequalities.

What is interesting and somewhat surprising about this condition is that such co-membership is itself arbitrary, so an arbitrary distinction is responsible for the scope of the presumption against arbitrariness. We do not deserve to have been born into a particular society any more than we deserve to have been born into a particular family. Those who are not immigrants have done nothing to become members of their society. The egalitarian requirement is based not on actual choice, consent or contract, but on involuntary membership. It is only the internal character of the system in which we arbitrarily find ourselves that gives rise to the special presumption against further arbitrary distinctions within it.

Since there are equally arbitrary extrasocietal distinctions that do not carry the same moral weight, the ground for the presumption cannot be merely that these intrasocietal inequalities have a profound effect on people's lives. The fact that they shape people's life prospects from birth is necessary but not sufficient to explain the presumption against them. So what is the additional necessary condition?

I believe it comes from a special involvement of agency or the will that is inseparable from membership in a political society. Not the will to become or remain a member, for most people have no choice in that regard, but the engagement of the will that is essential to life inside a society, in the dual role each member plays both as one of the society's subjects and as one of those in whose name its authority is exercised. One might even say that we are all participants in the general will.

A sovereign state is not just a cooperative enterprise for mutual advantage. The societal rules determining its basic structure are coercively imposed: it is not a voluntary association. I submit that it is this complex fact — that we are both putative joint authors of the coercively imposed system, and subject to its norms, i.e., expected to accept their authority even when the collective decision diverges from our personal preferences — that creates the special presumption against arbitrary inequalities in our treatment by the system.

Without being given a choice, we are assigned a role in the collective life of a particular society. The society makes us responsible for its acts, which are taken in our name and on which, in a democracy, we may even have some influence; and it holds us responsible for obeying its laws and conforming to its norms, thereby supporting the institutions through which advantages and disadvantages are created and distributed. Insofar as those institutions admit arbitrary inequalities, we are, even though the responsibility has been simply handed to us, responsible for them, and we therefore have standing to ask why we should accept them. This request for justification has moral weight even if we have in practice no choice but to live under the existing regime. The reason is that its requirements claim our active cooperation, and this cannot be legitimately done without justification — otherwise it is pure coercion.

The required active engagement of the will of each member of the society in its operation is crucial. It is not enough to appeal to the large material effects that the system imposes on its members. The immigration policies of one country may impose large effects on the lives of those living in other countries, but under the political conception that by itself does not imply that such policies should be determined in a way that gives the interests and opportunities of those others equal consideration. Immigration policies are simply enforced against the nationals of other states; the laws are not imposed in their name, nor are they asked to accept and uphold those laws. Since no acceptance is demanded of them, no justification is required that explains why they should accept such discriminatory policies, or why their interests have been given equal consideration. It is sufficient justification to claim that the policies do not violate their pre-political human rights.

That does not mean that on the political conception one state may do anything whatever to the citizens of another. States are entitled to be left to their own devices, but only on the condition that they not harm others. Even a nation's immunity from the need to justify to outsiders the limits on access to its territory is not absolute. In extreme circumstances, denial of the right of immigration may constitute a failure to respect human rights or the universal duty of rescue. This is recognized in special provisions for political asylum, for example. The most basic rights and duties are universal, and not contingent on specific institutional relations between people. Only the heightened requirements of equal treatment embodied in principles of justice, including political equality, equality of opportunity and distributive justice, are contingent in this way.

To be sure, even within a state, through economic competition for example, some members or associations of members may impose serious consequences on others without any implication that the others are asked to accept or authorize the actions that have those consequences. Citizens are not expected to treat each other equally in private transactions. But the broader legal framework that makes those actions possible and that legally sustains their results is subject to collective authority and justification and therefore to principles of social justice: not act by act, but for the system as a whole.

In short, the state makes unique demands on the will of its members — or the members make unique demands on one another through the institutions of the state — and those exceptional demands bring with them exceptional obligations, the positive obligations of justice. Those obligations reach no farther than the demands do and that explains the special character of the political conception.

VI

What is the overall moral outlook that best fits the political conception of justice? Although it is based on a rejection of monism and does not derive its content from a universal moral relation in which we stand to all persons, the political conception does not deny that there is such a relation. Political institutions create contingent, selective moral relations, but there are also non-contingent, universal relations in which we stand to everyone, and political justice is surrounded by this larger moral context.

The normative force of the most basic human rights against violence, enslavement and coercion, and of the most basic humanitarian duties of rescue from immediate danger, depends only on our capacity to put ourselves in other people's shoes. The interests protected by such moral requirements are so fundamental, and the burdens they impose, considered statistically, so much slighter, that a criterion of universalizability of the Kantian type clearly supports them. I say 'statistically' because the restrictions implied by individual rights can in particular cases be very demanding: you may not kill an innocent person to save your life, for example. But the importance to all of us of blanket immunity from such violation dominates the slight danger that we will be called on to lose our lives rather than violate the constraint. This is based not on a utilitarian calculation but on the great importance to each person of the kind of inviolability conferred by rights. Rights are a guarantee to each of us of a certain protected status, rather than a net benefit to the aggregate.

This minimal humanitarian morality governs our relation to all other persons. It does not require us to make their ends our own, but it does require us to pursue our ends within boundaries that leave them free to pursue theirs, and to relieve them from extreme threats and obstacles to such freedom if we can do so without serious sacrifice of our own ends. I take this to be the consequence of the type of contractualist standard expressed by Kant's categorical imperative and developed in one version by Scanlon. To specify it any less vaguely would require a full moral theory, which I will not attempt even to sketch here.

This moral minimum does not depend on the existence of any institutional connection between ourselves and other persons: it governs our relations with everyone in the world. However, it may be impossible to fulfil even our minimal moral duties to others without the help of institutions of some kind short of sovereignty. We do not need institutions to enable us to refrain from violating other people's rights, but institutions are indispensable to enable us to fulfil the duty of rescue toward people in dire straits all over the world. Further, it seems clear that human rights generate a secondary obligation to do something, if we can, to protect people outside of our society against their most egregious violation, and this is practically impossible, on a world scale, without some institutionalized methods of verification and enforcement.

The first of these roles, that of rescue, can be filled to some extent by NGOs that operate internationally but privately, providing individuals with the opportunity to contribute to relief of famine and disease. Even the second role, protection of rights, has its private institutional actors in the form of organizations like Amnesty International and Human Rights Watch. But successful action on a much larger scale would be possible through international institutions supported by governments, both with funds and with enforcement. The World Bank is in some respects such an institution, and the International Criminal Court aspires to be. The question is whether international developments will countenance the bending of national sovereignty needed to extend the authority of such institutions, both to command funds and to curb domestic rights violations with force, if necessary.

But even if this is the direction of global governance for the future, there remains a clear line, according to the political conception of justice, between the call for such institutions and a call for the institution of global socio-economic justice. Everyone may have the right to live in a just society, but we do not have an obligation to live in a just society with everyone. The right to justice is the right that the society one lives in be justly governed. Any claims this creates against other societies and their members are distinctly secondary to those it creates against one's fellow citizens.

Is this stark division of levels of responsibility morally acceptable, or is it too radical an exclusion of humanity at large from full moral concern? The answer from the point of view of the political conception must be that there is no single level of full moral concern, because morality is essentially multilayered.

Even within the framework of a just society special obligations arise from contingent personal relations and voluntary associations or undertakings by individuals. The whole point of the political conception is that social justice itself is a rise in exclusive obligation, but with a broader associative range and from a lower moral baseline than the personal obligations. And it depends on the contingency of involuntary rather than voluntary association.

Perhaps this move to a new moral level can be best understood as a consequence of the more basic obligation, emphasized by both Hobbes and Kant, that all humans have to create and support a state of some kind — to leave and stay out of the state of nature. It is not an obligation to all other persons, in fact it has no clear boundaries; it is merely an obligation to create the conditions of peace and a legal order, with whatever community offers itself.

This requirement is based not on a comprehensive value of equality, but on the imperative of securing basic rights, which can be done more or less locally. But once the state exists, we are in a new moral situation, where the value of equality has purchase. The difference between the political and the cosmopolitan conceptions is that the latter sees the formation of the state as answering also a universal demand for equality, even if as a practical matter it can be realized only locally. On the political conception, by contrast, the only universal requirement of equality is conditional in form: we are required to accord equal status to anyone with whom we are joined in a strong and coercively imposed political community.

Some standard of universalizability underlies even this conditional requirement. It is part of a multilayered conception of morality, shaped by the Kantian ideal of a kingdom of ends whose members do not share a common set of ends. The heightened obligations that arise from contingent particular associations do not subtract from a prior condition of universal concern, but rather move our moral relations selectively to a new level, at which more ends and responsibilities are shared. The universality of this morality consists in its applying to anyone who happens to be or to become a member of our society: no one is excluded in advance, and in that sense all persons are regarded as morally equal.

Such a morality also leaves space for voluntary combinations in the pursuit of common ends, which are not in general governed by standards of equality. But political institutions are different, because adherence to them is not voluntary: emigration aside, one is not permitted to declare oneself not a member of one's society and hence not subject to its rules, and other members may coerce one's compliance if one tries to refuse. An institution that one has no choice about joining must offer terms of membership that meet a higher standard.

VII

My thoughts about this subject were kindled by Rawls's treatment of the ethics of international relations in *The Law of Peoples*, but his approach is different, so let me say something about it. First of all, he poses the question not as a general one about international obligations or global justice, but as a question about what principles should govern the foreign policy of a liberal society. So it is an elaboration of his account of a just society, rather than an independent account of a just world. And he sees the answer to this question as having to do primarily with how such a society should deal with the other societies with which it shares the world, whether these be liberal, or non-liberal but still 'decent', in his term, or whether they be outlaw societies that fail to respect human rights and the restraints of international law.

As already noted, the moral units of this international morality are not individual human beings but separate societies, or 'peoples', and it is equality among these collective units that is the basis of Rawls's conception. For that reason Charles Beitz has given it the name *social liberalism*, to contrast it with his own view, which he calls *cosmopolitan liberalism* (Beitz 1979: 214–16; Beitz 2000). Our obligations as members of a liberal society toward the members of other societies are not direct, but are filtered through the relations between our societies. That is because, as Rawls puts it, societies have a 'moral nature', which deserves equal respect, provided they meet the basic conditions of decency. But individuals per se are not entitled to equal treatment internationally.

Rawls holds that the requirement of equal respect for other peoples is strong enough to impose on liberal societies a tolerance for non-liberal states that meet a minimal condition of decency, so that the foreign policy of a liberal state should not have the aim of moving all other societies toward liberalism, if possible. This is analogous to the restraint liberalism imposes internally against the use of state power to promote a particular comprehensive moral or religious view. It is surprising that internationally, equal respect should result precisely in toleration for the absence of such restraint in non-liberal societies. But Rawls believes that this consequence follows if we accord a moral nature and a moral right of equality to peoples, which are not themselves derived from the equality of individuals, and which take precedence over domestic liberal values in the international case.

The claims of individuals take over only at a much lower threshold, that of basic human rights. A society that does not respect the human rights of its subjects forfeits, in Rawls's view, the moral status that demands respect, equality and non-interference. But that is not necessarily true of a theocratic society with no elections, for example, provided it does not persecute minorities and observes due process of law (Rawls 1999b: 75–78).

This seems to me a mistake. The political conception of justice need not be based on the strong personification of peoples and need not imply the principled toleration of non-liberal societies. I would take a more individualistic position than Rawls does. The question of international toleration is difficult, but I believe that although there are obvious practical reasons for liberal societies not to try to impose liberal domestic justice universally, there are no moral reasons for restraint of the kind Rawls offers. It is more plausible to say that liberal states are not obliged either to tolerate non-liberal states or to try to transform them, because the duties of justice are essentially duties to our fellow citizens. But there seems nothing wrong with being particularly supportive of transformations in a liberal direction.

Whether other basic international obligations, such as those embodied in just war theory, can be accounted for without the moral personification of peoples is another question, but I would give a similar answer. People engaged in a legitimate collective enterprise deserve respect and non-interference, especially if it is an obligatory enterprise like the provision of security, law and social peace. We owe it to other people — considered as individuals — to allow them, and to some degree enable them, to collectively help themselves. So respect for the autonomy of other societies can be thought of as respect for the human rights of their members, rather than as respect for the equality of peoples, taken as moral units in their own right.

Rawls's conception is that sovereignty is constrained internally by the moral equality of individuals who are subjects of the state, but that the same force does not operate externally: from outside, sovereignty is constrained by the moral equality of other peoples, which imposes requirements even on a state that does not owe their members what it owes its own. I am prepared to accept the first part of this claim, about the source of internal constraints, but would offer universal human rights rather than the equality of peoples or societies as the source of the constraints on the external exercise of sovereign power.

VIII

The implications of the political conception for world politics tend to be conservative, but that is not the end of the story; the conservatism comes under pressure from powerful forces in the other direction. The source of that pressure lies both in existing global or international institutions and in the increasingly felt need to strengthen such institutions and to create new ones, for three types of purpose: the protection of human rights; the provision of humanitarian aid; and the provision of global public goods that benefit everyone, such as free trade, collective security and environmental protection. Institutions that serve these purposes are not designed to extend democratic legitimacy and socio-economic justice, but they naturally give rise to claims for both, in respect to their design and functioning. And they put pressure on national sovereignty by their need for power to be effective. They thus present a clearly perceived threat to the limits on claims of justice imposed by the political conception.

This poses a familiar dilemma: prosperous nations have reasons to want more governance on a world scale, but they do not want the increased obligations and demands for legitimacy that may follow in its wake. They do not want to increase the range of those to whom they are obliged as they are toward their own citizens; and this reflects the convictions of their citizens, not just of their governments.

Resistance to the erosion of sovereignty has resulted in the US refusal to join the Kyoto Treaty on atmospheric emissions and the International Criminal Court, decisions that have been widely criticized. Similar questions arise over who is to determine the policies of the International Monetary Fund and the World Bank, and over the authority of the United Nations in matters of international peace and security. But by far the most important institutions from this point of view are those of the international economy itself.

The global economy, within which the familiar inequalities are now generated, requires a stable international system of property rights and contractual obligations that provide the conditions for international commerce. These include: the rights of sovereign states to sell or confer legal title to the exploitation of their natural resources internationally; their right to borrow internationally and to create obligations of repayment on successor governments; the rights of commercial enterprises in one country to establish or acquire subsidiaries in other countries, and to profit from such investments; international extensions of antitrust law; regulation of financial markets to permit the orderly international flow of capital; the laws of patent and copyright; the rules of international trade, including penalties for violations of agreed restrictions on protective tariffs, dumping, preferential subsidies, and so forth. Many of the goods that contemporary persons consume, or their components, are produced in other countries. We are clearly in some kind of institutional relation — legal and economic — with people the world over.

This brings us to an issue that is internal to the political conception, rather than being about the choice between the political and the cosmopolitan conceptions. Some would argue that the present level of world economic interdependence already brings into force a version of the political conception of justice, so that Rawls's principles, or some alternative principles of distributive justice, are applicable over the domain covered by the existing cooperative institutions (Barry 1973: 128–33). This would be a very strong result, but I believe that it is not the case, precisely because such institutions do not rise to the level of statehood.

The absence of sovereign authority over participant states and their members not only makes it practically infeasible for such institutions to pursue justice but also makes them, under the political conception, an inappropriate site for claims of justice. For such claims to become applicable it is not enough that a number of individuals or groups be engaged in a collective activity that serves their mutual advantage. Mere economic interaction does not trigger the heightened standards of socio-economic justice.

Current international rules and institutions may be the thin end of a wedge that will eventually expand to seriously dislodge the dominant sovereignty of separate nation-states, both morally and politically, but for the moment they lack something that according to the political conception is crucial for the application and implementation of standards of justice: they are not collectively enacted and coercively imposed in the name of all the individuals whose lives they affect; and they do not ask for the kind of authorization by individuals that carries with it a responsibility to treat all those individuals in some sense equally. Instead, they are set up by bargaining among mutually self-interested sovereign parties. International institutions act not in the name of individuals, but in the name of the states or state instruments and agencies that have created them. Hence the responsibility of those institutions toward individuals is filtered through the states that represent and bear primary responsibility for those individuals.

But while international governance falls far short of global sovereignty, and is ultimately dependent on the sovereignty of separate states, international institutions are not all alike. Some involve delegation of authority, by states, to a supranational institution, generally by treaty, where this amounts to a partial limitation of sovereignty. Under NAFTA, for example, the domestic courts of the United States, Canada and Mexico are expected to enforce the judgements of its tribunals. And judgements of the European Court of Justice are enforced by the national courts of member states of the European Union.

Then there are the traditional international organizations, such as the UN, the WHO, the IMF, and the World Bank, which are controlled and financed by their member states and are empowered to act in various ways to pursue agreed-upon goals, but are not, with the exception of the Security Council, empowered to exercise coercive enforcement against states or individuals. Even the coercive authority of the Security Council is primarily a form of collective self-defence exercised by traditional sovereign powers, although there is some erosion of sovereignty in the move toward intervention to prevent domestic genocide.

Finally, there are a number of less formal structures that are responsible for a great deal of international governance — structures that have been enlighteningly described by Anne-Marie Slaughter in her recent book on government networks (Slaughter 2004). Such networks typically bring together officials of different countries with a common area of expertise and responsibility, who meet or communicate regularly, harmonize their practices and policies, and operate by consensus, without having been granted decision-making authority by any treaty. Examples are networks of environmental regulators, antitrust regulators, central bankers, finance ministers, securities commissioners, insurance supervisors, or police officials. The Basel Committee on Banking Supervision, for example, 'is now composed of the representatives of thirteen central banks that regulate the world's largest banking markets' (*ibid.*: 43).

It has developed standards for the division of tasks between home-country and host-country regulators, and has set uniform capital adequacy standards. Agreements are reached by consensus and implemented by the central banks themselves, acting under the sovereign authority of their several states. Slaughter argues that networks of this kind, which link the disaggregated subparts of sovereign states sharing common competences and responsibilities rather than the (notionally) unitary states themselves, will become increasingly important in global governance, and should be recognized as the wave of the future.

It is a convincing case. It is important to recognize that the traditional model of international organizations based on treaties between sovereign states has been transcended. Nevertheless, I believe that the newer forms of international governance share with the old a markedly indirect relation to individual citizens and that this is morally significant. All these networks bring together representatives not of individuals, but of state functions and institutions. Those institutions are responsible to their own citizens and may have a significant role to play in the support of social justice for those citizens. But a global or regional network does not have a similar responsibility of social justice for the combined citizenry of all the states involved, a responsibility that if it existed would have to be exercised collectively by the representatives of the member states. Rather, the aim of such institutions is to find ways in which the member states, or state-parts, can cooperate to better advance their separate aims, which will presumably include the pursuit of domestic social justice in some form. Very importantly, they rely for enforcement on the power of the separate sovereign states, not of a supranational force responsible to all.

Individuals are not the constituents of such institutions. Even if the more powerful states are motivated to some extent by humanitarian concerns to shape the rules in consideration of the weakest and poorest members of the international community, that does not change the situation fundamentally. Justice is not merely the pursuit of common aims by unequal parties whose self-interest is softened by charity. Justice, on the political conception, requires a collectively imposed social framework, enacted in the name of all those governed by it, and aspiring to command their acceptance of its authority even when they disagree with the substance of its decisions.

Justice applies, in other words, only to a form of organization that claims political legitimacy and the right to impose decisions by force, and not to a voluntary association or contract among independent parties concerned to advance their common interests. I believe this holds even if the natural incentives to join such an association, and the costs of exit, are substantial, as is true of some international organizations and agreements. There is a difference between voluntary association, however strongly motivated, and coercively imposed collective authority.

IX

A second, somewhat different objection to this limitation of justice to the nation-state is that it assumes an unrealistically sharp dichotomy between sovereign states and existing global institutions with respect to agency, authorization and authority. So even if economic globalization does not trigger the full standards of social justice, it entails them in a modified form.

In fact, according to this objection, there is a sliding scale of degrees of co-membership in a nested or sometimes overlapping set of governing institutions, of which the state is only the most salient. If we accept the moral framework of the political conception, we should conclude that there is a corresponding spectrum of degrees of egalitarian justice that we owe to our fellow participants in these collective structures in proportion to our degrees of joint responsibility for and subjection to their authority. My relation of co-membership in the system of international trade with the Brazilian who grows my coffee or the Philippine worker who assembles my computer is weaker than my relation of co-membership in US society with the Californian who picks my lettuce or the New Yorker who irons my shirts. But doesn't the first pair of relations as well as the second justify concern about the moral arbitrariness of the inequalities that arise through our joint participation in this system? One may even see an appeal to such a value in the call for standards of minimum compensation, fair labour practices and protection of worker health and safety as conditions on international trade agreements — even if the real motivation behind it is protectionism against cheap third-world labour.

Perhaps such a theory of justice as a 'continuous' function of degrees of collective responsibility could be worked out. It is in fact a natural suggestion, in light of the general theory that morality is multilayered.

But I doubt that the rules of international trade rise to the level of collective action needed to trigger demands for justice, even in diluted form. The relation remains essentially one of bargaining, until a leap has been made to the creation of collectively authorized sovereign authority.

On the 'discontinuous' political conception I am defending, international treaties or conventions, such as those that set up the rules of trade, have a quite different moral character from contracts between self-interested parties within a sovereign state. The latter may be part of a just socio-economic system because of the background of collectively imposed property and tax law in which they are embedded. But contracts between sovereign states have no such background: they are 'pure' contracts, and nothing guarantees the justice of their results. They are like the contracts favoured by libertarians, but unless one accepts the libertarian conception of legitimacy, the obligations they create are not and need not be underwritten by any kind of socio-economic justice. They are more primitive than that.

On the political conception, the same is true of the economic relation in which I stand to Brazilian or Philippine workers. Within our respective societies the contracts and laws on which this relation depends are subject to standards of social justice. Insofar as they transcend societal boundaries, however, the requirements of background justice are filtered out and commercial relations become instead something much thinner: instruments for the common pursuit of self-interest. The representatives of distinct societies that establish the framework within which such transactions can be undertaken will be guided by the interests of their own members, including their interest in domestic social justice. But a more comprehensive criterion of global socio-economic justice is not part of the picture.

By contrast a 'continuous' or sliding scale of requirements of justice would have to depend on a scale of degrees of collective engagement. I am related to the person who assembled my computer in the Philippines through the combination of US and Philippine property, commercial and labour law, the international currency markets, the international application of patent law, and the agreements on trade overseen by the World Trade Organization. The claim would have to be that since we are both participating members of this network of institutions, this puts us in the same boat for purposes of raising issues of justice, but somehow a different and perhaps leakier boat than that created by a common nation-state.

Leaving aside the practical problems of implementing even a weaker standard of economic justice through such institutions, does the idea make moral sense? Is there a plausible position covering this case that is intermediate between the political and the cosmopolitan conceptions? (The cosmopolitan conception would say that ideally, the full standards of justice should apply, but that practically, they cannot be implemented given the limited power of international institutions.) Although it is far from clear what the answer is, it seems to me that such a sliding standard of obligation is considerably less plausible than either the cosmopolitan (one-place) or political (two-place) standard. It is supposed to be a variation on the political conception, according to which one can be moved above the default position defined by human rights and collective self-interest through participation in the institutional structures that make complex economic interaction possible. But if those institutions do not act in the name of all the individuals concerned, and are sustained by those individuals only through the agency of their respective governments or branches of those governments, what is the characteristic in virtue of which they create obligations of justice and presumptions in favour of equal consideration for all those individuals? If the default really is a basic humanitarianism, permitting voluntary interaction for the pursuit of common interests, then something more is needed to move us up toward the higher standard of equal consideration. It will not emerge merely from cooperation and the conventions that make cooperation possible.

I would add two qualifications to this rather uncompromising claim. First, there are good reasons, not deriving from global socio-economic justice, to be concerned about the consequences of economic relations with states that are *internally* egregiously unjust. Even if internal justice is the primary responsibility of each state, the complicity of other states in the active support or perpetuation of an unjust regime is a secondary offence against justice.

Secondly, even self-interested bargaining between states should be tempered by considerations of humanity, and the best way of doing this in the present world is to allow poor societies to benefit from their comparative advantage in labour costs to become competitors in world markets. World Trade Organization negotiations have finally begun to show some sense that it is indecent, for example, when subsidies by wealthy nations to their own farmers cripple the market for agricultural products from developing countries, both for export and domestically.

X

That is more or less where we are now. But I said there was a dilemma, stemming from the need for more effective global institutions to deal with our collective problems, from global warming to free trade. It is not only the fear of tyranny but also the resistance to expanded democracy, expanded demands for legitimacy and expanded scope for the claims of justice that inhibits the development of powerful supranational institutions. Fortunate nations, at any rate, fear such developments. They therefore face the problem of how to create a global order that will have its own legitimacy, but not the kind of legitimacy that undermines the strict limits on their responsibilities.

The resistance to expanded democracy is sometimes explained on the ground that the right kind of *demos* does not exist internationally to permit democratic government beyond the nation-state. Even in the subglobal and much less unequal space of Europe this is a serious problem, which has given rise to significant debate. If there is not now a European civil society, is there nevertheless the hope of one? Is the possibility compatible with the linguistic diversity of Europe? Could it perhaps be brought into existence as the *result* of democratic European political institutions, rather than serving as a precondition of their creation?

But this, I believe, is not the main issue. Multilingual and multinational states have their problems, and they may have functioned most successfully before the era of democracy. But if there came into being a genuine European federation with some form of democratically elected representative government, politics would eventually develop on a European scale to compete for control of this centralized power. The real problem is that any such government would be subject to claims of legitimacy and justice that are more than the several European populations are willing to submit themselves to. That reflects in part a conviction that they are not morally obliged to expand their moral vulnerabilities in this way. (The recent expansion of the European Union, by increasing its economic inequality, will almost certainly inhibit the growth of its federal power for just this reason.)

Globally there are a number of ways in which greater international authority would be desirable. Resources for development aid and emergency relief could be more effectively obtained by a systematic assessment or tax than by the present system of voluntary contributions. Global public goods like atmospheric protection and free trade could obviously benefit from increased international authority. Both the protection of human rights and the provision of basic humanitarian aid would be easier if regimes found to be responsible for the oppression or destitution of their own subjects in these respects were regarded as having forfeited their sovereign rights against outside interference. Not only the prevention of genocide but the relief of famine may sometimes require a change of government, and the intervention of collective outside forces and agencies. This would mean establishing a link between internal and external legitimacy, as a qualification of the general right of non-interference (Barry 1999).

But all these types of increased international authority would bring with them increased responsibilities. An authority capable of carrying out these functions and imposing its decisions would naturally be subject to claims of legitimacy, pressures toward democracy and pressures to apply standards of justice in the distribution of burdens and benefits through its policies. There is a big difference between agreements or consensus among separate states committed to the advancement of their own interests and a binding procedure, based on some kind of collective authority, charged with securing the common good. The potential costs are much more serious than the risks that led to the US refusal to join the International Criminal Court.

This leaves us with the question whether some form of legitimacy is possible for the global or international case that does not depend on supranational sovereignty or democracy — let alone distributive justice — and yet can be embodied in institutions that are less cumbersome and feeble than those that depend for their creation and functioning on unanimous voluntary acceptance by sovereign states. For the moment, I do not see such a possibility, though perhaps it can be invented. The alternative to global sovereignty may not be global anarchy, but a clear and limited form of such governance remains elusive.

XI

Yet in thinking about the future, we should keep in mind that political power is rarely created as a result of demands for legitimacy, and that there is little reason to think that things will be different in this case.

If we look at the historical development of conceptions of justice and legitimacy for the nation-state, it appears that sovereignty usually precedes legitimacy. First there is the concentration of power; then, gradually, there grows a demand for consideration of the interests of the governed, and for giving them a greater voice in the exercise of power. The demand may be reformist, or it may be revolutionary, or it may be a demand for reform made credible by the threat of revolution, but it is the existence of concentrated sovereign power that prompts the demand, and makes legitimacy an issue. War may result in the destruction of a sovereign power, leading to reconfigurations of sovereignty in response to claims of legitimacy; but even in that case the conquerors who exercise power become the targets of those claims.

Even in the most famous case of the creation of a democratic federation, illegitimacy preceded legitimacy. The foundation of the United States depended on the protection of slavery, without which unanimity among the thirteen ex-colonies could not have been achieved. In fighting the civil war to preserve the Union, Lincoln knew that the preservation of sovereign power over the entire territory was the essential condition for progress in the pursuit of democratic legitimacy and justice. The battle for more political and social equality has continued ever since, but it has been possible only because centralized power was kept in existence, so that people could contest the legitimacy of the way it was being used.

So I close with a speculation. While it is conceivable in theory that political authority should be created in response to an antecedent demand for legitimacy, I believe this is unlikely to happen in practice. What is more likely is the increase and deployment of power in the interests of those who hold it, followed by a gradual growth of pressure to make its exercise more just, and to free its organization from the historical legacy of the balance of forces that went into its creation. Unjust and illegitimate regimes are the necessary precursors of the progress toward legitimacy and democracy, because they create the centralized power that can then be contested, and perhaps turned in other directions without being destroyed. For this reason, I believe the most likely path toward some version of global justice is through the creation of patently unjust and illegitimate global structures of power that are tolerable to the interests of the most powerful current nation-states. Only in that way will institutions come into being that are worth taking over in the service of more democratic purposes, and only in that way will there be something concrete for the demand for legitimacy to go to work on.

This point is independent of the dispute between the political and cosmopolitan conceptions. We are unlikely to see the spread of global justice in the long run unless we first create strong supranational institutions that do not aim at justice but that pursue common interests and reflect the inequalities of bargaining power among existing states. The question is whether these conditions can be realized by units established through voluntary agreement rather than by involuntary imposition. The path of conquest, responsible for so much of the scope of sovereign authority in the past, is no longer an option on a large scale. Other historical developments would have to create the illegitimate concentrations of power that can nurture demands for legitimacy, and provide them with something that is both worth taking over and not too easy to break up.

My conclusion, though it presupposes a conception of justice that Hobbes did not accept, is Hobbesian in spirit: the path from anarchy to justice must go through injustice. It is often unclear whether, for a given problem, international anarchy is preferable to international injustice. But if we accept the political conception, the global scope of justice will expand only through developments that first increase the injustice of the world by introducing effective but illegitimate institutions to which the standards of justice apply, standards by which we may hope they will eventually be transformed. An example, perhaps, of the cunning of history.

References

Barry, B. 1973. *The Liberal Theory of Justice*, Oxford University Press, Oxford.

———. 1999. 'Statism and Nationalism: A Cosmopolitan Critique', in Ian Shapiro and Lea Brilmayer (eds), *Global Justice*, Nomos 41, New York University Press, New York, 12–65.

Beitz, C. 1979. *Political Theory and International Relations*, Princeton University Press, Princeton.

———. 2000. 'Rawls's Law of Peoples', *Ethics* 110(4): 669–96.

Dworkin, R. 2000. *Sovereign Virtue*, Harvard University Press, Cambridge, MA.

Hobbes, T. 1976. *Leviathan*, John Wiley & Sons, London.

Murphy, L. 1998. 'Institutions and the Demands of Justice', *Philosophy and Public Affairs* 27(4): 251–91.
Pogge, T. 1989. *Realizing Rawls*, Cornell University Press, Ithaca.
———. 2002. *World Poverty and Human Rights*, Polity Press, Cambridge.
Rawls, J. 1999a. *A Theory of Justice*, Harvard University Press, Cambridge, MA (rev. edn).
———. 1999b. *The Law of Peoples*, Harvard University Press, Cambridge, MA.
———. 2001. *Justice as Fairness: A Restatement*, Harvard University Press, Cambridge, MA.
Singer, P. 2002. *One World*, Yale University Press, New Haven.
Slaughter, A.-M. 2004. *A New World Order*, Princeton University Press, Princeton.
Stiglitz, J. 2002. *Globalization and Its Discontents*, Penguin, London.

4

Beneficence, Justice and Demandingness

A Criticism of the Main Mitigation Strategies

Gianfranco Pellegrino

Giving alms to common beggars is naturally praised because it seems to carry relief to the distressed and indigent: but when we observe the encouragement thence arising to idleness and debauchery, we regard that species of charity rather as a weakness than a virtue.

— David Hume, *An Enquiry Concerning the Principles of Morals* (1975: II, §6)

If men were scrupulously just there would be no poor to whom we could give alms and think that we had realized the merit of benevolence. . . . It would be better to see whether the poor man could not be helped in some other way which would not entail his being degraded by accepting alms.

— Kant, *Lectures on Ethic* (1930: 455)

A number of people who stand round a shallow pond in which a child is drowning, and let it drown without taking the trouble to ascertain the depth of the pond, are, no doubt, shameful cowards, but they can hardly be said to have killed the child.

— Stephen, *A History of the Criminal Law of England* (1883: iii, 10)

1. The Anxiety of Demandingness in Western Debates

An ancient source of Indian ethics, a poem named *Thirukural*, warned us that

Those who are kind-hearted enter not
Into the terrible world of darkness.

Those who protect other life with kindness
Need not fear for their own lives.
This great earth and its biosphere declare
That sorrows are not for the merciful.
Those who do ill forsaking kindness, they say,
Must be oblivious of forsaking morality.
This world is not for the poor,
Nor the next for the unkind.

These verses strike us for their straightforward focus on kindness and its relation to poverty and morality. The message conveyed seems to be that kindness is the main virtue; lack of kindness is represented as altogether 'forsaking morality'. Moreover, kindness has to be displayed in the field of alleviation of poverty and protection of 'other life'. 'Kindness' is not a term-of-art in modern and contemporary moral philosophy (but see Barry 2009: 179–80; Cullity 1994: 108–9, 2004: 18–19); however, it seems plausible to identify kindness and mercy in the above-quoted verses with the virtues of 'beneficence' and 'justice' in the standard vocabulary of philosophical ethics — i.e., with a practical concern for the relative and absolute levels of others' wellbeing (see Buchanan 1996; Cullity 2004: 16–29; Frankena 1987; Julius 2003: 324n6, 2006: 176–77, 179; Kelly 1998; Nagel [this volume, pp. 59, 62–63]; Schneewind 1996).

Whether or not the serene simplicity of this framework is quintessential in Asian values or Eastern ethics is not my topic here. For my purposes, the relevant fact is that nothing similar to this attitude can be found in current Western debates on global poverty and morality. In contemporary Western discussions a focus on beneficence or justice toward the global poor is perceived as a stance in need of philosophical justification. Among the many issues of justification, particularly puzzling is the contention that both justice and beneficence, at least if assumed as purely impartial concerns for others' wellbeing, might turn out to raise *excessive demands*, and that their demandingness is morally objectionable (see Baier 1958: 203–4; Brandt 1979: 276).[1] This objection has been referred to as the

[1] Many authors would deny that the demands of justice could ever be excessive and objectionable. The common idea seems to be that justice is either a negative or a perfect duty, or both, and that negative and perfect duties cannot be puzzlingly demanding (on these ideas, see Buchanan [1987]). As a consequence, demandingness would raise an

'demandingness objection', and it comes in two different shapes, deriving from two different theoretical sources.[2]

In its first shape, demandingness is a consequence of impartiality (see Cullity 2004: 91–92; Kagan 1989: 389–90; Nagel 1991: 5–6, 50–51, 57; Scheffler 1994a: 8–13; Wolf 1982: 427–35). For instance, a strictly impartial assessment of wellbeing would lead to the conclusion that any pursuit of one's own interest is wrong, because only in very rare cases is it true that no one is worse off than the agent and no one could derive a great benefit, both in relative and in absolute terms, from a beneficent or equalizing behaviour (see Cullity 2009: 13). Then, the completely impersonal perspective required by beneficence and justice implies substantial costs in terms of significant personal relationships, fulfilment of and commitment to personal projects, integrity and self-respect (see Cottingham 1986, 1991; Kekes 1987; Murphy 2000: 21–23, 26–33; Railton 1984; Williams 1981; Wolf 1992).

However, it seems unreasonable to claim that in promoting certain personal values within our personal life when this is not extremely costly for others, we act wrongly. Likewise, it is morally objectionable to ask individuals to sacrifice what are substantial goods for them for the purpose of promoting even the smallest good for others. Morality cannot exact

---

issue only for beneficence-based views of morality. However, it is not so clear that socio-economic justice will never issue extreme demands. In conditions of extreme inequality, it seems plausible that the demands of distributive justice will rise very high, at least for very affluent agents. Accordingly, in what follows I shall assume that the demands of justice — especially those of an egalitarian cast — can extend so much as to be very demanding, and that there is no difference in this respect between socio-economic justice and beneficence. Despite not being widely stated, this view is affirmed in some recent treatments of the topic (see Ashford 2003; Cullity 2009: 9, 15–17, 18–19; Julius 2003: 326–27; Murphy 1999: 255–59, 262, 288–91, 2000: 8, 37, 95; Nagel 1991: 48–51, 54–55; Williams 1981: 14). Murphy (2000: 36–37) notices that in commonsense morality there are different attitudes to the demands of justice and those of beneficence. Justice is regarded as over-demanding only on rare occasions, whereas beneficence is very often felt as excessive. This could explain the views discussed at the beginning of this footnote. However, this differential treatment is not necessarily wrong (see Murphy 2000: 39–41, 74–76, 98).

The demandingness issue is not a recent discovery, even though the problem is mentioned in historical texts only in passing (see Cullity 2004: 244–45n4; Kagan 1989: 390; Murphy 2000: 136–37n2).

[2] Here, I am in part following Cullity (2004: 91–93, 2009: 8–9), but see also Mulgan (2001: 3–4).

sacrifices of one's own good life for the sake of insignificantly small gains in the general promotion of the good and the valuable. We can be asked to give *some* money and time to international aid organizations, for instance, but this request cannot be pushed to the point of asking for a *full* sacrifice of our personal projects and fulfilments and a life of *complete* dedication to global poverty relief. We can be asked to act for the direct rescue of any needy person in front of us, but, even in this kind of case, it is illegitimate to ask for any substantial sacrifice of our life and limbs for the purpose of saving others' lives.[3]

There are costs that cannot be asked, even in the name of morality. To pay these costs amounts to supererogatory conduct, i.e., a praiseworthy but not morally required course of action (see Heyd 1982; Urmson 1958; Wolf 1982: 438). As a consequence, any moral theory requiring such sorts of sacrifice is unbearably demanding and patently paradoxical. It is demanding because it does not distinguish saints and heroes from normal agents — in other words, it does not distinguish supererogatory conduct from normal obligations. It is paradoxical since it forbids patently permissible options, such as the pursuit of personal projects, the promotion of individual values and so on (see Cullity 2009: 13, 112).

In its second shape, demandingness arises out of the iteration of seemingly undemanding principles, such as 'Give your contribution to the well-being of others, when the cost is comparatively insignificant (other things being equal).' The first time this principle is applied to the conduct of a given agent, acting upon it may have comparatively insignificant costs, but the nth time that the principle requires the same agent to give up a small percentage of money or time, this may appear an enormous cost. Even an affluent person might be led to the edge of poverty by iterated small

[3] The two cases mentioned in the main text — contribution to international aid organizations and direct rescue — might arguably be different, both in their nature and in their moral significance. A great part of the current discussion on the demandingness objection deals with the so-called 'life-saving analogy', i.e., with the contention that there are no substantial moral differences between these two cases (see Singer [this volume, p. 17], 2007: 475, 480). I shall not consider this issue here. In the rest of this article, I shall assume that in both cases beneficence and justice require helping the victims, and that the analogy between directly saving a life and contributing to international aid organizations holds. Moreover, I shall not consider the conceptual differences that, even assuming the life-saving analogy, may distinguish contributions to international aid organizations from cases of direct rescue (see Cullity 2004: 10–12).

contributions in money and time. This is a perfect general problem: no matter which reasons are cited for contributing to others' wellbeing, no matter whether the required contributions are aimed at equalizing relative differences or at raising absolute levels of wellbeing, small iterated contributions might be legitimate in isolation, but absurdly demanding overall (see Cullity 2004: 70–73, 78–80, 86–88, 92–93, 132–34, 2009: 13, 17, 18–19).

Theorists disagree about the meaning and interpretation of the demandingness objection, as well as about its connections with similar objections.[4] Moreover, many different reactions have been voiced to the objection itself. Some authors simply dismiss it. Two main dismissal strategies have been employed. According to some theorists, the difficulty of meeting the demands of morality constitutes a problem for human agents and their motivations, rather than a puzzle for morality itself, and we can cope with this difficulty through a mixture of reasoning, policy, moral educations, and moral sanctions (see Glover 1977: 107–12; Kagan 1989: 386–403; Rachels 1979; Singer [this volume], 1979: ch. 8, 2009: chs 5, 9, 10; Unger 1996: 56–59; Wolf 1982: 426). For others, the issue itself is misplaced, because there are no settled levels of acceptable demands against which the allegedly excessive demands of morality can be assessed (see Murphy 2000: 34–62, 64–70; see also Cullity 2004: 90–102).

Many theorists have engaged seriously with the objection, with the common aim of devising a principled standard to limit the demands of morality. Two recent strategies are the following:

I. *Just institutions and collective beneficence*: It has been argued that a focus on institutions aimed at realizing egalitarian justice, or on collective

[4] In the main text, the demandingness objection has been presented as an issue concerning the *content* of morality. It is a puzzle arising from the specific tenets voiced in certain moral views, and from the contradiction between the demands of partiality and those of impartiality, between agent-relative reasons and agent-neutral reasons (Nagel [1991] is the most comprehensive statement of this way of framing the issue). According to some theorists, the demandingness issue has rather to do with the *authority* of morality and its relationship with practical rationality. The demands that morality makes on us might be *practically* irrational (at least if practical rationality embodies non-moral but prescriptive ideals) — and this is what creates the problem of demandingness (see Brink 1986; Scheffler 1994b: ch. 2; Singer 2007: 478, 482; Wolf 1982: 426–27). See also Cullity (2004: 90).

beneficence, might provide the means for limiting excessive demands on individuals (see Murphy 2000: ch. 5; Nagel 1991: 14–15, 38, 43, 53–60, 85; Scheffler 2005: 236–40).

II. *Argument from presuppositions*: Extreme demands might be contradictory with the very presuppositions of beneficence and justice. As a result, demands of beneficence and justice may be limited in a principled way by imposing on them side-restraints derived from the presuppositions of justice and beneficence (see Cullity 2004: chs 8–10, 2009: 21–32).

Unfortunately, both these strategies will prove to be ineffective — or at least, so I shall argue in this essay. First, I shall claim that the duties arising from, and connected to, just institutions will turn out to be as demanding as the duties of justice when they are addressed directly to individuals (section 3). Second, I shall show that collective beneficence in its various senses sets limits to the demands of beneficence only by assuming the moral insignificance of non-compliance. However, such a move rests on a wrong conception of beneficence, according to which beneficence is not a full-fledged moral requirement, and its demands are very weak by default. This is not a solution to the demandingness objection, since it simply begs the question (section 5).

Finally, the arguments from the presuppositions of beneficence and justice rest on a contentious assumption, according to which beneficence and justice protect *permissible* pursuits and aims. According to these arguments, since beneficence and justice presuppose that certain pursuits, projects and aims are permissible ones, the demands of beneficence and justice cannot jeopardize the permissibility of those pursuits, projects and aims for beneficent and just people. However, it is plausible that beneficence and justice concern *good* or *right* pursuits, aims and projects. Since the realm of goodness and rightness is narrower than the area of permissible action, much of the mitigating effect of the arguments of presuppositions gets lost (section 6).

2. Institutional Solutions: Mitigating Justice

In many conceptions, socio-economic justice dictates actions aimed at implementing an equal or fair distribution of at least primary goods or basic resources for large sectors of society (see Dworkin 1981; Rawls 1999: §15).

As may easily be imagined, in any historical society in the present and past conditions of humanity, to comply with justice so conceived would certainly be very demanding for large sectors of society. Whoever is placed at a socio-economic level even slightly superior to the position of those worst off might be required to give up shares of her own goods in order to redistribute them. This might be very demanding, also because after the redistribution people belonging to socio-economic levels only slightly superior to those of the worst off can find themselves placed at the level below. But even focusing on citizens placed many levels above the worst off, redistribution might still impose severe demands on large groups of them. Accordingly, a problem of over-demandingness exists for any theory concerning socio-economic justice in the domestic context.[5] In the international context as well, the problem holds, and it might increase. The amount of redistribution needed to compensate existing inequalities across the world would be large enough to impose even more severe demands on many people in affluent countries.

Two different strategies have been pursued in order to mitigate the excessive demands of socio-economic justice. First, it has been argued that certain inequalities are not to be discarded, since they are morally unobjectionable for various reasons — such as their role in giving incentives to efficiency, or by virtue of their origin in the free actions of the victims (see Rawls 1999: 68). Here, I shall not consider this strategy.

---

[5] It might be argued that insofar as justice requires the better off to make substantial sacrifices for the sake of the worst off, but those sacrifices do not bring the latter to a level superior to that of the better off, this demand is not excessive. But socio-economic justice asks only this kind of sacrifice; therefore, its demands are never excessive: 'it is an extreme demand to have to accept the *greater* advantages of others — in the sense of *advantages greater than one enjoys oneself* — as a sufficient reason for lower expectations over the whole course of one's life.' However, it is not 'an extreme demand to have to accept lower expectations for the sake of others who will be better off than they would otherwise have been, but still not as well off as you are. That is accepting lower life prospects for the *advantage* of others, but not for the *greater* advantages of others' (Nagel 1991: 54). This argument relies on the idea that a demand of justice is excessive only when it places its addressee below the threshold of whoever benefits from the sacrifice required. However, this is a trivial claim. It is obvious enough that such tough requests are excessive and moral objectionable. What is less clear is whether less severe demands would be acceptable. What about a demand of redistribution that leaves its addressees only minimally better than their beneficiaries? It seems plausible enough that such levelling-down demands are morally objectionable, too.

A second strategy relies on institutions. As per this strategy, socio-economic justice is viewed as a virtue of the main institutions of a given society — more precisely, justice is, or derives from, an arrangement of the basic institutions of our society. On this view, institutions are considered just when they bring about just outcomes and rectify existing inequalities. In addition, individual obligations of justice amount to the duty to support and to give the required contribution to the working of just institutions (see Beitz 1999: 131; G. Brock 2009: chs 3–5; Moellendorf 2002: 30–36, 39–40, 43, 48, 53, 62, 73; O'Neill 1994: 81–83, 1996: 105–6, 112–13; Pogge 1992: 90–101, 1994: 90–98, 1995: 113–19, 2002: 20–26, 169–77; Rawls 1999: §§2, 10, 19: 99–100).

This focus on institutions mitigates the demands of justice in two ways. First, since institutions are a better means of promoting justice and repairing injustice than any individual, uncoordinated action, any institutional promotion of justice is more efficient than any kind of individual action. Second, individuals are not asked anything else apart from supporting and contributing to just institutions. Hence, once just institutions are in place and once citizens have provided what is needed for their support and working (for instance, once citizens have performed basic civic duties such as voting, tax paying and so on), any individual is free to pursue her self-interested or partial aims.

This focus on just institutions leaves a large sphere of actions free from any moral requirement, thereby guaranteeing substantial room for personal projects, self-interested pursuits and legitimate partiality. Therefore, this institutional strategy provides a safe means of mitigating the demands of socio-economic justice. The core of the strategy lies in a division of labour between institutions and individuals: institutions bring about justice, while citizens limit themselves to enabling the existence and functioning of justice-producing institutions (see Nagel 1991: ch. 6; Rawls 1996: 268–69, 1999: §10: 47; Scheffler 2005).[6]

[6] I am not claiming that the mitigation of severe demands from justice is the only aim or justification of institutional views. An institutional approach to justice might be employed for many different purposes, and it may descend from several distinct premises. The huge impact that institutions have on daily life, as well as the fact that injustice deriving from institutional arrangements is particularly difficult to eliminate, can justify institutionalism as well (see Rawls 1996: 265–71). Likewise, the idea that injustices deriving from institutions are particularly objectionable when those institutions are coercive might require an institutional approach to justice (see Blake 2001).

The following assumptions, taken together, are required in order to achieve mitigation through a focus on institutions.

I. Dualism

Institutional action and individual conduct differ in kind and in mode of operation. Accordingly, the moral and political principles that are used to regulate institutions do not hold for individual conduct. The requirements of socio-economic justice concern institutions, not individual actions (see Rawls 1999: §10: 47). Therefore, when institutional action leaves spaces of inequality, no individual may be required to act in reparation. As said previously, individuals may be required to support and give their due to institutions, not to substitute them — and this is the main mitigating device. Dualism is an essential tool in blocking extreme demands, because it provides the only principled way of avoiding the idea that individual actions are required in the reparation of injustices that institutions fail to remedy. If dualism is a false assumption, then citizens might legitimately be required to act directly in the promotion of justice, notwithstanding their support to just institutions.

II. Institutional efficiency

Institutional promotion of justice is more efficient than individual action, because institutions have a deeper and more far-reaching impact on daily life, and also an all-encompassing power to rectify and eliminate the main factors of injustice in society. At the same time, to support institutions and to contribute to their working is less demanding than any individual action aimed at promoting socio-economic justice. As a consequence, institutions are not only the best means, but also provide the most economic route to justice, and for this reason they permit the required mitigation of the demands that otherwise justice would impose upon individuals. If institutions were an awkward means of promoting justice, then of course any appeal to them would be inappropriate. More importantly, if support to just institutions were more demanding than the direct promotion of justice, the institutional strategy of mitigation of the demands of justice would be self-defeating.[7]

[7] Murphy (1999) addresses an important set of criticisms against dualism, to which this article is deeply indebted. He claims that dualism is not a necessary move for gaining the mitigating outcomes of an institutional approach to justice, and this is one of his main

III. Institutional bordering

Institutions can be delimited in a clear way — their mode of working, their impact on daily life, and the requirements for support and contribution to their functioning can be clearly specified. There is a clear-cut distinction between areas of social life that are affected by institutions and that in their turn affect institutions, and areas where no institutional features are present — even though in those areas we could face some form of collective action performed by groups, associations and similar collective entities. This distinction serves the function of locating the area of individual conduct that is unaffected by the demands of justice: outside the institutional realm, no demands of justice are made, in virtue of assumption I. Absent a sharp boundary between institutional and non-institutional realms, no areas would remain untouched by the demands of justice, and over-demandingness would ensue.

---

arguments against dualism (*ibid.*: 289–91). I disagree with this. As stated in the main text, dualism appears to me the only principled way of claiming that individuals are not required to undertake further actions to eliminate injustices, over and above their support of and contribution to just institutions. If the principle dictating the elimination of inequalities holds for both institutions and individuals, then both institutional action and individual conduct can be assessed in terms of justice. In a sense, dualism makes possible a kind of indirect theory of justice, along lines similar to many kinds of indirect utilitarianism. By virtue of dualism, individual actions are assessed indirectly, and not directly in terms of justice. This indirect assessment amounts to claiming that any individual action is right insofar as it supports and contributes to just institutions and it does not undermine the working and existence of just institutions. Actions that do not qualify as being against or in favour of just institutions are not regulated, and therefore they are morally permissible.

Murphy might be conflating two points that I am trying to keep separate in this essay. A mitigating effect of the demands of justice arises from the effectiveness of the institutional promotion of justice. The point conveyed in assumption II (regarding institutional efficiency) is precisely that institutions are the best means of promoting justice, in economic and efficiency terms. Since those means are different from individual action, their employment both alleviates the demands of justice upon individuals, and ensures that the goal of justice is achieved. However, individuals cannot be saved from possible demands of justice only by appeal to an instrumental view of institutional justice, contrary to what Murphy believes. Indeed, even institutions might not be perfectly efficient, and individuals can be called upon to contribute when there are cases of institutional failure. Only dualism can block this appeal to individual action, declaring it morally objectionable. Accordingly, dualism performs a mitigating function, contrary to Murphy's contention.

3. Against Institutionalism

Institutionalists claim that the only legitimate demand that justice may address to individuals is to support and give their due contribution to the working of just institutions. Complying with this duty is much less demanding than any individual promotion of justice, while just institutions can achieve as much justice as — and possibly more than — individual just conduct.

Unfortunately, the institutionalist strategy fails because the very duty to support just institutions turns out to be very demanding.[8] The excessive extent of the demands issued by a duty to support just institutions can be shown through the following reasoning — a reasoning that will result in challenging assumptions I and II.

It seems obvious enough that the duty to support just institutions includes something more than the support of *existing* just institutions. A plausible conception of this duty amounts to at least three different obligations:

a. a duty to support *existing* just institutions;
b. a duty to rectify unjust *existing* institutions; and
c. a duty to give one's own individual contribution to the creation of just institutions where they are absent.

There are no apparent reasons to reject *c* while endorsing *a* and *b*. Indeed, the intuitive and historical idea of a natural duty of justice seems to amount precisely to the idea of a duty to *create* just institutions (see Rawls 1999: §19: 99). However, it has been claimed that no duty to create new just institutions is incumbent on individuals and that the only duty one has is to support, and possibly rectify, the just institutions under which one is living. In favour of this claim, a *relational argument* is usually given, to the effect that only shared institutionalized relationships can trigger individual duties of justice. Accordingly, individuals have the duty to support only their shared institutions, and to rectify only injustices obtaining within the scope of their shared political institutions. However, there is no duty either to rectify unjust institutions or to contribute to establishing just institutions abroad (see Nagel [this volume, p. 65]).

---

[8] This point is made also in Murphy (1999: 289–90).

Still, the rejection of *c* may undermine the whole institutionalist strategy. If there is no duty to contribute to the creation of just institutions where and when they are absent, a consequence might be that the overall efficiency of institutions in terms of justice would be greatly diminished. As a matter of fact, just institutions are not widespread all over the world. If only just institutions that are already present and settled should be supported, and there is no duty to create new just institutions, then it is likely that great injustices will continue and even increase. The amount of justice brought about by just institutions whose scope is very limited, as it would be if there were no duty to create new ones, would be minimal. But, if the mitigating power of a focus on institutions is to be morally legitimate, it seems that the promotion of justice through institutions should not be grossly inferior to the individual promotion of justice.[9] Then, the institution-based mitigation strategy is to be interpreted in terms of the three duties just listed.

Unfortunately, if so viewed, institutional justice may be as demanding as the individual promotion of justice, or even more. Think about the actions demanded of any affluent citizen of the first world in order to promote and enhance just institutions across the whole globe, and especially in poor countries. It is apparent enough that a life of political activism devoted to encouraging and enhancing international institution-building would be as demanding as a life devoted to individual contribution to famine relief. Possibly, in some cases, the life of the political activist may be even more demanding than a life-long programme of individual monetary contributions to international aid organizations.

It might be argued that the duty to create new institutions is in itself an institutional one, and that for this reason it is not very demanding. It might be contended that every citizen of the affluent world has the duty to support, contribute to and possibly rectify her own domestic institutions, while

[9] A common assumption of any mitigation strategy is that the moderation of the duties of justice or of beneficence thereby obtained should not come at the expense of justice and beneficence themselves. To put it otherwise, an acceptable mitigation of the demands of justice or beneficence is not simply a reduction of the amount of justice or beneficence accorded, but an attempt to have an acceptable level of justice or of beneficence while imposing less burdensome demands on agents. A simple drop of the demands going beyond a given threshold would be, if proposed as a mitigation strategy, both trivial and arbitrary.

the duty to create new just institutions abroad is an obligation incumbent on the just institutions already existing and so supported.[10]

This contention might be justified by appealing to institutional efficiency. It might be argued that institutional action is more efficient than individual efforts in creating new just institutions. Be that as it may, this does not rule out demandingness. For it seems plausible enough that by assigning to existing institutions the further task of creating new institutions across the world, the extent and the burden of the individual duty to support institutions will increase accordingly. Imagine that each liberal-democratic state has the duty to do what is necessary to build just institutions wherever they are lacking. It is easy to imagine that the duties of the citizens of many liberal democracies would be much greater than the actual ones. In sum, by assigning to existing institutions the duty to create new just institutions, the liberating effect of the division of the labour between individuals and institutions might be greatly reduced.

It might be claimed that dualism, not institutional efficacy, is the background justification of the claim that the creation of new just institutions abroad is a task for institutions. Assumed as a methodological principle, dualism debars any extension of principles concerning institutions to individual conduct. Since institutions and individuals are different in kind, they should be regulated by different principles. Hence, individuals cannot be required to create new just institutions in the name of justice, or as a way to achieve more justice, because individual conduct is simply outside the reach of the demands of justice. Hence, if creating new just institutions is a matter of justice, then it is a duty incumbent upon institutions.

However, if dualism in this shape holds, it follows not only that there is no individual duty to create new institutions, but also that the duty to support and contribute to existing just institutions is not a demand of justice at all. People cannot be required to give their support and contribution to just institutions in the name of justice, because justice concerns only institutions. A different rationale for the duty of individuals toward their just institutions should be indicated. Justice is the function of institutions, and it provides the rationale for their existence. But it cannot be invoked in order to ask individuals to support just institutions. This move risks jeopardizing any individual duty to support institutions.

---

[10] This is Rawls's claim concerning international duties of assistance, in Rawls (2001: §15).

Thus interpreted, the institutionalist approach is no longer a mitigation strategy. It is not a way of mitigating the demands of justice upon individuals, but rather a way of cancelling any demand made in the name of justice. Institution-based justice does not concern individuals. Citizens have duties of loyalty or of responsibility toward their institutions, perhaps, but they do not have any obligation in terms of justice. This is not necessarily objectionable. Still, it is sufficient to conclude that institutionalism is not a mitigation strategy at all.

As a consequence of this line of reasoning, it might be claimed that the best option would be to reject dualism and to find a different argument that could be employed to deny that individuals have a general duty to create new just institutions. Unfortunately, this option faces two difficulties. First, it seems that no easy or plausible argument has been found to rule out a general duty to create new just institutions incumbent upon individuals. Natural duties of justice have an immediate plausibility. Second, dualism is an essential mitigation device, since it has the effect of isolating parts of individual conduct from the demands of justice. If dualism does not hold, there are no arguments that are able to block the demands of justice. Even though institutions might be the best means of achieving justice, if it is not established that they are the only site and subject of justice, then there is no principled way to exclude the demand that in some cases individuals could be asked to effect justice when institutions fail to do so, or when institution-produced justice is greatly suboptimal.

The line of reasoning presented in this section might be summarized as follows. Institutional justice requires of individuals not only support to existing just institutions, but also efforts to create new just institutions when and where they are absent. This natural duty of justice cannot be ruled out and it concerns individuals, not institutions. Unfortunately, a life of political activism in favour of just institutions is very demanding. Accordingly, a focus on institutional justice is not a good mitigation strategy.

4. Collective Requirements: Mitigating Beneficence

There are no doubts that the demands of beneficence on individuals might often be very excessive. By virtue of its focus on absolute levels of well-being, under the actual circumstances of our world, beneficence would require (even slightly) affluent individuals living in the first world to give their greatest available contribution in order to raise the wellbeing of the global poor. As has been claimed, only the possibility that the giver could be reduced below the subsistence threshold might set a legitimate barrier to the demands of beneficence (see Cullity 2004: 70–73; Murphy 2000: 67, 76). It is absolutely patent that to demand individuals to donate their substance, effort and time till they are reduced to the edge of poverty is extreme, excessive and possibly absurd.[11] Accordingly, attempts have been made to mitigate the request of beneficence, and they have been even more numerous than the mitigation arguments in the field of socio-economic justice.

A very well-developed mitigation strategy focuses on the plausible intuition that, after all, beneficence is a collective affair, and that the bad predicament of the global poor is a shared responsibility of many individuals in the first world. More precisely, the collective nature of beneficence seems to derive from three assumptions.

I. Can implies ought

Contrary to keeping promises, parental duties and other special or relational duties,[12] beneficence is not connected to the previous actions or relations of the agent. Rather, it seems that beneficence is at stake any time that one has the possibility of alleviating the condition of a needy person. In the case of beneficence, there is no matter of responsibility. One is asked to help the needy simply because of their needs and because the potentially beneficent person is in a condition where helping is available to her. In the sphere of beneficence, factual possibilities are a source of duty (see Goodin 1985: 117–44; Griffin 2008: 101–4, 181–82).

[11] To beneficence applies the second kind of demandingness listed in §1. The demands of beneficence may not be excessive in isolation: in single instances, to ask affluent people to contribute to relieving global poverty when this is not too costly for them is not over-demanding. The fact is that by iterating this request, affluent people may be led to the edge of poverty — and this is obviously excessive.

[12] For some theorists, justice works as a special or relational duty, in being connected to previous actions or relations (see Beitz 1999; Blake 2001: 261–66; Dworkin 2000: 6; J. Horton 2006, 2007; Moellendorf 2002: 30; Nagel [this volume, p. 65]; Pogge 1992: 90–101; Sangiovanni 2007: 5–8; Simmons 1996). Famously, Pogge (2002: 15–26) claims that the duties of global justice arise from past and present responsibilities of the affluent countries towards the global poor. In this essay, I shall not consider these views, and try to remain neutral on these topics.

II. Equality of moral status

Since past actions, shared relations and responsibilities are not at stake, there are no principled ways of selecting among the potential addressees of the demands of beneficence, apart from their factual possibility of acting beneficently. Accordingly, everyone is equally entitled, and requested, to act beneficently. There is an equality of moral status among the group of potential benefactors. The most famous argument in this field, the life-saving analogy, exploits this assumption. It is plausible enough that a bystander in front of a drowning child ought to act in order to save her. Since in our current technological conditions there is no difference in costs incurred and actions needed between saving a drowning child in front of us and giving our contribution to international aid organizations, we have the same duty of beneficence toward a single drowning child in front of us and toward millions of children threatened by avoidable diseases and famines in the third world.[13]

III. Cumulative effects (efficiency of collective beneficence)

Yet, it is conceivable that, even accepting the extreme demands of beneficence, no single person would be able to relieve each and every needy person around the globe. By contrast, it seems plausible enough that collective efforts are needed to raise the global poor to the level of a decent subsistence. Moreover, it is also likely that the coordinated and cooperative pursuit of beneficence will be more effective than any individual uncoordinated and non-cooperative effort (see Cullity 2004: 60).

As with justice, it turns out that a collective pursuit of beneficence is less demanding than individual, uncoordinated and non-coordinative beneficence. It is empirically obvious that when all, or many, individuals from the affluent world give their contribution in time and money to the relief of global poverty, the average individual share of contribution will decrease rapidly and greatly. Accordingly, a mitigation strategy addressed to the demands of beneficence can rest on the idea that the only legitimate demands would be those imposed on individuals if beneficence was

[13] See note 3.

pursued collectively and in conditions of full compliance (see Cullity 2004: 74; Murphy 2000: 86–87, 96–101).

Two different strategies of this kind have been proposed. First, an *ideal collective consequentialist view* of beneficence has been put forward, according to which the unobjectionable amount of beneficent behaviour is that demanded by the set of rules of conduct, or of motives, whose effective internalization by all, or by an overwhelming majority in a given society, would produce the best overall outcome in terms of beneficence. There is a duty to promote the internalization of and compliance to those rules through examples, reproaching non-compliers, discussions of related issues, and moral education, and this duty is included in the area of beneficence (see Hooker 2000: 29–37, 72–92, 159–74; Mulgan 2001: part II; Murphy 2000: 85–86; Parfit 1984: 30–31). This secondary duty concerning the promotion of optimal rules performs the role of the duty to support and create just institutions in institutionalist views of justice (see section 3 above).

A different approach is the *fair share view of collective beneficence* (see Cohen 1981: 76; Murphy 2000: 89–93; Parfit 1984: 30). This view equates the required share of beneficence with that needed to relieve global poverty if every potential benefactor would give her own contribution. Accordingly, the morally right conduct consists in giving one's own fair share of beneficence, calculated with reference to the total contribution guaranteed by a universal beneficent behaviour.

Ideal collective consequentialism and the fair share view of collective beneficence rest on the same interpretation of the demandingness objection. From assumption III, it follows that a collective pursuit of beneficence is both more efficient and less demanding than individual beneficent conduct. From this empirical observation, a normative consequence may be drawn. Higher levels of demandingness are linked to individual failures in cooperating with collective pursuits of beneficence. In other words, the demands of beneficence increase proportionally to rates of non-compliance. It seems that the greater the number of people who fail to comply with the demands of beneficence, the greater the contribution that compliers are required to give. But requiring certain individuals to do more because of others' failures in discharging their duties is unfair (see D. Brock 1981: 912; Cohen 1981; K. Horton 2011) or at least unreasonable (see Cullity 2004: 241n10; Murphy 2000: 88–93). People cannot be held responsible, and made victims, of others' wrongness. Consequently, the morally legitimate demands of beneficence ought to bracket the facts about actual compliance. Rather, they should be regulated by facts concerning ideal compliance. Ideal compliance, not actual compliance, is to be employed to establish the acceptable extent of the demands of beneficence.

5. Against Collective Beneficence

In the previous section, two mitigation strategies were presented that rest on the idea that increased demands of beneficence are objectionable because they are produced by non-compliance. Increased demands of beneficence aimed at compensating the effect that non-compliance with beneficence would have upon needy peoples are unfair or unreasonable, according to the supporters of these mitigation strategies. Accordingly, an assessment of this answer to the demandingness objection requires a clear understanding of why and how unfairness or unreasonability crops up in such cases.[14]

When the demands of beneficence are increased as a consequence of partial compliance, the ensuing unfairness includes, and amounts to, two distinct elements. First, by connecting the demands of beneficence with facts about actual compliance, non-compliers have been given the power to increase the demands addressed to compliers. In a sense, non-compliers, as it were, have the power to institute *new* duties addressed to compliers (see, for similar remarks, Cullity 2004: 76–77). Possibly, it is not literally so — perhaps non-compliers merely have a power to increase the extent of already existing duties of beneficence. However, even this increase seems a move they ought not to be allowed to make. New duties or increased duties ought not arise from impermissible behaviours. Wrongdoers ought not to be permitted to give rise to duties, since they have neither rights nor legitimate powers (see Hohfeld 1923: 36, 50–60). Second, due to the increased demands of beneficence created by non-compliance, there are obvious and illegitimate inequalities among compliers and non-compliers. Compliers are more burdened than non-compliers.

Ideal collective consequentialism and fair share views of beneficence react in the same way to these two factors of unfairness. Unfairness is

[14] An explanation of this unfairness is attempted in Murphy (2000: 88–93). In the main text of the present essay, an alternative, and hopefully better, explanation is provided.

to be eliminated, and the demands of beneficence moderated. This purpose can be achieved by breaking the connection between non-compliance and the size of the demands of beneficence. This connection is morally objectionable. The amount of beneficence is to be linked to ideal compliance, not to actual non-compliance. Non-compliance has no moral significance.

Many objections have been levelled against both ideal collective consequentialism and fair share views of beneficence (Cullity 2004: 74–77; Mulgan 2001: 59–65, 67–89, 107–21). Here, a particular objection will be directed against the assumption that non-compliance has no moral significance.

In many moral realms, non-compliance does have moral significance. For instance, when non-compliance amounts to encroachment on established rights or entitlements, it seems that it has a distinctive moral import. Also, the disappointment of legitimate expectations, or the breaking of moral rules aimed at protecting spheres of autonomy, liberties and morally relevant personal goods, may elicit new duties and strengthen old ones. As a result, it might be affirmed that non-compliance with norms regulating expectations, or with norms dictating respect for autonomy and liberties, has genuine moral significance. Non-compliance with rules of fair distribution is surely morally significant, too.

In such cases, it is also conceivable that new duties of compensation and reparation would arise as a consequence of non-compliance. Likewise, it is plausible that the duties that one has failed to comply with remain valid and binding ones. It might be argued that the duty of compensation of and reparation toward victims adds to the already existing duty that non-compliers fail to discharge, and that this might give the impression that, due to non-compliance, certain obligations have increased their extent and demandingness. When someone fails to do her duty, thereby encroaching upon a right,[15] it is plausible that other agents are invested with the original duty, and to this a new duty of compensation is added. In this perspective, the increased duties of beneficence imposed on compliers as a consequence of others' non-compliance might be accounted for as a result of the summation of their original duties and the compensation to be ensured to the victims of denied beneficence. Since compensation for

[15] On the correlativity between rights and duties, see Hohfeld (1923: 36–50).

denied beneficence obviously assumes the form of beneficence, the result of partial compliance with the duty of beneficence toward the global poor amounts simply to increased demands upon the compliers.[16]

It might be objected that the duty to compensate the victims of non-compliance is incumbent on the non-complying agent, and not on innocent agents. Accordingly, compliers do not have their duties increased. No analogy, then, might be established between non-compliance concerning rights, legitimate expectations and similar areas, and partial compliance in the field of beneficence.

Still, it is not the case that the victims, if the non-compliers fail to compensate them, can legitimately remain uncompensated. It seems plausible enough that agents who are not responsible for the wrongdoing are invested with the duty to compensate the wrongs ensuing from others' faults — at least when no compensation from the wrongdoer is likely to obtain. To put it otherwise, innocent victims have a right to compensation, not to retaliation — i.e., to extort compensation from wrongdoers. In other words, in such cases compensation does not coincide with punishment.[17] Wrongdoers are to be punished and others cannot be punished in their place; yet, this rule does not hold with respect to compensation. Wrongs might be compensated by innocent agents. For instance, in most states, innocent tax-payers contribute with their tax revenue to compensations given to victims of criminal offences, not only in the form of legal assistance in trials but also in terms of financial aid to unemployed or otherwise destitute victims. Whatever the rationale of this duty imposed on tax-payers might be, it entails that normal citizens have their ordinary duties increased by virtue of non-compliance. In a sense, they have their normal negative duties of abstaining from criminal offences, and an extra

[16] A similar line of reasoning is defended in Goodin (1985: 134–35).

[17] And even in cases of coincidence, it might be argued that the points of the two reactions are not the same. Punishment aims at the prevention of future crimes, or at retribution, whereas compensation aims at relieving the disadvantages of victims and restoring the initial situation. Accordingly, punishment and compensation may concern different agents. From a different perspective, it might be argued that we are facing two distinct species of the ascription of responsibility: in partial compliance situations, compliers are not *at fault* for denied beneficence, but still they are vicariously *liable* for compensation (see Feinberg 1970: 136–37). Since beneficence is simply the duty to benefit people in need, compensation for denied beneficence amounts simply to taking upon one's own shoulders increased amounts of beneficent actions.

burden that is the outcome of the fact that other citizens failed to abstain from injuring others. Increased demands of beneficence arising from non-compliance can be read along the same lines. As a consequence, even in the case of beneficence, non-compliance retains its moral significance, and no mitigation strategy may be obtained by bracketing facts about actual compliance.

A rejoinder to this objection might go as follows. Denied beneficence is not to be equated with encroachments on rights, or with offences, injuries or the disappointment of legitimate expectations. Despite its praiseworthiness, beneficence is less strict as a demand than respect for rights, protection from serious offences or the satisfaction of legitimate expectations. In a sense, denied beneficence is a less serious fault. Accordingly, no compensation is required for its victims, or at least compensation may be required only on the part of wrongdoers. In the field of beneficence, compensation is not a social responsibility. To put it otherwise, when people do not have a right to our assistance, it is not morally wrong withholding it: we are not 'slaves to the badly off' (Narveson 1999: 156; see also Narveson 2003).

These claims may underlie the mitigation strategy based on bracketing facts about actual compliance with beneficence. Still, if this is the case, it turns out that this strategy rests on a contentious conception of beneficence, according to which beneficent behaviour is supererogatory, and beneficence as an ideal is less binding than justice, or respect for rights or protection of legitimate expectations. This mitigation strategy assumes that beneficence is nothing but charity (see Narveson 1999).

If so, it seems that the very project of mitigating the demands of beneficence is void. If beneficence is so weak a requirement, there is no danger that its demands might become extreme. In other words, this mitigation strategy begs the question, since its success turns on the assumption that beneficence's demands are very weak by default. A real mitigation strategy should not assume that the demands to be moderated are, by their very definition, very weak ones. Demands from justice and beneficence may be very high and extreme. This is what makes the demandingness objection a genuine issue. To equate beneficence with charity and supererogatory assistance is a frequent move in the debate (see Murphy 2000: 5, 63, 71–72). However, it is not an answer to the demandingness objection, but simply a dismissal of it.

Of course, this line of reasoning is not to be taken as suggesting that beneficence is necessarily a matter of rights or of legitimate claims (as in Cullity 2004: 250n8; Gewirth 1982; O'Neill 1986, 2008; Sen 1984; Shue 1980). Simply, failures of beneficence are morally wrong actions: the idea that people have a right to assistance is not necessary to account for this, even though a rights-based view might be one way to argue in favour of beneficence (see Griffin 2008: 88–90). Still, no significant conception of the demandingness objection may be obtained by denying that failures of beneficence are morally wrong actions and by equating beneficence and supererogatory charity. However, this denial seems to be implicit in the mitigation strategy based on bracketing the moral significance of actual non-compliance.

In conclusion, the mitigation strategy considered in this section begs the question it is aimed at answering. Either beneficence is a genuine moral requirement or it is only a matter of supererogatory action. In the first case, failed beneficence cannot be put into brackets, and mitigation of the demands of beneficence cannot be based on such a bracketing. In the second case, the question of demandingness does not even arise, since the demands of charity cannot be stringent enough to overcome the threshold of acceptability.

6. Against Arguments from Presuppositions

Recently, a different kind of argument has been employed to mitigate the demands of beneficence and justice. This mitigation strategy rests on the idea that any acknowledgement of the requirements of justice and beneficence entails commitment to presuppositions that establish limits to those very requirements (see Cullity 2009: 22–30).[18] Accordingly, demandingness may be avoided on account of the fact that a mitigation of certain demands is necessary to have a consistent compliance with the requirements that those very demands express.

This argument from presuppositions assumes that beneficence and justice find their grounds in reasons of promoting interests that it is *not*

[18] In his more recent treatment of the issue, Cullity picks out three different sources of moral requirements — concern, respect and cooperation (see Cullity 2009: 10–19). I shall not endorse this framework here. For the purposes of this essay, what Cullity labels as concern amounts to beneficence, and cooperation, in his language, corresponds at least to a part of what has been here called socio-economic justice.

wrong to have or to pursue — beneficence and justice express a practical concern for interests whose furthering is *morally permissible* (Cullity 2004: 17, 134–49, 2009: 20–21).[19] If the pursuit of certain interests and goods is permissible, i.e., not wrong, for beneficed people, it cannot be wrong for benefactors to pursue them in their own lives as well. If a good grounds a requirement to help others to have it, it cannot be wrong for me to have it as well. Accordingly, it cannot be the case that beneficence or justice require actions such that the pursuit of permissible interests by the benefactors is jeopardized. It cannot be the case that beneficence requires giving up the goods and perspectives of life that one is striving to ensure to others. If an agent refrains from further beneficence, or from a higher level of justice, in order to pursue such interests and goods, that cannot be wrong. Beneficence and justice cannot lead to too hard and sober lives, if one only acknowledges that what is good in life is not only what is needed to do beneficent or just actions.

To devote money and time to leisure and culture, to friendship and personal commitments and projects, if of a valuable type, cannot be considered a failure of beneficence or of justice, because in many cases beneficence and justice require one to provide help to other people in their pursuit of these very kinds of goods. Accordingly, the pursuit of partial goods such as friendship and personal projects and commitments cannot be wrong, nor can lives spent in pursuing them be wrong. But if this is the case, it cannot be wrong for benefactors to limit their beneficence in order to guarantee to themselves those very goods and the lives focused on them. This reasoning provides a principled way of limiting the demands of beneficence and justice, and to block the iteration process that leads to absurd demandingness (see Cullity 2004: 128–29, 137–66, 2009: 21–30).[20]

[19] With some qualifications, though. There could be reasons for helping people in doing something wrong, provided the reason for helping is not the wrongness itself. As Cullity explains, 'As an electoral officer, I may be required to declare you the winner in an election even though your interest in getting elected is to use your office for bad ends. But the reason grounding this requirement on me is not that it serves your interest in doing what is wrong. Rather, it is that fairness dictates that I act impartially' (Cullity 2009: 21). See also Cullity (2004: 143–45).

[20] Cullity (2004: 103–4) traces this argument from the presuppositions of beneficence back to Kant's *Metaphysics of Morals*, Ak. 6.393, 6.450–51, and to Williams (1981: 12, 18).

The argument above rests on two assumptions. The first assumption is that beneficence and justice protect aims and goods that are *merely permissible*, i.e., not wrong. When an interest is not wrong, then we are required to help people to have it — at least when this is possible at no substantial cost to us.

Now, this assumption suggests a very permissive perspective, according to which any possible interest whose pursuit is not immoral is beneficence-requiring. This seems to imply, for instance, that failing to help an amateur to amass a great private art collection is a failure of beneficence as well as other more striking cases, such as failing to help people in dire need. To mitigate this consequence, Cullity suggests two integrations of this assumption. First, he emphasizes the difference between gaining and losing, and between choosing at the outset an entire life focused on certain expensive pursuits and continuing one's life. Cullity maintains that the costs of losing previously possessed goods and interrupting an already structured life may be high enough to ground requirements of beneficence. Second, if it is the case that a cheaper option is available to the agent, at no substantial costs for her, then the agent has no legitimate claim to being helped in pursuing the more expensive option. Accordingly, many of the most expensive and futile goods are not beneficence-requiring (Cullity 2004: 152–55).

The second assumption is that there are certain specific kinds of goods, that Cullity calls 'commitment goods', that are (*a*) intrinsically irreplaceable; and (*b*) ground demands of beneficence. Those goods are things such as friendship, personal integrity or commitment to personal projects and the ensuing achievements. Their specific feature is not being available when one is willing to replace them with cheaper alternatives. As Cullity explains,

> a willingness to replace your friendship with cheaper ones that are just as good for you would involve a very unappealing detachment from your friends. Indeed, the fullest kind of friendship is a good which this sort of willingness would prevent me from possessing. . . . A similar point applies to the good of integrity: living in conformity with one's convictions. It may be the case that if I had different convictions, it would be cheaper to live in conformity with them. But in relation to many convictions, to regard myself as having the choice of replacing them with cheaper ones would be to lack those convictions altogether. (Cullity 2004: 155–56)

From these two assumptions, Cullity draws his conclusion. Pursuit of commitment goods is permissible, because they are irreplaceable and ground demands of beneficence. Accordingly, beneficence itself cannot require us to give up those goods (see *ibid.*: 156).[21]

To this argument might be addressed the following objection. It seems implausible to claim that any permissible good or permissible life is a ground of beneficence's demands. Even assuming the limitations to the first assumption listed earlier (the distinction between the cost of losing goods and that of gaining them, the fact that only the cheaper option is a ground for beneficence), it seems that Cullity's focus on mere permissibility enlarges too much the realm of beneficence. In other words, it seems counter-intuitive to claim that failures to help very affluent people keep (some of) their goods, or to go on leading their lives, have the same moral significance, and are as wrong as, failures to help destitute people in dire need. On the other hand, it seems that there should be a difference between goods and lives that are merely permissible and goods and lives that should be guaranteed to any individual. And it seems that, in conditions of partial compliance with beneficence or justice, it is plausible enough to ask people to give up goods or lives that are permissible but not necessary in order to ensure others the possibility of having goods or lives of minimal decency.

To reject this point and to block the demands of beneficence and justice, one needs to claim not merely that certain goods or lives are permissible, but that they are the *only* good or right ones. However, absent an independent argument against sacrifice, it is quite conceivable that the beneficent and just agent has a good enough life even when she gives up many of the interests and goods she is striving to ensure to others. It seems quite conceivable that *both* altruistic lives *and* lives devoted to partial projects and commitments are good ones — and this seems also to fit commonsense judgements.[22] To argue otherwise, one needs to claim that the goods whose pursuit is incompatible with certain degrees of beneficent

[21] Cullity claims also that if certain kinds of lives focused on commitment goods are shown to be permissible ones, other sorts of goods of different kinds might also be permissible, because they are necessary to leading those lives (see Cullity 2004: 160–65). I shall not consider this claim, here; however, the objections presented in the main text apply also to this further claim.

[22] Cullity (2004: 134, 157) acknowledges this point.

and just conduct (for instance, commitment goods) are *uniquely necessary* to making a good life, and that purely altruistic lives are not good enough.[23]

However, if both altruistic lives and non-altruistic lives are good, it seems that beneficence may require benefactors to give up some of their goods and to lead more altruistic lives. This is not contradictory, because what the beneficent agent loses in terms of non-altruistic goods may be gained in terms of the good of an altruistic life.

It might be argued that the second assumption of the argument from the presuppositions of beneficence and justice might block this demand, and make contradictory the requests of beneficence and justice when they jeopardize the enjoyment of commitment goods. According to this assumption, commitment goods and the lives focused on them cannot be replaced by other goods and lives, even when the latter are cheaper and of equal goodness, because the very nature of those goods prevents any replacement. As a consequence, beneficence and justice cannot demand that agents give up commitment goods.

This argument is wrong. For the claim that to be willing to replace one's friendships, or personal convictions, with cheaper goods amounts to losing friendship or integrity does not entail that this loss is worse for the agent, or that it cannot be compensated. But if the loss of those goods can be compensated by goods of equal value, then commitment goods do not ground beneficence. In other words, the friends and commitments typical of a non-altruistic life will be lost in altruistic lives; however, this is not a genuine loss, if other similar friends and commitments substitute them. Accordingly, failing to help people engaged in non-altruistic lives is not a failure of beneficence, at least if the alternative of an altruistic life is at their disposal. By contrast, failure to help people in dire need, unable to live any decent life, altruistic or not, is an obvious failure of beneficence.

In sum, the argument from presuppositions is unable to mitigate the demands of beneficence and justice, because it rests on wrong assumptions about the reasons for helping people and about the value of lives.

7. Conclusion

Demandingness turns out to be a recalcitrant issue. Three attempts to block extreme demands made in the name of justice and beneficence have

---

[23] In fact, Cullity (2004: 114, 129–31, 134, 136, 141, 144, 165–66) states this view, but rejects it.

been considered here, and they have been found unconvincing. Those strategies fail in two respects: either they fail in mitigating the demands of beneficence and justice (this is the case of the institutionalist strategies), or they rest on wrong assumptions (this is the case of collective beneficence and the argument from presuppositions). The struggle with the demandingness objection still cannot be considered won.[24]

References

Ashford, Elizabeth. 2003. 'The Demandingness of Scanlon's Contractualism', *Ethics* 113(3): 273–302.

Baier, Kurt. 1958. *The Moral Point of View*, Cornell University Press, Ithaca.

Barry, Brian. 2009. 'Humanity and Justice in Global Perspective', in Thomas Pogge and Darrel Moellendorf (eds), *Global Justice: Seminal Essays*, Paragon House, St Paul, 179–209.

Beitz, Charles. 1999. *Political Theory and International Relations*, Princeton University Press, Princeton.

Blake, Michael. 2001. 'Distributive Justice, State Coercion, and Autonomy', *Philosophy and Public Affairs* 30(3): 257–96.

Brandt, Richard B. 1979. *A Theory of the Good and the Right*, Clarendon Press, Oxford.

Brink, David O. 1986. 'Utilitarian Morality and the Personal Point of View', *The Journal of Philosophy* 84(8): 417–38.

Brock, Dan W. 1991. 'Defending Moral Options', *Philosophy and Phenomenological Research* 51(4): 909–13.

Brock, Gillian. 2009. *Global Justice: A Cosmopolitan Account*, Oxford University Press, Oxford.

Buchanan, Allen. 1987. 'Justice and Charity', *Ethics* 97(3): 558–75.

———. 1996. 'Charity, Justice, and the Idea of Moral Progress', in Jerome B. Schneewind (ed.), *Giving: Western Ideas of Philanthropy*, Indiana University Press, Bloomington, 94–116.

Cohen, L. Jonathan. 1981. 'Who Is Starving Whom?' *Theoria* 47(2): 65–81.

Cottingham, John. 1986. 'Partiality, Favouritism and Morality', *Philosophical Quarterly* 36(144): 357–73.

———. 1991. 'The Ethics of Self-Concern', *Ethics* 101(4): 798–817.

Cullity, Garrett. 1994. 'International Aid and the Scope of Kindness', *Ethics* 105(1): 99–127.

———. 2004. *The Moral Demands of Affluence*, Clarendon Press, Oxford.

———. 2009. 'Demandingness and the Arguments from Presuppositions', in Timothy Chappell (ed.), *The Problem of Moral Demandingness: New Philosophical Essays*, Palgrave Macmillan, London, 8–34.

[24] Michele Bocchiola read previous drafts of this paper, providing helpful suggestions and insightful comments. I am very grateful to him. Previous versions of this paper were presented at various conferences. I received many comments and suggestions from the audiences, in particular from Ian Carter, Neera Chandhoke, Marcello Di Paola, Elisabetta Galeotti, Sebastiano Maffettone, and Daniele Santoro. Of course, the conclusions defended here should be considered my exclusive responsibility.

Dworkin, Ronald. 1981. 'What Is Equality? Part 2: Equality of Resources', *Philosophy and Public Affairs* 10(4): 185–246.

———. 2000. *Sovereign Virtue: The Theory and Practice of Equality*, Harvard University Press, Cambridge, MA.

Feinberg, Joel. 1970. *Doing and Deserving: Essays in the Theory of Responsibility*, Princeton University Press, Princeton.

Frankena, William K. 1987. 'Beneficence/Benevolence', *Social Philosophy and Policy* 4(2): 1–20.

Gewirth, Alan. 1982. 'Starvation and Human Rights', in Alan Gewirth, *Human Rights: Essays on Justifications and Applications*, University of Chicago Press, Chicago, 197–217.

Glover, Jonathan. 1977. *Causing Death and Saving Lives*, Penguin, Harmondsworth.

Goodin, Robert E. 1985. *Protecting the Vulnerable*, University of Chicago Press, Chicago.

Griffin, James. 2008. *On Human Rights*, Oxford University Press, Oxford.

Heyd, David. 1982. *Supererogation: Its Status in Ethical Theory*, Cambridge University Press, Cambridge.

Hohfeld, Wesley N. 1923. *Fundamental Legal Conceptions as Applied in Judicial Reasoning and Other Legal Essays*, Yale University Press, New Haven.

Hooker, Brad. 2000. *Ideal Code, Real World: A Rule-Consequentialist Theory of Morality*, Clarendon Press, Oxford.

Horton, John. 2006. 'In Defence of Associative Political Obligations: Part One', *Political Studies* 54(3): 427–43.

———. 2007. 'In Defence of Associative Political Obligations: Part Two', *Political Studies* 55(1): 1–19.

Horton, Keith. 2011. 'Fairness and Fair Shares', *Utilitas* 23(1): 88–93.

Hume, David. 1975. *An Enquiry Concerning the Principles of Morals*, Oxford, Clarendon Press.

Julius, A. J. 2003. 'Basic Structure and the Value of Equality', *Philosophy and Public Affairs* 31(4): 321–55.

———. 2006. 'Nagel's Atlas', *Philosophy and Public Affairs* 34(1): 176–92.

Kagan, Shelly. 1989. *The Limits of Morality*, Clarendon Press, Oxford.

Kant, Immanuel. 1930. *Lectures on Ethics* (trans. Louis Infeld), Methuen, London.

Kekes, John. 1987. 'Benevolence: A Minor Virtue', *Social Philosophy and Policy* 4(2): 21–36.

Kelly, Paul J. 1998. 'Contractarian Justice: An Overview of Some Contemporary Debates', in Paul J. Kelly and David Boucher (eds), *Social Justice: From Hume to Walzer*, Routledge, London and New York, 185–202.

Moellendorf, Darrell. 2002. *Cosmopolitan Justice*, Westview Press, Boulder.

Mulgan, Tim. 2001. *The Demands of Consequentialism*, Clarendon Press, Oxford.

Murphy, Liam B. 1999. 'Institutions and the Demands of Justice', *Philosophy and Public Affairs* 27(4): 251–91.

———. 2000. *Moral Demands in Nonideal Theory*, Oxford University Press, Oxford.

Nagel, Thomas. 1991. *Equality and Partiality*, Oxford University Press, New York.

———. 2005. 'The Problem of Global Justice', *Philosophy and Public Affairs* 33(2): 113–47 (reprinted in this volume, Chapter 3).

Narveson, Jan. 1999. 'Feeding the Hungry', in Jan Narveson, *Moral Matters*, Broadview Press, Peterborough, 143–56.

Narveson, Jan. 2003. '"We Don't Owe Them a Thing!" A Though-Minded but Soft-Hearted View of Aid to the Faraway Needy', *Monist* 86(3): 419–33.

O'Neill, Onora. 1986. *Faces of Hunger: An Essay on Poverty, Justice and Development*, Allen & Unwin, London.

———. 1994. 'Justice and Boundaries', in Chris Brown (ed.), *Political Restructuring in Europe: Ethical Perspectives*, Routledge, London, 69–88.

———. 1996. *Towards Justice and Virtue: A Constructive Account of Practical Reasoning*, Cambridge University Press, Cambridge.

———. 2008. 'Lifeboat Earth', in Thomas Pogge and Darrel Moellendorf (eds), *Global Justice: Seminal Essays*, Paragon House, St Paul, 1–20.

Parfit, Derek. 1984. *Reasons and Persons*, Clarendon Press, Oxford.

Pogge, Thomas. 1992. 'An Institutional Approach to Humanitarian Intervention', *Public Affairs Quarterly* 6(1): 89–103.

———. 1994. 'Cosmopolitanism and Sovereignty', in Chris Brown (ed.), *Political Restructuring in Europe: Ethical Perspectives*, Routledge, London, 89–122.

———. 1995. 'How Should Human Rights Be Conceived?' *Jahrbuch fur Recht und Ethik* 3: 103–20.

———. 2002. *World Poverty and Human Rights: Cosmopolitan Responsibilities and Reforms*, Polity, Cambridge.

Rachels, James. 1979. 'Killing and Starving to Death', *Philosophy* 54(208): 159–71.

Railton, Peter. 1984. 'Alienation, Consequentialism and the Demands of Morality', *Philosophy and Public Affairs* 13(2): 134–71.

Rawls, John. 1996, *Political Liberalism*, Columbia University Press, New York.

———. 1999. *A Theory of Justice*, Harvard University Press, Cambridge, MA (rev. edn).

———. 2001. *The Law of Peoples*, Harvard University Press, Cambridge, MA.

Sangiovanni, Andrea. 2007. 'Global Justice, Reciprocity, and the State', *Philosophy and Public Affairs* 35(1): 3–39.

Scheffler, Samuel. 1994a. *The Rejection of Consequentialism: A Philosophical Investigation of the Considerations underlying Rival Moral Conceptions*, Clarendon Press, Oxford.

———. 1994b. *Human Morality*, Oxford University Press, Oxford.

———. 2005. 'Egalitarian Liberalism as Moral Pluralism', *Aristotelian Society Supplementary Volume* 79(1): 229–53.

Schneewind, Jerome B. 1996. 'Philosophical Ideas of Charity: Some Historical Reflections', in Jerome B. Schneewind (ed.), *Giving: Western Ideas of Philanthropy*, Indiana University Press, Bloomington, 54–75.

Sen, Amartya K. 1984. 'The Right Not to Be Hungry', in Paul Alston and Katarina Tomasevski (eds), *The Right to Food*, Martinus Nijhoff, Dordrecht, 69–81.

Shue, Henry. 1980. *Basic Rights: Subsistence, Affluence and US Foreign Policy*, Princeton University Press, Princeton.

Simmons, A. John. 1996. 'Associative Political Obligations', *Ethics* 106(2): 247–73.

Singer, Peter. 1972. 'Famine, Affluence and Morality', *Philosophy and Public Affairs* 1(3): 229–43 (reprinted in this volume, Chapter 1).

———. 1979. *Practical Ethics*, Cambridge University Press, Cambridge.

Singer, Peter. 2007. 'Review Essay on *The Moral Demands of Affluence*', *Philosophy and Phenomenological Research* 75(2): 475–83.

———. 2009. *The Life You Can Save: Acting Now to End World Poverty*, Random House, New York.

Stephen, James Fitzjames. 1883. *A History of the Criminal Law of England*, MacMillan, London.

Unger, Peter. 1996. *Living High and Letting Die: Our Illusion of Innocence*, Oxford University Press, New York.

Urmson, James O. 1958. 'Saints and Heroes', in A. Melden (ed.), *Essays on Moral Philosophy*, University of Washington Press, Seattle, 198–216.

Williams, Bernard. 1981. 'Persons, Character and Morality', in Bernard Williams, *Moral Luck*, Cambridge University Press, Cambridge, 1–19.

Wolf, Susan. 1982. 'Moral Saints', *The Journal of Philosophy* 89(8): 419–39.

———. 1992. 'Morality and Partiality', *Philosophical Perspectives* 6: 243–59.

Part II

DEPAROCHIALIZING THE DEBATE

5

Global Justice

Amartya Sen

'Injustice anywhere is a threat to justice everywhere,' said Dr Martin Luther King, Jr, forty-five years ago in April 1963, in a letter from Birmingham Jail. It would be hard to find a more urgent intellectual agenda today than the demands of world justice. But world justice is not an easy subject. I think I should begin with a few remarks on the idea of justice in general and that of world justice in particular.

It is, I would argue, useful to distinguish between: (*a*) an organization-focused understanding of justice; and (*b*) the basic idea of realized justice. Sometimes justice is conceptualized in terms of certain organizational requirements — some institutions, some regulations, some rules (for example, free speech, or free trade, or progressive taxation, depending on a particular understanding of the structural demands of justice). This can be fine enough as far as it goes, but, going beyond institutions and structures, we also have to examine what actually does emerge, influenced by institutions and organizations, but also by other features of the society (such as behaviour modes, social norms and practices and so on).

In classical Sanskrit, two distinct words — *niti* and *nyaya* — help to differentiate two separate concentrations. Words such as *niti* and *nyaya* have been used in many different senses in different legal theories in ancient India, but one of the main uses of the term *niti* is organizational propriety. In contrast, the term *nyaya* stands for a more comprehensive concept of realized justice. In this line of vision, the role of institutions, important as it is, takes a subsidiary and partial role. For example, the ancient Indian legal theorists talked disparagingly of what they called *matsyanaya*: 'justice in the world of fish' — a society of fish where a big fish can freely devour a small fish. This is outlined as what is to be avoided, and it is seen as imperative that the 'justice of fish' cannot invade the world of human beings. So *nyaya* is the subject-matter of the kind of society that the social institutions and practical rules should aim at, working with other influences. The realization of justice in the sense of *nyaya* is not just a matter of judging institutions and rules, but of judging the societies themselves. Whatever the propriety of established organizations, if a big fish remains free to devour a small fish, then this is a violation of human justice, no matter to what the causation of that transgression is traced.

In the inclusive perspective of *nyaya*, there is little room for judgements like Ferdinand I's famous 16th century maxim: 'Fiat justitia et pereat mundus' ('Let justice be done, though the world perishes'). If the world does perish, there would not be much to admire in this development in the perspective of *nyaya*, even though the austere *niti* leading to this result could be defended with very sophisticated arguments of different kinds. The distinction is important, even when *niti* and *nyaya* complement each other. For example, setting up many more schools for children in educationally deprived countries would be an important *niti*, but what would be celebrated in the perspective of *nyaya* is the achievement that boys and girls are actually educated and have the freedom that comes from that accomplishment. Similarly, reforming the counterproductive patent laws for medicine to make urgently needed drugs against preventable diseases affordable by the poor of the world would be an excellent departure in *niti*, but it is the actual overcoming of those diseases (through the combination of cheaper drugs, more targeted research, better delivery and use, and so on) that would demand inclusion in the vision of *nyaya*.

It is easy to see that the pursuit of world justice would need a great many institutional developments and organizational changes around the globe, but underlying our interest in institutional analysis must be some idea of the overall demands of global justice itself. The distinction between *nyaya* and *niti* is, thus, important for the subject of world justice.

Contemporary Political Philosophy

We are not, of course, working in an intellectual vacuum, for these subjects have engaged attention over a very long period of time. There are also well-developed bodies of literature on the theory of justice in political philosophy, in jurisprudence and legal philosophy, and in welfare economics. Even though the inspiration for contemporary works on justice goes back to classic contributions of the stalwarts of the European Enlightenment, for example the contributions of Jean Jacques Rousseau, Immanuel Kant, Jeremy Bentham, and Thomas Jefferson, the modern discipline of the theory of justice has been most strongly influenced by the writings of John Rawls, whose path-breaking book, *A Theory of Justice*, published in 1971, has set the stage for much of the present-day animation in the theory of justice. Even those of our leading contemporary political philosophers, such as Ronald Dworkin, Thomas Nagel, Robert Nozick, and Thomas Scanlon (to name a few), who have proposed rather different ways of dealing with issues identified by Rawls in his famous contribution, have tended to a great extent to see the requirements of a theory of justice in basically Rawlsian coordinates. John Rawls is clearly the dominant influence in the contemporary philosophy of justice.

I must admit that I too have, until fairly recently, tended to agree on the centrality of the Rawlsian perspective on justice, seeking departures mainly in the form of different answers to essentially Rawlsian inquiries. I now believe that this is a serious mistake, despite the profundity of Rawls's ideas and the debt that we owe to him. It is, I believe, quite useful to examine why the scepticism of the Rawlsian basic framework may be justified, and why there is an urgent need for foundational departures from the prevailing theories of justice in contemporary political philosophy. These departures are necessary for the theory of justice in general, but they are particularly important for addressing the challenges of world justice.

Rawlsian Theory of Justice as Fairness

The starting-point of Rawls's formulation of the theory of justice is his insistence that the idea of justice — and the institutions needed for it — should be based on the demands of a more foundational concept than justice, namely, fairness. It is on the foundations of fairness (as characterized by Rawls) that the Rawlsian principles of justice are developed. Fairness involves a demand to avoid bias in our assessments, and in particular the need to escape being influenced by our respective vested interests or personal advantages. It is, in this sense, a demand for impartiality. Rawls's explication of the demands of impartiality makes use of an imaginary device, which he calls the 'original position'. The original position is a postulated situation of primordial equality, when the parties involved have no knowledge of their respective personal identities *within* the group as a whole. They have to choose, under this devised 'veil of ignorance', what exact rules should govern the society they are, as it were, 'establishing'. The influence of individual vested interest or personal gain is 'kept out' through the insistence that the deliberations on the choice of rules occur under ignorance of each person of his or her own personal interests and particular desires. This is how Rawls gets to his principles of justice.

Rawls's principles of justice, thus chosen, are used to set up, as it were, the basic institutional structure of the society. He characterizes in the following way the exact principles that he expects would emerge in the 'original position', with a priority for the first principle over the second, in the case of any conflict.

> (1) Each person has an equal right to a fully adequate scheme of equal basic liberties which is compatible with a similar scheme of liberties for all.
>
> (2) Social and economic inequalities must satisfy two conditions. First, they must be attached to offices and positions open to all under conditions of fair equality of opportunity; and second, they must be to the greatest benefit of the least advantaged members of society. (Rawls 1993: 291)

It will be readily seen that the principles of justice, which are aimed at setting up 'just institutions', take the form of specifying organizational requirements mainly in the sense of *niti*, rather than judging the societies as a whole, in the sense of *nyaya*. That, as will emerge, is indeed a problem, but I must also emphasize that despite this rather limited focus, Rawls does also provide plentiful discussion of the kind of just society we might hope to see as emerging from these appropriate institutional choices.

More substantively, it can be seen that the principles of justice identified by Rawls include the priority of liberty (the 'first principle') giving precedence to maximal liberty for each person subject to similar liberty for all. Other issues of institutional choice are taken up through a compound set of requirements that are combined in the 'second principle', but the 'priority of liberty' comes first.

The first part of the second principle is concerned with the institutional requirement of making sure that public opportunities are open to all, without anyone being excluded or handicapped on grounds of, say, race or ethnicity or caste or religion. The second part of the second principle (called the 'difference principle') is concerned with distributive equity as well as overall efficiency, and it takes the form of making the worst-off members of the society as well off as possible.

Rawls's analysis of equity in the distribution of resources is done through an index of what Rawls calls 'primary goods', which are *general-purpose means* to achieve a variety of ends (whatever resources would be generally helpful in getting what people would want, varied as they might be). Rawls sees primary goods as including such things as 'rights, liberties and opportunities, income and wealth, and the social bases of self-respect' (Rawls 1971: 60–65).

Some Questions

The Rawlsian theory of justice has been a major constructive force in political philosophy, welfare economics and legal theory. Even though I must argue for the need for several radical departures from the Rawlsian understanding of the theory of justice, I must also emphasize how much our thinking on justice has benefitted from Rawls's constructive work — both affirmatively and dialectically. Also, there are elements of Rawls's theory that, I would argue, cannot but be central to any plausible theory of justice. For example, I would strongly support Rawls's chosen starting-point, to wit, the need to consider the demands of fairness as a prelude to the scrutiny of justice. Even though I shall presently suggest that the particular way Rawls proceeds to characterize fairness has several difficulties, I concur with his general belief that some exacting demands of impartiality must be incorporated in the foundations of justice.

The discipline of comparison

I proceed now to a number of critical issues that are problematic in the Rawlsian framework. The first question is extremely simple but, I would argue, rather far-reaching: *what do we want from a theory of justice?* In his analysis of justice, Rawls takes the principal task of a theory of justice to be aimed at identifying the 'just society'. This leads to what can be called a 'transcendental' approach to justice that focuses on identifying perfectly just societal arrangements, rather than offering a way of comparing not entirely just societies against each other (the kind of societies we might actually encounter in the world — to decide on what we should actually do — rather than pine for the perfectly just). The transcendental approach goes back at least to the writings of Thomas Hobbes, and to his insistence that we cannot talk about justice without invoking a sovereign state, since we cannot fulfil the exacting requirements of a perfectly just society without the help of unimpeded sovereignty. So this is in line with a transcendental approach (focusing on the unsurpassably just), but there were, in fact, many other approaches in political philosophy that emerged during the Enlightenment which did not take the transcendental route (for example, those proposed by Adam Smith, or Condorcet, or Mary Wollstonecraft, or William Godwin, or Jeremy Bentham, or John Stuart Mill).

However, in Rawls's work, and in the theories that have followed his identification of the requirements of a theory of justice, the attention of modern political philosophy has tended to be relentlessly focused on addressing the transcendental question (and quite often *only* that question). In contrast, what can be called a 'comparative' approach would have concentrated instead on ranking alternative societal arrangements (whether some arrangement is 'less just' or 'more just' than another, so that we get guidance on what to do), rather than focusing exclusively — or at all — on the identification of a fully just society. Modern social choice theory takes a robustly comparative approach.[1] I shall call this 'the comparison question'.

Room for disagreement

The second question concerns the type of agreement that can reasonably be expected to emerge from public reasoning under conditions of fairness (in Rawls's case, through his device of the 'original position'). Can we really expect that everyone in the original position would proceed to accept some one specific set of rules — principles of justice — as the only way to go? Is it sensible to assume that all our disagreements really arise from our respective vested interests (so that once they are taken out of action, we would all come to exactly the same conclusion)?

[1] Social choice theory, in its modern form, has been pioneered by Kenneth Arrow (1951). See also Sen (1970). The analytical priority of the comparative can also be seen in the early formulations of social choice theory in the 18th century, particularly by Marquis de Condorcet (1785).

Could it be that some of our differences are linked with basically different conceptions of justice, focusing on different grounds of justice? I shall call this the 'room for disagreement question'.

Individual interest, social parochialism and open impartiality

The third issue concerns Rawls's way of characterizing the demands of fairness. How do we specify these demands so that evaluation of justice and the choice of principles of justice, under those conditions, guarantee the necessary impartiality? The issue of impartiality relates both to eliminating the influence of vested interest across the board, and also to eradicating the impact of local parochialism — an issue of some importance not only for global justice, but also for local or national justice in a global world. Rawls keeps his exercise of fairness confined to the limits of each polity on its own, that is, roughly speaking, separately for each nation-state, or what we can roughly think of as a nation-state. While fairness in the treatment of all the persons in a nation (or 'a people', as Rawls calls that collectivity) is pursued by Rawls through vigorous elimination of individual vested interests, others who do not belong to this nation or people, do not come into consideration in the same way at all.

That is problematic enough, but there is in addition a second problem as well. The exclusive focus on eliminating the influence of individual vested interest, as opposed to that of community-based parochialism, makes the pursuit of impartiality and fairness in the Rawlsian framework that much more limited. I shall call this 'the impartiality question'.

Freedoms and capabilities

Fourth, since Rawls concentrates on a person's holding of 'primary goods' (like income, wealth, etc.) to judge the overall advantage that he or she enjoys compared with others, there is some serious overlooking of the fact that different persons, for reasons of personal characteristics or environmental influence, can have widely varying 'conversion' opportunities of external objects (like income and wealth) to their respective capabilities — what they can or cannot actually do. A person with a proneness to illness, or living in an epidemiologically challenged environment, may get far less out of a given amount of income than another who is not similarly afflicted.

Rawls does talk about the eventual emergence of special provisions for 'special needs' (for example, for the blind or for those who are otherwise clearly disabled), at a later phase — the 'legislative phase' — of his multi-stage story of Rawlsian justice. This is good rectification as far as it goes, but (*a*) these corrections occur (if they do) only after the basic institutional structure has been set up through the Rawlsian 'principles of justice' (which are not influenced by such 'special needs'); and (*b*) even at a later stage, when special note is taken of 'special needs', there is no attempt to come to terms with the *pervasive* variations in conversion opportunities between any two different persons.

Transcendental versus the Comparative

The transcendental and comparative approaches are quite distinct, and neither approach, in general, subsumes the other (Sen 2006). This is unfortunate for the transcendental approach, since no matter what other characteristics a theory of justice might sensibly have, it must also, for use in practical reasoning, help us to address comparative assessments of justice, such as: how can we make a country, or the world, less unjust? The pursuit of justice in the world can never take the form of jumping in one go to some perfectly just society. Despite that, the Rawlsian framework, and nearly all the theories of justice in contemporary political philosophy, are exclusively devoted to identifying 'the perfectly just', rather than being concerned in any direct way with comparative assessments.

The intellectual interest in, and practical relevance of, comparative questions about justice are hard to deny. Investigation of different ways of advancing justice in a society (or in the world), or of reducing manifest injustices that may exist, demands comparative judgements about justice, for which the identification of fully just social arrangements is neither necessary nor sufficient. To illustrate the contrast involved, it may well turn out that in a comparative perspective, the introduction of social policies that eliminate widespread hunger (or remove rampant illiteracy) is widely seen as a manifest advancement of justice. But the implementation of such policies would still leave the societies involved far away from the transcendental — or unsurpassable — requirements of a fully just society (since transcendence would have many other demands regarding equal liberties, distributional equity and so on).

To take another example, instituting a system of health insurance in the United States that does not leave tens of millions of Americans without any guarantee of medical attention at all may be judged to be an advancement of justice, but such an institutional change would not turn the United States into a 'just society', since there would remain a thousand other transgressions to remedy. Some non-transcendental articulation is clearly needed.

But, it can be asked, do we not need a transcendental pure theory to have an intellectually adequate theory of comparative assessment of justice? There seems to be fairly widespread belief among many of the practitioners of Rawlsian and other transcendental theories of justice that comparative questions can be answered only with the help of a transcendental identification of a perfectly just society. It is, however, not at all easy to see why this should be the case. Indeed, the two exercises are quite distinct and neither need throw much light on the other. You cannot get anything like the richness of a comparative approach from identifying a transcendental possibility. For example, you may firmly conclude that Leonardo da Vinci is the best painter ever in the world (including Picasso, Braque and so on), but it won't tell you how to rank Picasso against Braque. Conversely, you could not necessarily get the unsurpassable (or the transcendental) alternative from the totality of our comparative judgements. We may be able to make a great many pair-wise comparisons, but not quite all. We may be able to rank, say, Picasso against Braque, or Dali, and make many other such judgements, and yet we may fail to identify the 'very best', or the 'absolutely right' choice, because of an inability to rank some pairs of alternatives, say Picasso against Van Gogh (if the two are competing for the top position).

This is not to reduce in any way the importance of the inspiration that Rawls's transcendental theory has provided in drawing general attention to many issues of practical importance, such as the critical role of social institutions, the special status of personal liberty, or the centrality of poverty removal as a social concern. And yet if we want to use that theory not just for inspiration, but for guidance for making judgements about the enhancement of justice through institutional reform or behavioural transformation, we would not, alas, get any specific comparative implications from the identification of a transcendental alternative.

Disengagement from World Justice in Transcendental Theories

It is not hard to see that world justice demands many reforms and many new institutions and practices. But the mere identification of the 'perfectly just society' would not tell us much about what to do to pursue the advance of justice in the world in which we live. Indeed, the concentration on the transcendental approach has had, I would argue, a seriously negative effect on practical discussion of justice in general and global justice in particular. We can think of many changes that would manifestly advance world justice as we see it, without getting us to 'the perfectly just world'. However, that kind of discussion would appear to be just 'loose talk' to those who are persuaded by the Hobbesian–Rawlsian claim that justice is about the perfectly just society, and that we need a fully sovereign state to apply the principles of justice with its extensive institutional requirements, which is a consequence of taking questions of justice to be exclusively issues of transcendental justice.

Consider the strongly argued dismissal of the relevance of 'the idea of global justice' by one of the leading contemporary philosophers, Thomas Nagel (from whose work I have learned so many things). His argument draws on his understanding that there are extensive institutional demands to think cogently about justice which cannot be met at the global level at this time. As Nagel puts it, 'it seems to me very difficult to resist Hobbes's claim about the relation between justice and sovereignty,' and 'if Hobbes is right, the idea of global justice without a world government is a chimera' (Nagel 2005: 115 [see this volume, p. 60]). In the global context, Nagel concentrates, therefore, on clarifying other demands, distinguishable from the demands of justice, such as 'minimal humanitarian morality' (Nagel 2005: 130–33, 146–47 [see this volume, p. 74]).

In the Rawlsian approach too, the application of a theory of justice requires an extensive cluster of institutions that determines the basic structure of a fully just society. Not surprisingly, Rawls actually abandons his own principles of justice when it comes to the assessment of how to go about thinking about global justice. In a later contribution, *The Law of Peoples*, Rawls invokes a 'second original position', with a fair negotiation involving representatives of different polities — or different 'peoples' as Rawls calls them — who serve as parties under this second veil of ignorance (Rawls 1999). However, Rawls does not try to derive principles of justice that might emanate from this second original position and concentrates instead on certain general principles of humanitarian behaviour.

Thus, the theory of justice, as formulated in this transcendental approach, reduces many of the most relevant issues of justice in the world as being simply inadmissible when it would seem to be most strongly needed. This is a pity: when people across the world agitate to get more global justice, they are not clamouring for some kind of 'minimal humanitarianism'.

Incomplete Orderings and the Use of Comparative Judgements

Am I overstretching the dichotomy between the transcendental and the comparative? The former may be neither necessary nor sufficient for the other, but should not a sequence of pair-wise comparisons invariably lead us to the very best? That presumption has some appeal, since the superlative might indeed appear to be the natural end-point of a robust comparative. But this is, in fact, a non sequitur. It is only with a 'well-ordered' ranking (for example, a complete and transitive ordering over a finite set) that we can be sure that pair-wise comparisons must ultimately identify a 'best' alternative. We must, therefore, ask: how complete should the assessment be, for it to be a systematic discipline of evaluation? In what can be called a 'totalist' approach that characterizes the standard theories of justice (including Rawls's), incompleteness tends to appear as a failure, or at least as a sign of the unfinished nature of the exercise. Indeed, the survival of incompleteness is sometimes seen as a defect of a theory of justice, which calls into question the positive assertions that such a theory makes. In fact, however, a theory of justice that makes systematic room for incompleteness allows one to arrive at possibly quite strong judgements (for example, about the injustice of continuing famines in a world of prosperity, or of persistently grotesque subjugation of women), without having to find highly differentiated assessments of every political and social arrangement in comparison with every other arrangement (e.g., addressing such questions as: is a top income tax rate of 39 per cent more just or less just than a top rate of 38 per cent?). I have discussed elsewhere why a systematic and disciplined theory of normative evaluation, including assessment of social justice, need not take a 'totalist' form (Sen 2000; *cf.* Sen 1970, 1997, 1999, 2004).

Incompleteness may be of the lasting kind for several different reasons, including unbridgeable gaps in information, and judgemental unresolvability involving disparate considerations that cannot be entirely eliminated, even with full information. For example, it may be hard to resolve the overall balance of the comparative claims of equity considerations, when different considerations conflict in subtle ways. And yet, despite such durable ambiguity, we may still be able to agree readily that there is a clear social injustice involved in the persistence of endemic hunger or exclusion from medical access, which calls for remedying for the *advancement* of justice (or reduction of injustice), even after taking note of the costs involved. Similarly, we may acknowledge the possibility that liberties of different persons may, to some extent, conflict with each other (so that any fine-tuning of the demands of equal liberty may be hard to work out), and yet strongly agree that torturing people in custody would be an unjust violation of liberty, and such policies demand immediate rectification.

There is a further consideration that may work powerfully in the direction of making political room for incompleteness of judgements about social justice, even if it were the case that every person had a complete ordering over the possible social arrangements. Since a theory of justice invokes agreement between different parties (for example in the 'original position' in the Rawlsian framework), incompleteness can also arise from the possibility that different persons may continue to have some differences, even after agreeing on a lot of the comparative judgements. Even after vested interests and personal gains have been somehow 'taken out' of consideration through such devices as the 'veil of ignorance', there may remain possibly conflicting views on social priorities, for example in weighing the claims of need over entitlement to the fruits of one's labour.

Room for Disagreement: An Illustration

Conflicts of distributive principles that are hard to eradicate can be illustrated with an example. The illustration is concerned with the problem of deciding which of three children should get a flute about which they are quarrelling — you have to adjudicate between these different claims.

Child A claims it on the ground that she is the only one of the three who knows how to play the flute (the others don't deny this). If that is all you knew, the case for giving it to the first child would be strong.

However, child B expresses his claim to the flute on the ground that he is the only one among the three who is so poor that he has no toy of his own, and that the flute will give him something to play with (the other two concede that they are much richer and well supplied with engaging amenities). If you had only heard child B and none of the others, the case for giving it to child B would be strong.

Child C, on the other hand, argues that she has been working for many months to make the flute with her own labour (the others confirm this), and just when she had finished her work, she complains, 'these Johnnies came along trying to snatch the flute away from me.' You might have given it to child C if her statement was all you had heard.

However, having heard all three you do have a problem. Theorists of different persuasions — utilitarian or egalitarian or libertarian — may believe that a just resolution can be readily spotted here, though, alas, they would respectively see totally different resolutions as being 'obviously right'.

The main point to note in the present context is that the different resolutions all have serious arguments in support of them, and we may not be able to identify, without some arbitrariness, one of the alternative arguments as being the only one that must invariably prevail. Different impartial judges may take different views in this decisional problem (unrelated to their respective vested interest or hope of personal gain). And the problem of choice in this case is ultimately one of priorities in the principles of justice, so that the decisional dilemma reflects a deeper problem of conflict of unrejectable principles that would need to be accommodated.

And yet in many particular cases, there will be no decisional dilemma to resolve, even when none of the underlying reasons is summarily rejected. It may turn out that the child who has made the flute is also the poorest, or the only one who knows how to play the flute. Or it might be the case that child B's deprivation is so extreme, and his dependence on something to play with so important for a plausible life, that the poverty-based argument might come to dominate the judgement of justice. There could be what can be called 'circumscribed congruence' despite the varying weights that different impartial judges apply to the conflicting considerations.

Rawls has shown, rather convincingly in my view, why liberty has a special place that cannot be ignored when comparing the claims of liberty against other considerations, including the avoidance of inequality and poverty. Rawls went on to argue for giving total priority to liberty in *all* cases. It is much easier to be persuaded that such a priority would be quite right when the violations of personal liberty happen to be extremely serious, whereas issues of economic inequality are not at all matters of life and death. And yet when the transgressions against liberty are rather marginal, and the inequalities involved can cause extremely tragic deprivations, then, as Herbert Hart, the Oxford legal philosopher, argued in a famous critique of Rawls, the case for giving invariable priority to liberty would be hard to defend (Hart 1973). In his later writings, Rawls was willing to make some concessions to Hart's argument (Rawls 1993: lecture 8), and yet his theory makes that very hard to do.

Open Impartiality and Global Public Discussion

I turn now to the third issue, the impartiality question. The role of impartiality in the evaluation of social judgements and societal arrangements is well recognized in moral and political philosophy. There is, however, a basic distinction between two quite different ways of invoking impartiality. With what I would call 'closed impartiality', the procedure of making impartial judgements invokes only the members of a given society or nation or what Rawls calls a 'people'. The Rawlsian method of 'justice as fairness' uses the device of an 'original contract' between the citizens of a given polity. No outsider is involved in such a contractarian procedure, or is a party to the original contract (either directly, or through representatives). For the members of the focal group, the 'veil of ignorance' requires them to be ignorant of their respective identity *within* the focal group, and this can be an effective procedure for overcoming *individual partialities* within the focal group.

However, even under the veil of ignorance a person does know that she belongs to the focal group, and is not someone outside it — indeed he or she could be anyone in that particular group — and there is no insistence at all that perspectives from outside the focal group be invoked.

As a device of structured political analysis, the procedure is not geared to addressing the need to overcome group prejudices or parochialism.

In contrast, in the case of 'open impartiality', the procedure of making impartial judgements can (and in some cases, must) invoke judgements inter alia from outside the focal group. For example, in Adam Smith's use of the device of 'the impartial spectator', the requirement of impartiality requires the invoking of disinterested judgements of 'any fair and impartial spectator', not necessarily (indeed sometimes ideally not) belonging to the focal group (Smith 1976).

Adam Smith was particularly concerned about avoiding the grip of parochialism in jurisprudence and moral and political reasoning. In a chapter entitled 'On the Influence of Custom and Fashion upon the Sentiments of Moral Approbation and Disapprobation', Smith gives various examples of how discussions confined within a given society can be incarcerated within a seriously narrow understanding:

> the murder of new-born infants was a practice allowed of in almost all the states of Greece, even among the polite and civilized Athenians; and whenever the circumstances of the parent rendered it inconvenient to bring up the child, to abandon it to hunger, or to wild beasts, was regarded without blame or censure. . . . Uninterrupted custom had by this time so thoroughly authorized the practice, that not only the loose maxims of the world tolerated this barbarous prerogative, but even the doctrine of philosophers, which ought to have been more just and accurate, was led away by the established custom, and upon this, as upon many other occasions, instead of censuring, supported the horrible abuse, by far-fetched considerations of public utility. Aristotle talks of it as of what the magistrates ought upon many occasions to encourage. Plato is of the same opinion, and, with all that love of mankind which seems to animate all his writings, nowhere marks this practice with disapprobation. (Smith 1976: 210)

Adam Smith's insistence that we must inter alia view our sentiments from 'a certain distance from us' is, thus, motivated by the object of scrutinizing not only the influence of vested interest, but also the impact of entrenched tradition and custom. While Smith's example of infanticide remains sadly relevant in some societies even today, many of his other examples have relevance to other contemporary societies. This applies, for example, to Smith's insistence that 'the eyes of the rest of mankind' must be invoked to understand whether 'a punishment appears equitable' (Smith 1982: 104). Scrutiny from a 'distance' may be useful for practices as different as the stoning of adulterous women in Taliban's Afghanistan, selective abortion of female foetuses in China, Korea and parts of South Asia (Sen 2001), and plentiful use of capital punishment in China, Singapore or parts of the United States (with or without the opportunity for celebratory public jubilation).

While we are not likely to have a global state or a global democracy any time soon, Smith's emphasis on the use of the impartial spectator has immediate implications for the role of global public discussion in the contemporary world, to arrive at some important comparative judgements. Global dialogue, which I believe is central for world justice, comes today not only through institutions like the United Nations or the WTO, but much more broadly through the media, through political agitations, through the committed work of citizens' organizations and many NGOs, and through social work that draws not only on national identities but also other commonalities, like trade union movements, cooperative operations or feminist activities.

Primary Goods versus Capabilities

I turn, finally, to the capability question. In comparing the relative advantage of two persons in applying the difference principle of Rawls, we are directed by Rawls to proceed on the basis of the holdings of primary goods the two persons respectively have. But he focuses on command over general-purpose resources, rather than the actual ability of the person to do this or be that. In a series of contributions, the Rawlsian approach of focusing on primary goods has been fairly extensively challenged in recent years by the alternative perspective of what is called the 'capability approach' (Sen 1985; Sen and Nussbaum 1993). In that line of vision a central role is given to the person's actual ability to do the different things she has reason to value. These attainments in human living (like being well nourished, avoiding premature mortality, taking part in the life of the community, and so on) are called human functionings. We have to concentrate on those functionings which we value and have reason to value, and the focus is specifically on a person's capability to achieve particular combinations of valued functionings. All the achievable combinations of functionings are called a person's capability set, and it is on this that the capability approach concentrates.

Through this elementary procedure, the capability approach focuses on human life, and not just on some detached objects of convenience, such as incomes or commodities that a person may possess, which are often assumed to be the main criteria of human success. Since the income-oriented approach is quite standard in economics in particular, the capability approach proposes a change — a serious departure — away from concentrating on the means of living, to the actual opportunities of living.

It is not hard to see the reasoning underlying the understanding that the departure in favour of capability can make a significant — and constructive — difference. For example, if a person has a high income but is also very prone to persistent illness (for inherited, acquired or environmental reasons), then the person need not necessarily be seen as being very well off, on the mere ground that her income is high. She certainly has more of one of the means of living well (that is, a lot of income), but she has difficulty in translating that into good living (that is, living in a way that she has reason to value) because of the adversities of illness and physical handicap. We have to look instead at the extent to which she can actually achieve, if she so chooses, being healthy and well, and doing various things she would value doing.

To understand that the *means* of satisfactory human living are not themselves the *ends* of good living helps to bring about a momentous extension of the reach of the evaluative exercise, especially for world justice. And the use of the capability perspective helps to pursue these extensions.

It is important to emphasize that the focus of the capability approach is not just on what a person actually ends up doing, but also on what she is in fact capable of doing, whether or not she chooses to make use of that opportunity. For example, in terms of being undernourished, a famine-stricken victim may be just as deprived of food and nourishment as a person who voluntarily fasts, for political or religious reasons (despite having the ability to buy and eat plenty of food). Their manifest undernutrition may be much the same, but the capability of the well-off person who chooses to fast to be actually well nourished (if she were to choose to go that way, instead) is much larger than that of the person who starves involuntarily because of poverty and destitution. The idea of capability is, thus, oriented towards freedoms and opportunities (to wit, the capability to live the kinds of lives that people have reason to value), rather than being concerned only with the one particular life that the person chooses to live.

Conclusion

The focus of this essay has been on linking the understanding of justice to the nature of the society and the kind of opportunities and freedoms that people actually have, not just to institutions and practices (that too, but not just that). In this sense my concentration has been on *nyaya,* rather than only on *niti.* Terrible things happen in the world in which we live — from illiteracy and starvation to torture and violence. They arise from a variety of causes, which demand investigation, but the ultimate test of success is not whether the rules or institutions we can dream up are plausible, but what opportunities, what real capabilities people actually have in the world in which they live, based on all the influences that work on society.

To conclude, I have argued against giving the theory of justice a transcendental form — concerned only with characterizing 'the just society'. We have reason to try to address as many questions of comparative assessment as we can. Agreement on many major issues of world justice can emerge even when there are other matters in which we continue to differ and disagree. When Adam Smith and Condorcet argued for the abolition of slavery, or for free public education for all, including for women, they were not claiming that these changes would make the world perfectly 'just' — but only *more just* in an identifiable way, than the world they saw around them. A comparative perspective that makes use of incomplete rankings (with the discipline of using partial orders that modern social choice theory has extensively explored) has much more to offer to the understanding of the demands of world justice (strictly, the removal of world injustice) than the transcendental approach of Hobbes and Rawls, which is forced to abstain from judgements of world justice to concentrate on the fluffy characteristics of 'minimal humanitarianism'.

I have also argued against considering the question of impartiality in the fragmented terms that apply only within nation-states — never stepping beyond the borders. This is important not only for being as inclusive in our thinking about justice in the world as possible, but also to avoid the dangers of local parochialism against which Adam Smith warned nearly two-and-a-half centuries ago. Indeed, the contemporary world offers much greater opportunity of learning from each other, and it seems a pity to try to confine the theorization of justice to the artificially imposed limits of nation-states. This is not only because (as I earlier quoted Martin Luther King as saying) 'injustice anywhere is a threat to justice everywhere' (though that is hugely important as well). But in addition we have to be aware how our interest in others across the world has been growing, along with our growing contacts and increasing communication.

Already in the 1770s, David Hume noted the importance of increased intercourse in expanding the reach of our sense of justice. He had put the issue thus:

> again suppose that several distinct societies maintain a kind of intercourse for mutual convenience and advantage, the boundaries of justice still grow larger, in proportion to the largeness of men's views, and the force of their mutual connections. History, experience, reason sufficiently instruct us in this natural progress of human sentiments, and in the gradual enlargement of our regards to justice, in proportion as we become acquainted with the extensive utility of that virtue. (Hume 1966: 25)

The search for world justice is a central challenge in the world today not merely because our lives are interconnected, but also because the very presence of our interconnections makes us inescapably interested in and involved with each other. The 'natural progress of human sentiments' and 'the gradual enlargement of our regards to justice', which David Hume saw in the 1770s, did not come to an end in the 18th century.

References

Arrow, Kenneth. 1951. *Social Choice and Individual Values*, Wiley, New York.

Hart, H. L. A. 1973. 'Rawls on Liberty and Its Priority', *University of Chicago Law Review* 40(3): 534–55.

Hume, David. 1966 [1777]. *An Enquiry Concerning the Principles of Morals*, Open Court, La Salle, Illinois.

Marquis de Condorcet. 1785. *Essai sur l'Application de l'Analyse a la Probabilité des Décisions rendues a la Pluralité des Voix*, L'Imprimerie Royale, Paris.

Nagel, T. 2005. 'The Problem of Global Justice', *Philosophy and Public Affairs* 33(2): 113–47 (reprinted in this volume, Chapter 3).

Rawls, John. 1971. *A Theory of Justice*, Harvard University Press, Cambridge, MA.

———. 1993. *Political Liberalism*, Columbia University Press, New York.

Rawls, John. 1999. *The Law of Peoples*, Harvard University Press, Cambridge, MA.
Sen, Amartya. 1970. *Collective Choice and Social Welfare*, Holden-Day, San Francisco.
———. 1985. *Commodities and Capabilities*, North-Holland, Amsterdam.
———. 1997. 'Maximization and the Act of Choice', *Econometrica* 65(4): 745–79.
———. 1999. 'The Possibility of Social Choice', *American Economic Review* 89(3): 349–78.
———. 2000. 'Consequential Evaluation and Practical Reason', *Journal of Philosophy* 97(9): 477–502.
———. 2001. 'The Many Faces of Gender Inequality', *The New Republic*, 17 September.
———. 2004. 'Incompleteness and Reasoned Choice', *Synthese* 140(1–2): 43–59.
———. 2006. 'What Do We Want from a Theory of Justice?' *Journal of Philosophy* 103(5): 215–38.
Sen, Amartya, and Martha Nussbaum. 1993. *The Quality of Life*, Clarendon Press, Oxford.
Smith, Adam. 1976 [1759]. *The Theory of Moral Sentiments*, Clarendon Press, Oxford.
———. 1982. *Lectures on Jurisprudence*, Liberty Press, Indianapolis.

6

Who Owes Whom, Why and to What Effect?

Neera Chandhoke

It is not very difficult to answer the first of the three questions posed in the title. Increasingly, a number of political philosophers are convinced that the developed/affluent world has duties of justice toward the poor/developing world that is wracked by ill health, poverty and starvation. They, however, differ on who this duty-bound agent is. For instance, theorists of *international* justice hold that since only permissible inequalities between governments can be allowed, governments of the richer countries should transfer some portion of their resources to the governments of the poor countries. This will enable the scaling down of inequalities (Miller 2007). Theorists of *global* justice argue, on the other hand, that it is not only the state but persons that stand squarely at the centre of any theory of justice for the following reasons. One, the individual is the prime unit of moral concern, rights and duties. Two, no person should suffer for reasons that are morally arbitrary such as gender, class, race, and nationality. Three, if persons do suffer from multiple ills of the human condition for entirely avoidable reasons, or for reasons outside their control, others who are more fortunate have duties toward them, irrespective of where both categories of persons live and work. Two implications follow from these basic presuppositions of global justice. The first implication is that since, like other morally arbitrary factors, national boundaries are irrelevant, the span and the constituency of justice cannot but be global. The second implication is that not only Western governments, but also ordinary citizens who live in the richer countries, have obligations of justice toward the global poor. These obligations may or may not be as strong as the obligations they owe their fellow citizens, but the principle that persons have duties beyond borders is incontrovertible.

When it comes to the *why* of justice, different philosophers justify their conviction that the richer world has duties toward the global poor in distinctive but often overlapping ways. The first part of this essay, which maps some of these positions, concentrates mainly on liberal egalitarian theories of global justice. In the succeeding section I engage critically with these theories from the perspective of the developing world. I argue that there is an important component of justice that is more or less missing in these theories. The identification of this component might help us address the third question asked in the title — to what effect?

Let me spell out the logic of asking and negotiating the third question. The debate on global justice, which has now been around for almost twenty years, commands a great deal of attention. A number of distinguished philosophers have joined in the debate; conferences and special editions of reputed journals are dedicated to an exploration of the issue; a veritable publishing industry has developed around the theme; and, no academic course in political science and philosophy departments can now afford to leave out this topic. This is, of course, not the first time that scholars have been preoccupied with the phenomenon of an unjust global order marked by the domination of the West on the one hand, and deep poverty that blights the lives of millions of people in the developing world on the other. The intellectual stage for theories of imperialist exploitation was set early in the 20th century by Rosa Luxemburg and Lenin. These theories were rediscovered and reinvented in the 1970s, when scholars belonging to the dependency school took on the modernization theorists (Amin 1974; Baran 1973; Frank 1969; Wallerstein 1974). In a frontal attack on modernization theory, the dependency theorists charged that countries of the developing world could neither replicate the path taken by the West, nor compete with the advanced capitalist world. Though formal colonialism had more or less ended by the 1960s, the experience had succeeded in casting a rather long shadow. South America, Sub-Saharan Africa and South Asia had been so thoroughly impoverished, that they were fated to infinite dependence on the advanced capitalist world. As Andre Gunder Frank was to put it memorably, what we see and will continue to see in the indefinite future is the 'development of underdevelopment' in the former colonies. Development and underdevelopment are, he was to suggest, two sides of the same coin.

Though dependency theory had a fairly short life in academia, there was a time when it attracted a lot of scholarly and political attention. The message that colonialism revealed enormous capacity to constantly reinvent itself in new guises, proved particularly attractive for scholars trying to explain development, or the lack thereof. More significantly, dependency theory provided a theoretical space for scholars from the developed as well as from the developing world to come together to deliberate on the future of a 'third world' whose history had been sadly crippled by the historical legacy of colonialism (Amin 1977; Banaji 1972; Chattopadhya 1972; Patnaik 1986).

The contemporary debate on global justice is confined largely to Western intellectuals. The reason for this one-sided transaction of theory should be fairly obvious. Since these theories concentrate mainly on the duties of justice that the richer West has toward the global poor who live in the developing world, scholars from the latter part of the world are excluded from the debate by definitional fiat. Though the question whether the not-so-poor in the developing world also have obligations to the global poor is an interesting one, I do not address it here. I merely want to register the point that theories of global justice stop short on one count: these theories just do not conceive of a universal and reciprocal humanity in which all of us have duties of justice to each other. Are we, who live and work in the developing world, fated to remain consumers of acts, whether these acts are those of harm, or of duty, performed by the West? But this point is perhaps minor compared to the larger issue of what the moral status of the global poor in theories of global justice is. Let me hasten to add that it is not as if the poor are not of moral concern, or that they do not possess moral standing, in these theories. Yet the poor, who live mainly in countries of South Asia, Sub-Saharan Africa and South America, somehow remain faceless, as if they do not possess moral agency or the capacity to make their own histories, or as if they are mere recipients both of processes as well as obligations that emanate from elsewhere.

Steven Smith has argued in another context that, despite accommodating the value of responsibility in its negative form, contemporary egalitarian teleology, and liberal egalitarian compassion-based theories of social relations, devalue the rational perspective and agency of those who are defined as having 'bad fated' conditions through no fault of their own. The distinction between 'choice' and 'circumstance' is important for liberal egalitarians because this determines the extent of obligations. Yet this approach ignores the concept of human agency based on a more positive notion of responsibility. That is, it does not conceive of persons as rationally *responding* to certain conditions, as distinct from merely *experiencing* them. Smith accordingly suggests that distributive principles of justice must also include centrally but paradoxically the 'possibility of an individual agent-based response to misfortune that transforms adverse contingencies, such that the consequences of this response is that the "initial bad luck" becomes a positive part of the "sufferer's" identity' (Smith 2005: 70). In this essay, I want to take this sort of critique of liberal egalitarian theory in a different direction, and argue that human agency, which is a *constitutive* aspect of justice, might well be sidelined by these theories. Given the egalitarian credentials of the philosophers who have launched the global justice debate, the sidelining is surely unintended. Yet a focus on what has been left out, even if unintentionally, might answer to some extent the third question raised in the title — to what effect?

I. Mapping the Debate on Global Justice

Since the publication of Peter Singer's influential 1972 essay 'Famine, Affluence and Morality' (Singer 1972, reprinted in this volume), the belief that the inhabitants of the richer countries (the developed world) have an obligation to transfer a part of their resources to the poorer parts of the world (the developing world) that shudder under the combined effect of disasters and need, has gained tremendous ground. Today, theories of global justice have taken a direction that is different from that of Singer's concept of individual choices and moral responsibility, but his argument has framed the debate in significant ways. Focusing on the gap between the moral principles cherished by the West, and starvation and scarcity in major parts of the world, Singer suggested that suffering and death from lack of food, shelter and medical care are simply bad. If it is within the power of the citizens of the affluent West to prevent something bad from happening, without sacrificing anything of comparable moral importance, they are morally obliged to do so. It does not matter that people who suffer from avoidable misery are distant or proximate, or whether they are fellow nationals or needy foreigners. The need of strangers is as morally compelling as the need of neighbours or fellow citizens. It also does not matter that other people do or do not contribute their mite to the alleviation of poverty and misery; individuals should take on this moral responsibility. And finally, morality demands a radical revision of conceptions of moral duties. Donating to famine relief is a matter not of charity but of duty.

Basically, Singer held that the rich West should be giving much more toward famine relief (in Bangladesh) than it generally does. But focusing as he did on agents making moral choices between spending on personal desires and helping the needy, Singer did not address the larger scope of global political morality. Normative political theory is, however, concerned not only with moral choices made by individuals, but with the political contexts in which people make these choices; that is, with political institutions and practices. Subsequent theories of global justice have focused on precisely these factors and these contexts. In the process they have addressed the issue of *why* the richer world owes the global poor in a different way.

This turn in liberal theory holds a significant implication. Despite the fact that liberalism has traditionally claimed that its values are universal in scope, political philosophers have, more or less, proceeded to design just institutions for communities that are bounded by territory. On the other hand, theories of global justice seek to reinstate the universality of liberalism. Therefore, debates on the subject revolve around the 'why' and the 'to what extent' aspects of global justice. Simon Caney, for instance, suggests in his *Justice Beyond Borders* that, given the presumption of universal morality, there is no reason to defend the civil and political rights of one's fellow citizens and not be concerned about the rights of other people wherever they may live. This position, suggests Caney, is simply incoherent (Caney 2005: 77). Darrel Moellendorf similarly argues that if there are good reasons to support justice within the nation-state, these reasons also apply to supporting justice across the globe (Moellendorf 2002: 28).

The broadening of liberal concerns to issues that lie outside the territorial boundaries of the nation-state has not gone unchallenged. Thomas Nagel, for instance, distinguishes between obligations to fellow citizens and obligations to the distant needy. The least controversial claim we could make in political theory, suggests Nagel, is that we do not live in a just world. At the global level, the facts about poverty are so grim that justice here might be a side issue. These are humanitarian disasters. Poverty brings home the realization that

> there is some minimal concern we owe to fellow human beings threatened with starvation or severe malnutrition and early death from easily preventable diseases. . . . Although there is plenty of room for disagreement about the most effective methods, some form of humane assistance from the well off to those in extremis is clearly called for apart from any demand of justice if we are not simply ethical egoists. (Nagel 2005: 118; see this volume, p. 63)

However, at the same time, argues Nagel, justice requires more than mere humanitarian assistance to those in desperate need. Humanitarian duties hold in virtue of the absolute rather than the relative need of the people 'we' are in a position to help. But justice, according to Nagel, depends on the relationship between the value of justice and the existence of institutions that sovereign authority makes possible (Nagel 2005: 119; see this volume, p. 63). In sum, though citizens have a duty of justice toward one another through the legal, social and economic institutions established by the sovereign power, this duty is not owed to everyone in the world. Others in the world are owed the duty of humanity. 'Justice is something we owe through our shared institutions only to those we stand in a strong political relation. It is, in the standard terminology, an *associative* obligation' (*ibid.*: 121; see this volume, p. 65). It is clear that for Nagel the claims of fellow nationals on justice are much stronger than the claims of foreigners. To the distant needy the West owes only humanitarian assistance.

On the other hand, taking their cue from John Rawls's *Theory of Justice* (1972), Charles Beitz and Thomas Pogge argue that the institutional preconditions for a global theory of justice exist at the global level. According to Rawls, justice is a property of schemes of social and economic cooperation within a single territorial and politically bounded community. His theory of justice focuses on the way in which major social institutions distribute fundamental rights and duties and determine the division of advantages from social cooperation in a social environment. Rawls stipulated institutional preconditions for the applicability of his principles of justice; therefore, this theory cannot apply to persons who do not share relationships and institutions. In a later work (Rawls 1999),

Rawls had specifically suggested that the responsibility of members of affluent societies extends no further than helping 'burdened' societies, which are neither well ordered nor capable of sustaining justice, to reach a plane where they can be so capable.

Charles Beitz in his earlier work (1979, 1999) extended the concept of the basic structure to the global arena, and argued that economic, trade and cultural links across the world had generated and consolidated a global system of social cooperation. In the same vein, Pogge (2002) was to hold that the concept of the basic structure includes rules that shape the interaction of individuals in the public arena. For both philosophers, interdependence in the global arena cancels out the idea that national societies are sufficiently discrete, or that they can be treated as separate entities. Therefore, Rawls's theory of justice must dictate the just allocation of advantages and burdens from such cooperation in the global arena. It follows that the difference principle — that social and economic inequalities must work for the good of the least advantaged — also applies to this arena (Beitz 1979: 151).

Further, nationality, as Pogge wrote, is just

> one further deep contingency (like genetic endowment, race, gender, and social class), one more potential basis of institutional inequalities that are inescapable and present from birth. Within Rawls's conception, there is no reason to treat this case differently from the others. And so it would seem that we can justify our global institutional order only if we can show that the institutional inequalities it produces tend to optimize (against the backdrop of feasible alternative global regimes) the worst social position. (Pogge 1989: 247)

Similarly, Beitz held that there is no reason to extend Rawls's original position to the world as a whole. If the parties in the original position do not know morally arbitrary facts about themselves, such as talents and race, then they ought also to be ignorant of their nationality. That is, they should be ignorant of whether they live in a country that is rich or poor, well endowed in resources or not so well endowed. The recognition that nationality is one of the factors that are morally arbitrary, and that therefore should not be dictating the life chances of individuals, bears significant implication. If people are ignorant about their nationality when they decide on principles of justice, there is more likelihood that a distributive framework that minimizes the risks that come from living in a poor country can be established.

Moreover, as Pogge points out, the colonial past has given to Western countries an unfair advantage in global forums, and systemically disadvantaged the developing world. 'We', rues Pogge, are harming the global poor by imposing an unjust global order in which Western markets are closed by protectionist policies, in which local agriculture is subsidized, and in which anti-dumping measures are introduced in many sectors in which the developing world is best able to compete, such as agriculture, clothing and textiles. Moreover, the better off enjoy significant advantages in appropriating wealth from the planet, such as crude oil. At the same time, the worse off are largely, and without compensation, excluded from the gains of the appropriations (Pogge 2002: 201–3). An application of Rawls's conceptions of justice, which make the life prospects of the least advantaged the primary standard of assessing social institutions, testifies that global institutions are clearly unjust and need to be improved upon. Above all, since Western governments dominate the decisions of global institutions, the negative duties of the citizens of wealthy countries, duties not to cause harm, are violated (*ibid.*: 23).

Of crucial significance to Pogge's argument in his *World Poverty and Human Rights* (2002) is the claim that citizens of the affluent world are morally responsible for the starvation, malnutrition and deaths that take place in the developing world. Because their representatives have participated in, and even determined decisions that have inflicted harm on the global poor, the negative duty of the citizens of the affluent West — the duty not to cause harm — has been violated. (For Pogge, human rights impose, not a fundamental positive duty to help realize the good to which a particular right entitles a rights-holder, but rather a fundamental negative duty *not* to cause harm.) It follows that those who are involved in upholding the institutions of the state should discontinue their involvement, challenge the policies of their own government, and compensate for injustice by either working for the reform of institutions, or working for the protection of the victims.

Let me now sum up briefly the debate on global justice. Broadly speaking, the debate has generated two sorts of theoretical positions. The first of these is the position that citizens of the rich West have the same obligations to the global poor as they have to their own compatriots.

Larry Temkin, for instance, holds that natural misfortunes across societies are every bit as bad as natural misfortunes within societies, and there are reasons of justice for addressing the former that are every bit as strong as the corresponding reasons of justice for addressing the latter. This holds even if 'we' are not responsible for the needy's plight in other countries. There will still be agent-neutral reasons of justice to help (Temkin 2004: 182). The second position is that the citizens of the affluent West owe duties of humanitarian assistance to the poorer parts of the world, but justice to their own compatriots.

Undeniably, these sophisticated philosophical formulations on why the West owes the distant needy have marked a marvellous transformation in the ways justice has traditionally been conceptualized. Yet the proposed resolutions may well stop short of what is needed to meet the challenge of global poverty. What I want to do now is to approach the issue of global justice from the vantage point of the 'distant needy' that live and work in the developing world. What does the rendering of obligations by the West mean to them? As an aside, people who suffer from hunger and ill health do not only belong to the abstract category of the global poor. These are persons who respond to their situation in particular sorts of ways and who might even acquire agency in the process. There may be more to justice than conceived of in theories of global justice. As Hamlet in Shakespeare's immortal play was to advise, 'There are more things in heaven and earth, Horatio, than are dreamt of in your philosophy.' What those things are is elaborated in the section that follows.

Claiming Rights, Realizing Justice

Let me put forward the following propositions as the broad context for the argument that follows.

- The modern democratic state is many things, but above all it is a *condensate* of power. This state possesses an unparalleled capacity to gather, generate, codify, implement, and arbitrate power through a variety of means, technologies of surveillance, and opacity of governance. Above all, the modern democratic state has revealed an enormous capacity to *legitimize* power through, say, authorization of permissible forms of dissent.

- States that possess democratic credentials are likely to be *imperfectly* just.
- At the same time, the democratic state recognizes and grants equal rights to citizens, paramount among which is the right to participate in politics, the right to be represented in forums of decision making, the right to hold governments responsible, the right to form associations, and the right to protest. Collectively, this set of rights may be termed civil and political rights.
- Justice has to be *realized*, even wrested, from imperfectly just states through forms of collective action that are enabled by the grant of civil and political rights.
- In a globalized world, the lives of people wherever they might live and work are affected not only by decisions taken by global institutions, but also by factors such as patterns of investment, trade, media, and transmission of communications and information across borders. Therefore, the policies of global institutions and global capitalism can only be countered through the formation of global coalitions of resistance.
- These global coalitions of resistance have managed to build bridges of solidarity among the poor and the oppressed.
- Collective action in global forums to claim, reclaim and realize rights is a constitutive aspect of justice. These political acts not only contribute to the realization of rights that lie at the core of justice, but also to the realization of human agency.
- The main agent that can realize rights and thus justice remains the national state, upon which demands can be made and from which accountability can be demanded.
- A transfer of resources from the affluent West to the needy in the developing world might contribute only one, and not necessarily the most significant, component to the basket of resources as well as to the range of strategies available to the poor.

This sketchy framework is not meant to suggest that we should privilege the national over the global. The option is implausible given the interconnections that globalization has wrought, and given that the lives of ordinary people over the world are affected by tangible decisions taken by global institutions. These decisions range from the lifting of subsidies to the agricultural sector to the reduction of emissions to halt climate change. Rather, the framework is merely to suggest that the global and the national constitute a series of overlapping relationships. In these relationships, sometimes the global dominates and at other times the national becomes more important. Sometimes they work in tandem. Therefore, whereas much of the poverty that has wrecked the lives of people in distant lands can clearly be traced to the working of global institutions dominated by Western countries, and though coalitions in the space of global civil society have mounted large-scale protests against these policies, when it comes to *realizing* justice and *reclaiming* rights, the national state acquires significance for reasons spelt out below.

In order to elaborate the argument that is only implicit in the bullet points registered at the beginning of this section, I draw upon one particular development in India's recent biography. Whereas 94 per cent of India's workforce is in the unorganized sector, the Indian government had, for at least four decades after independence, failed to take the rights of this section of the workforce into account. Policies were enacted for this sector only in the 1980s; that is, at the time when India liberalized, and subsequently globalized. Ratna Sudershan (2007) has argued that the decade of the 1980s witnessed two paradoxical developments. One, despite the large differences in the situation of the old and the new informal workers, and between workers in the developed and the developing countries, the forging of associative networks between them resulted in the formulation of a definite approach to social protection. Two, although globalization has expanded the informal sector, the process has also provided the space for serious discussion on how to ensure the rights of informal workers to social protection. A number of such discussions in global forums led to the creation of international networks such as Women in Informal Employment: Globalizing and Organizing (WIEGO). Over time, the network began to advocate the adoption of the right to social protection across the world.

Notably, members of WIEGO, who include representatives of several membership-based organizations from different countries, have been engaged in advocating the rights of informal workers *not as an act of duty* toward the informal workers of the developing world, but as a technique for *securing the rights* of all workers who eke out a living in precarious work situations. At the very time globalization has created more workers in the informal sector, international advocacy has played an important role in increasing the visibility of informal workers, and in generating commitment to providing universal social protection. This strategy seems to have been successful in India. For in December 2008 the Government of India finally passed the Unorganized Sector Workers Social Security Bill. The bill aims to provide social security and job protection to at least 375 million workers in the unorganized sector.

I mention this example to illustrate the point that even democratic states are likely to be imperfectly just. Justice has to be realized and sometimes wrested from a powerful state through modes of protest through collective action. In the context of globalization, it is more than obvious that we can no longer insulate political struggles for the realization of rights within a country, from global coalitions across countries, simply because trans-border investment patterns dictate labour conditions. In recent years, a space has been created for the articulation of global coalitions of the poor and of the oppressed, because globalization, like other political processes, is double-edged. On the one hand, globalization has knit the world into a single structure, and on the other hand it has given rise to global civil society, which has forcefully brought home not only the illegitimacy of global capitalism but also the issue of peoples' rights. Focused on resistance to the imposition of a new liberal orthodoxy across the world, global coalitions have protested against the privatization of basic services and of the economy, curbs on subsidies, financial deregulation, the opening up of fragile economies to financial and trade flows, and denial of the rights of workers. Networks of resistance have also brought onto political agendas significant issues such as debt relief for poor countries, development, the illegitimacy of global finance capital, criticism of the policies of the advanced capitalist world and of global financial institutions, interests of small farmers, peasants, informal labour, and indigenous people, and human rights, within a general critique of dominant modes of domination and exploitation. Helped by the international media, these coalitions have succeeded in putting onto domestic political agendas issues that have been neglected by national governments. But there is more. These webs of solidarity and networks of advocacy may not lead to a (minimal) transfer of resources from the rich to the poor as theorists of global justice suggest, but they do something equally significant; they can lead to the grafting of social policy onto government agendas, and they can heighten awareness of what is due to human beings.

In the process, global coalitions have had a *constitutive* impact on justice in two ways. One, they have challenged the legitimacy of decisions taken by global institutions, and in many instances forced a rethink. For instance, at the end of November 1999, massive protests involving some 700 organizations and about 40,000 students, workers, NGOs, religious groups, and representatives of business and finance, brought the third ministerial meeting of the World Trade Organization (WTO) at Seattle to a halt. The WTO was to set in motion a new multilateral round of trade negotiations. Collective anger at the relocation of industries to the developing world, at the unsafe and abusive work conditions in the factories and sweatshops found there, at environmental degradation, at the elitist structure of the organizations, at the under-representation of poor countries in global institutions, at the absence of transparency, and at the widespread exploitation of working people, exploded in a series of angry demonstrations.

Though large-scale protests against the WTO, the International Monetary Fund (IMF) and the World Bank were not new, the scale of mobilization as well as the intensity of protest were. Livid demonstrations by student unions, environmentalists or 'tree-huggers', economic and xenophobic nationalists, church groups, anarchists, protectionists, consumer groups, NGOs, and even business and financial groups validated the new concept that had been catapulted into transnational vocabularies at the Earth Summit in Rio in 1992, when about 2,400 representatives of non-governmental organizations came to play a central role in the deliberations — the concept of global civil society.

The unprecedented agitation in 1999 compelled the WTO to create a 'development round' of talks that were initiated in Doha. The objective of this initiative is to address structural lacunae within the organization, and to ensure that the less developed countries are equal partners in the organization (Chandhoke 2002).

The other way in which global coalitions have had a constitutive impact upon justice is the following. Global civil society actors, which act as the guardians of a morally informed consensus on the minimum that is due to human beings, have engaged in norm setting (Chandhoke 2002). These norms dictate what should be done for human beings (access to basic rights), and what should not be done to them (torture).

Through these processes, not only have global and national civil society actors forced a change in the content of justice, they have also expanded the constituency of and for justice. Nancy Fraser has made an important point in this context. She argues that political actors have transformed the monological debate on justice into a dialogue. Earlier, Fraser comments, theorists of justice did not imagine that those who will be subjected to these principles of justice might have a role to play in determining these requirements.

> Today however, monological theories of social justice are becoming increasingly implausible. . . . as the circle of those claiming a say in frame-setting expands, decisions about the 'who' are increasingly viewed as political matters, which should be handled democratically, rather than as technical matters, which can be left to experts and elites. . . . No longer content to ascertain the requirements of justice in a monological fashion . . . [some] theorists are looking increasingly to dialogical approaches, which treat important aspects of justice as matters for collective decision-making, to be determined by the citizens themselves, through democratic deliberation. (Fraser 2008: 28)

Fraser's argument that now justice has become dialogical rather than monological because of the expansion of the constituency of justice is a compelling one. But even if the constituency of and for justice has expanded because global civil society agents have inserted their own agendas and critiques into dominant agendas, of particular relevance is the question — on which agent are demands for the realization of justice to be placed? Let me phrase the point in another way. We have realized that political action that lays claims to certain goods has to be collective. In a globalized world where decisions taken by powerful actors impact the lives of people wherever they live, it follows that this action has to be global in scope. The objective of collective action is to realize justice through claim making. But the idea that justice has to be realized through purposeful collective action does not tell us *which agent* has to take on the duty of enabling access to the goods the rights claimed are rights to.

Let us, therefore, shift the focus of this discussion from duties to rights in order to highlight the issue at stake. The proposition on rights holds that P (persons) has R (rights) to some G (good). If P has the right to G, then she ought to be given G, and it would be wrong not to give her G.

Therefore, the assertion of a right places an obligation on other agents. However, all agents are not in a position to enable the realization of G that P has R to. My family, for instance, cannot help realize my right to an adequate income, unless of course the family owns a business, and is thus in a position to generate and distribute profits in the shape of an assured salary, or a dividend. But not all families are in such a happy position, and we will have to look elsewhere, to some agent that is in a *position* to realize my right to an income. The said agent must have the resources and the power to enable my access to the good that I have a right to. Therefore, let us assume that rights place obligations on *relevant* agents, relevant agents being those agents that are in a position to affect the realization of the right. Relevant agents can affect rights negatively by placing limits on the right, or in deciding that the claim made by the right is not strong enough to generate an obligation. These agents can create a positive environment for the realization of the right on offer, both by acknowledging the salience of the right, and by enabling access to a good the right is a right to through the establishment of appropriate institutions and policies.

We still have to identify this agent. The idea that crucial rights can be claimed, reclaimed or realized from global institutions appears unfeasible and, therefore, unrealizable, at least for the foreseeable future. Whatever be the power of global institutions, these institutions simply do not have the mandate to realize rights. Nor are they obliged to do so. Global institutions might be compelled by civil society activism to moderate and modify policies that have the potential of wreaking havoc on the lives of the global poor. The process of realizing rights, however, demands other preconditions. Apart from possessing power and resources, the institution that is in a position to realize rights should be (*a*) proximate in a metaphorical sense; (*b*) accessible; (*c*) possess the capacity to garner resources through policies of taxation; (*d*) have the power to legislate, implement and monitor social policy; and (*e*) be responsible to the constituency that it is accountable to. Certainly, interlocking structures and institutions of global governance have been set in place, such as international bureaucracies, world trade regimes, regulatory authorities, a rule-making process, and international judiciaries. But the hope that these institutions can legislate and implement a just world order, or engage in the intricate business of realizing rights that remain unfulfilled, is but a dream on our collective political horizon. As of now this is not the mandate of whatever global institutions that exist.

We are left with the recognition that, whereas collective action that is both global and national in scope can demand the realization of rights, the only agent that can possibly enable access to the goods the right is a right to remains the national state. The democratic state is determinate, it is metaphorically speaking proximate, and it can be held to account. Moreover, the state is best able to secure the good a right is a right to, simply because it has, or at least can garner, the resources to do so. It is only the state that can tax its citizens and redistribute revenues in a fair and just manner, and establish the preconditions for enabling access to the good the right is a right to. And this is important, because redistributive justice requires as its essential preconditions institutions, policies, distributive mechanisms, tribunals, regulatory agencies, a vibrant civil society, a free press, and a judiciary that can be appealed to if these rights have not been fulfilled. Civil society agents cannot establish these institutional preconditions.

The first inference we can draw from the preceding argument is that rights and justice can be realized through collective action that is both national and global. The second inference is that the realization of a right presupposes a determinate agent, which is in a position to enable access to the good the right is a right to. Moreover, this agent must be *obliged* to enable access to the right on offer. Which other agent apart from the democratic state can the poor or their representatives in civil society approach? We can concur with the proposition that affluent citizens of the Western world are obliged to transfer some portion of their resources to the global poor. But are the global poor in a position to approach citizens of affluent states, and claim that they have a right to a portion of the resources the said citizens command, because these resources have been unjustly accumulated through actions of global institutions, in which Western governments were dominant? Can poverty-stricken peasants in much of the developing world even *afford* to wait for realization to dawn on Western governments and citizens that their actions have wronged people living in this part of the world, and that the wronged have to be compensated? The more significant point is whether the global poor should even be doing so — that is, waiting for first-world largesse. There *is* a qualitative difference between being given something as a matter of duty, and demanding something by reasons of right. If we agree that democracy is based upon the presumption that all citizens possess equal moral worth, then persons whose moral status has been compromised by poverty, ill health and illiteracy must approach the system as the bearers of a right that has been denied to them or that remains unfulfilled, not as victims or as complainants of forces unleashed from outside.

The act of claiming what is our due bears an important implication: persons realize human agency in and through political practices and claim-making. The concept of human agency can be interpreted in two ways. The quintessential liberal take on agency is that just political institutions should enable human beings to craft and revise projects that make their life worthwhile. In a second and a more radical sense, persons realize agency when they address the historical constraints that prevent them from formulating, pursuing and revising projects. If one of the main objectives of political practices is to realize justice, which is embedded in the democratic state but which is often unrealized or partially realized, the political context is reshaped. Politics, in other words, has a determinate objective — that of shaping and reshaping the political context in which we live and work. If political philosophers focus on the political context that shapes moral choices, they must also take cognizance of how political struggles that try to reshape those contexts that inhibit the making of choices, allow human beings to make their own history, even if the histories they make are not the histories they wanted to make in the first place. Whether the histories we make are not the ones we wanted to make is not the constitutive aspect of agency; the constitutive aspect of agency is that collective action allows human beings to realize what is their due by right, and to place claims for the realization of rights, and thereby justice.

To What Effect?

To sum up the argument so far: in the first part of the essay, I concentrated on answering the first two of the three questions asked in the title, who owes whom, and why. Let me now proceed to address the question, to what effect? The debate on global justice concerns primarily the question of why the affluent West owes the global poor. The problem is that it is not easy to discern the moral status of those who should be receiving transfers of resources from the affluent West. Pogge suggests that the global poor are rights-bearers, since they possess negative rights not to be harmed. But it appears that the global poor have no role to play in the *realization* of this right not to be harmed. Of course there is no reason, given the objectives of theories of global justice, that these issues should be addressed. Yet any comprehensive theory of global justice has to deal with a related issue, the realization of moral agency. Otherwise there is a real danger that the moral status of persons whose condition is sought to be remedied will be reduced to that of beneficiaries of transfer of resources from the West. Should human beings be reduced only to the status of beneficiaries?

It is in this context that I have argued that the capacity of ordinary human beings to extract justice from often recalcitrant elites and modes of power is a *constitutive* aspect of justice. This is not to rule out the idea that people in different parts of the world have a duty toward those who suffer for no fault of their own, and whose rights have been thus violated. It is to suggest that the realization of justice demands things other than merely a transfer of resources.

Therefore, theorists of global justice may rightly insist on the rendering of duties or obligations to the global poor; however, because multiple transactions have constituted a single world to which principles of justice should apply, such obligations can constitute only *one* component of an entire range of strategies that concentrate on the realization of goods to which human beings have rights. Let me hasten to add that different strategies of helping the poor need not be mutually exclusive; they can, equally, complement each other. If citizens of the affluent world contribute to, say, Oxfam so that the organization can invest in development activities in poor countries, this has to be welcomed. If concerned citizens across the world come together in and through networks that consolidate solidarity for and with the poor, and compel national governments to take up the issue of poverty, it is equally good. And if, in tandem, these different agents can bring about the reform of global institutions, as well as the reform of national governments, it is even better. But it is best that human beings realize agency by standing up to demand what is due to them.

Indisputably, the elimination of global injustice is an essential precondition for the realization of justice within the country. A country can hardly institutionalize processes and institutions that deliver justice if it is hampered by unequal and exploitative international trade; if its decisions are constrained by unjust policies of global institutions such as the WTO; if it has to spend a major part of its revenues on paying back interest on debts; and if it is condemned to primary forms of economic activity because technology and expertise is not available to it. Injustice on a global scale is increasingly being challenged. The forging of coalitions within and across borders has placed onto the political agenda challenges to the profound injustice that globalization has brought in its wake. Political coalitions within national borders need global networks to bring home sharply the illegitimacy of deprivation and poverty. But ultimately, it is the national state that is responsible for the way its citizens' lives are going. People who have been denied rights ultimately have to claim these rights from the state, at least as long as a system of global governance is not set in place. But there is more to claiming rights from states. The act of claiming what is due to human beings simply because they are human realizes agency. And that is of value because ultimately we have to reach planes where we do not have to rely only on the good intentions of others.

References

Amin, Samir. 1974. *Accumulation on a World Scale*, Monthly Review Press, New York.

———. 1977. *Imperialism and Unequal Development*, Harvester Press, Hassocks, and Monthly Review Press, New York.

Banaji, Jairus. 1972. 'For a Theory of Colonial Modes of Production', *Economic and Political Weekly*, 7(52): 2498–2502.

Baran, Paul. 1973. *The Political Economy of Growth*, Penguin, Harmondsworth.

Beitz, Charles. 1979. *Political Theory and International Relations*, Princeton University Press, Princeton, NJ.

———. 1999. *Political Theory and International Relations*, Princeton University Press, Princeton, NJ (rev. edn).

Caney, Simon. 2005. *Justice Beyond Borders: A Global Political Theory*, Oxford University Press, Oxford.

Chandhoke, Neera. 2002. 'The Limits of Global Civil Society', in Marlies Glasius, Mary Kaldor and Helmut Anheier (eds), *Global Civil Society 2002*, Oxford University Press, Oxford, 35–54.

Chattopadhya, P. 1972. 'On the Question of the Mode of Production in Indian Agriculture: A Preliminary Note', *Economic and Political Weekly* 7(13): A39, A41–A46.

Frank, Andre Gunder. 1969. *Capitalism and Underdevelopment in Latin America*, Modern Reader Paperbacks, London (rev. edn).

Fraser, Nancy. 2008. *Scales of Justice: Reimagining Political Space in a Globalizing World*, Polity, Cambridge.

Miller, David. 2007. *National Respect and Global Justice*, Oxford University Press, Oxford.

Moellendorf, Darrel. 2002. *Cosmopolitan Justice*, Westview Press, Boulder, CO.

Nagel, Thomas. 2005. 'The Problem of Global Justice', *Philosophy and Public Affairs* 33(2): 113–46 (reprinted in this volume, Chapter 3).

Patnaik, P. (ed.). 1986. *Lenin and Imperialism*, Sangam, London.

Pogge, Thomas. 1989. *Realizing Rawls,* Cornell University Press, Ithaca.
———. 2002. *World Poverty and Human Rights,* Polity, London.
Rawls, John. 1972. *A Theory of Justice,* Oxford University Press, New York.
———. 1999. *The Law of Peoples,* Harvard University Press, Cambridge, MA.
Singer, Peter. 1972. 'Famine, Affluence and Morality', *Philosophy and Public Affairs* 1(3): 229–43 (reprinted in this volume, Chapter 1).
Smith, Steven R. 2005. 'Keeping Our Distance in Compassion-Based Social Relations', *Journal of Moral Philosophy* 2(1): 69–87.
Sudershan, Ratna. 2007. 'Social Protection, the Informal Economy, and Globalization', unpublished paper prepared for the Ford project 'Globalization and the State in India' directed by Neera Chandhoke.
Temkin, Larry. 2004. 'Thinking about the Needy, Justice and International Organizations', *The Journal of Ethics* 8(4): 349–95.
Wallerstein, Immanuel. 1974. *The Modern World System,* Academic Press, New York.

7

The Romance of Global Justice

Sen's Deparochialization and the Quandary of Dalit Marxism

Aakash Singh Rathore

The Problems of Global Justice

In his influential paper entitled 'The Problem of Global Justice', Thomas Nagel concluded that 'the idea of global justice without a world government is a chimera' (Nagel 2005; see this volume, p. 60). The link between justice and sovereignty along Hobbesian lines, as arguably taken up by John Rawls and certainly by post-Rawlsians like Nagel, results in this trenchant problem of accommodating global justice in contemporary liberal thought. But to call this, as Nagel does, *the* problem of global justice is, it seems to me, both too hasty and too optimistic; for global justice throws up many more and possibly even greater problems than just this — let us call it as Amartya Sen does — *institutional* one (Sen 2009).

The institutional problem of global justice (in a nutshell, and in the Rawlsian vernacular, there is no 'basic structure' at the global level, and thus no possibility for justice — strictly speaking — at the global level), can be matched by perhaps an even more primitive *conceptual* problem of global justice: disentangling the unique phenomenon of global justice from the ostensibly discrete notions of international justice, transnational justice or even local, social justice[1] is not easy, especially when we take into account that the cause(s) of the injustice or unjust scenario may be concretely attributable (Collier 2007). To put it in another way, the well-established

[1] Rawls himself identified 'three levels of justice': 'local', 'domestic' and 'global'; they were, however, incompatible out of their own places (Rawls 2001).

juridical principle of *subsidiarity* may also be relevant in our assessment of whether a situation is regarded as a global-justice issue (e.g., world poverty, environmental degradation, pandemics, violent ethnic discrimination) or more locally as simply a regional (transnational) phenomenon (e.g., the Kurdish problem primarily of Turkey, Iran and Iraq) — where is the threshold? What are the criteria for deciding? And, who gets to decide?

This essay will take up a unique case that illustrates that, beyond and outside the institutional problems posed by political philosophers like Nagel, even the very conceptual problems of 'global justice', at least as it is currently theorized, are profound and perhaps insurmountable. The specific case considered herein, that of Indian untouchables, would seem to establish that 'global justice' may be conceptually problematic, and that the distinction between a global-justice issue and a local- or social-justice issue is an unstable one, like a Gestalt figure switching to and fro. It is crucial to keep in mind that the Indian untouchables constitute some 10 per cent of the total chronic global poor (Kumar 2009), and thus — given that global poverty is an essential problematic of global justice (Pogge 2002) — this fundamentally social-justice dilemma in India must simultaneously be regarded as a global-justice priority. My intuition is that there is something amiss in the present global justice debate, that is, the debate as it is currently very monologically conducted, and the case-study presented here simply follows one of many possible leads to try to tease out and display some aspects of the parochial quandary.

The idea of global justice, as an academic thematic, is said to arise around the time of Peter Singer's controversial but extremely influential essay on 'Famine, Affluence and Morality' from 1972 (see Chapter 1). One can easily dispute this and point back to innumerable precursors, recent or distant — salient ones such as Kant's *Perpetual Peace,* and less salient ones such as Kautilya's *Arthashastra.* But not only more germane but indeed more urgent than excavating and identifying the possible historical origins of this thematic is noting, with astonishment, the narrowness of contemporary voices taking part in it. A survey of *Books in Print* confirms what Neera Chandhoke refers to as a veritable global justice 'publishing industry', and yet, despite the quantity of work, 'contemporary debate on global justice is confined largely to Western intellectuals' (Chandhoke, this volume, p. 145). The reasons for the monological character of the contemporary global justice debate are diverse.

They include, inter alia, the fact that it is largely refracted quite specifically through the thought and work of one political philosopher in particular, John Rawls. A great deal of the global justice literature is a Rawlsian and post-Rawlsian literature, and thus it appears to others as an internalist problem being worked out by specialists — with a quite narrow and wholly theoretical horizon. However, given that Peter Singer's touchstone essay on famine fails even to mention Rawls — Rawls's major work, *A Theory of Justice*, predates Singer's essay by only a few months — it is evident that the global justice debate even within the Western world need not necessarily be pegged to the specifically Rawlsian framework. It is telling that someone as firmly placed within the literature just mentioned as Amartya Sen himself finds this literature imbalanced: 'the contemporary — and largely Western — pursuit of political philosophy in general and of the demands of justice in particular has been, I would argue, limited and to some extent parochial' (Sen 2009). More about Sen and parochialism in a moment.

Another reason for the monological character of the global justice debate is that one can discern in non-Western scholarship, political philosophy included, a reluctance to decontextualize itself and make bold and brash speculative gestures about the global, given the often clinging complexity of the local in these areas. As a trite illustration, the Bangladeshi famine about which Singer writes, moving from the concrete tragedy to speculative heights within a couple of pages, could hardly be so coolly theorized by political philosophers at that time in Dhaka, or even in Delhi or Lahore, for that matter. Deparochializing the global justice debate, then, would not only require the Western elite who control its discursive horizon to pluralize its monological character, but would also require from them a willingness to recontextualize it, or think it through its local (pre)conditions (Chandhoke, this volume). And, on the other side, if the hitherto voiceless quasi-participants of this problematic are to be granted the conditions sufficient to be recognized and heard, they must for their part be willing to speak up. Till now, neither side has made a significant move toward the other. Thus we find ourselves in this risible situation not wholly dissimilar to the Congress of Berlin; here we have a couple of hundred primarily US northeast-coast intellectuals debating the possibility, claims and scope of justice on a globe of some six billion persons. But if contextualizing global justice turns out to be a necessary ingredient in globalizing global justice, we are faced with a daunting task indeed. Luckily, Amartya Sen has recently cleared a great deal of brush for us.

Amartya Sen's Deparochialized Approach to Global Justice

Amartya Sen is a scholar well known to have contributed in numerous ways toward the advancement of the humanities and social sciences. The nearly 500-page *The Idea of Justice,* which was completed when Sen was aged around 76, is surely the author's last great work, though there is disagreement whether it may be counted among his best.

It is at least a *great* one in every sense: capacious, innovative, expansive, multidisciplinary, comprehensive, pioneering, captivating, and — like this description — wordy. It is also Sen's definitive and final break with the Rawlsian approach to political philosophy, which, as he correctly points out, is hugely influential in contemporary (especially Anglo-American) academia. Sen had been under the influence of Rawls for decades, although he has critiqued aspects of Rawls's thought all along (Sen 1999). Till now, though, those were always immanent critiques, attempts to critically contribute to the basic idea of justice as conceived by Rawls and within the liberal framework. Now, however, Sen substitutes an altogether new conception of justice (rather, an altogether *old* one, as becomes apparent through discussions of classical Indian philosophy) and abandons the Rawlsian vehicle, in all its obsolescence, by the side of the road.

While Sen identifies several deep problems with the Rawlsian theory of justice, the central and most fundamental one seems to be that it is transcendent and pursues perfection. Given the indisputable and widespread presence of intolerable injustice throughout the world, Sen argues that the transcendent theorization of justice is functionally redundant in the current global context, where persons everywhere seek to redress specific problems of (in)justice in an effective manner. He thus proposes a 'comparative' rather than a perfectionist theory of justice, one that is grounded in actual and relevant circumstances rather than transcendent of all politics. Working out the constituents of this comparative theory of justice, Sen articulates each in contrast with Rawls's (or Rawlsians') own components: Sen seeks a comprehensivist (and thus necessarily consequentialist, though not utilitarian[2]) account, not a deontological or purely principled one; he seeks an approach based on *open* impartiality (here favouring Adam Smith's 'impartial spectator' rather than Rawls's 'veil of ignorance', which he calls 'closed' impartiality, since in Rawls's account, only members of the polity being constructed are considered); he borrows from social choice theory and reconstructs his own capabilities approach as elements of his theory of (evaluative/comparative) justice, in contrast to Rawls's traditional conception of 'primary goods'; and, above all, he draws from his decades-long experience as a uniquely global(ized) intellectual to insert into the heart of his idea of justice not just a *possibility* for conceiving of justice at the global level (which Rawlsians debate and Nagel, as we saw already, denies), but the fundamental *precondition* of global justice.

And this brings us to the real motivation behind, and virtue of, his book: it is not just a conception of justice; it is a framework for *global justice*.

Although Rawlsians (e.g., Sebastiano Maffettone) and post-Rawlsians (e.g., Thomas Pogge) have made heroic attempts to stretch the Rawlsian fabric enough to cover the possibility, if not the plausibility, of global justice, the definitive statement of the impossibility of global justice in the Rawlsian theory comes from Thomas Nagel. Because Sen in his *Idea of Justice* agrees with Nagel's interpretation of Rawls, and as it follows from this interpretation of Rawls that global justice is a chimera, Sen is forced finally to choose between *either* a Rawlsian approach *or* global justice. A half-century after Rawls's 1958 essay 'Justice as Fairness' laying out the basics of his theory of justice, an essay that had inspired and motivated Sen's vocation, the world has changed too much for Sen to be able to be blind toward the urgent need for global justice — *thus* he breaks with Rawls definitively, in this great work dedicated to the memory of John Rawls.

In the steadily growing critical and secondary literature on Sen's recent work, there is seldom mention of what I have claimed to identify as its *central* motivating feature.[3] However, to read *The Idea of Justice* as a

---

[2] Or so Sen claims. Sebastiano Maffettone, however, argues that Sen's consequentialism is functionally tantamount to utilitarianism, and moreover that it suffers from the same defects (Maffettone 2011).

[3] Including, surprisingly, even Samuel Freeman's recent review (Freeman 2010).

framework for global justice rather than simply as a rival theory of justice is hermeneutically advantageous in many respects. For a start, it provides the opportunity to understand Sen's abundant use of Indian literature, history and philosophy as methodologically consistent with his attempt to formulate a non-parochial conception of justice that can operate at the global level, rather than, as often snidely remarked, as merely the eccentricity of an author who is ethnically Indian. Moreover, such a reading also provides centripetal organizational force for coping with the multidisciplinary and chromatically themed essays, from epistemology to sustainable development and human rights, from reflections on famine prevention, to a full chapter devoted to an interpretation of the ancient Indian epic, the *Bhagavadgita,* to a restatement of the capabilities approach in economics, and so on. Everyone knows that Sen is a polymath, but that alone is not sufficient grounds for such a display of knowledge as appears in this book, much of it superfluous toward a rival theory of justice. Readers may therefore choose to read this work as a particularly prolix break-away liberal theory of justice, but I think it is more accurate to read it instead as the very first, experimental, searching sketch of a comprehensive framework for global justice beyond and outside of the institutional (Rawlsian) approach.

If truth be told, critics have not been too impressed by Sen's book (Gray 2009; Poole 2009). Scholars see it as his last *major* work, but lacking in comparison with his best ones (Romano 2009). While this may perhaps be true, it neglects to take into account that Sen's book is not just a mediocre ending-work when evaluated against his oeuvre; rather, when evaluated against what (little) the rest of us political philosophers are doing in the current context of the global justice debate, Sen's *The Idea of Justice* is surely a profound and most welcome beginning.

It is, however, far from adequate. Among the most disturbing features of Sen's monumental work is its complete silence on the subject of caste-based discrimination in India and the past and present plight of the untouchables. Indeed, the Dalit problem has been something of a blind spot within the literature of the global justice publishing industry, and even its often-cited reference works, such as Paul Collier's *The Bottom Billion,* fail to mention this sizable portion of that bottom billion (Collier 2007). Surprisingly, Sen's major works — such as *Development as Freedom* (1999) or even *Inequality Reexamined* (1992) — also fail to mention the persistence of problems associated with untouchability and the chronic poverty of that sizable community. Thus, we turn now to a certain aspect of the Dalit problem — a peculiarly perplexing one wherein the notion of global justice gets ironically reflected in an antagonistic position toward the more direct and local goal of (social) justice.

Dalit Marxism: A 'Contextualization' Quandary?

In 2004, the economist Bhalchandra Mungekar, current member of the Rajya Sabha (the upper house of the Indian parliament) and former Planning Commission member, drafted a significant paper on the effects of globalization on the Indian untouchable community, or 'Dalits' (Mungekar 2004).

Mungekar analyzes Ambedkarian economic philosophy, presents the socio-economic condition of the Dalits, outlines the direction of economic reforms in post-1991 India, and clarifies what impact the said reforms have had and will continue to have on the Dalits, the most vulnerable sector of Indian society. Mungekar shows that the impact of the reforms has largely been negative, making the already impossibly difficult life of the majority of Dalits even less bearable. Mungekar is not satisfied with simply pointing out problems; he also suggests a set of well-thought-out remedial measures, each inspired by Ambedkarian economic philosophy, aimed at alleviating some of the added burden weighing down on Dalits as a result of liberalization. Mungekar selected the topic because he felt that 'the Dalits, till recently, remained largely preoccupied with the socio-political and religious-cultural problems . . . [and] that the economic dimensions of these problems remained overlooked and neglected' (2004: 2); I have, on the contrary, headed in the direction returning from the economic dimension back again toward the socio-political, religious–cultural problems, or what political philosophers refer to as the 'theologico-political problem' (Strauss 1965).

We begin by assenting to the common activist premise that all social justice movements arguably require some sort of ideology in order to provide cohesiveness for their members and unity of purpose for the group as a whole (Oakeshott 1975); however, the ideology employed need not be an *idealism*. Ideologies are (relatively) attainable; idealisms are not. Classical Marxist ideology is inherently an idealism, if its practice in history can be relied upon as evidence — and indeed, it is central to Marxist thought that actual historical experience trumps speculative theory (Marx 1966). Thus it follows that while the Dalit movement may need an ideology in order to succeed, it does not necessarily need Marxism.

As Mungekar points out, 'Dr. Ambedkar considered *Brahmanism* and *Capitalism* as the main enemies of the labouring classes' (2004: 4) — and surely he was correct in that supposition. But while the Dalits and the labouring classes are overlapping groups, they are not identical (Bhowmik 1992). There are many ways to formulate the significance of this point. For example, this suggests that the Dalit problem could be tackled without the inherent contradictions of capitalism (to use Marx's phrase [1966]) having to be solved. Otherwise — albeit unpleasantly — formulated: it is conceivable to envisage an exploited labouring class which has few Dalits within it, even in India.

The 'exploited labouring classes' in developed Western countries have no Dalits; indeed, they have nothing remotely similar to Dalits, as Mungekar has shown:[4] 'There may be iniquitous social systems elsewhere in the world, but the caste system in India has no parallel' (2004: 4). That is, developed Western countries may indeed suffer from the inequities endemic to capitalism, but they are free from the scourge of untouchability. But notice: despite being free of the theologico-political problem of Brahmanism, these countries have nevertheless been incapable of solving the politico-economic problems of extractive capitalism (Habermas 1975).[5]

In short, extractive capitalism could be regarded as a universal problem for the labouring classes, whereas untouchability is a particular problem for Dalits. The Dalit movement, insofar as it adheres to Marxism, expends energy on addressing the (possibly insoluble) global or universal problem, whereas this energy might be channelled toward the more urgent particular problem. To solve the problem of untouchability requires *achievable* societal change; to solve the problem of extractive capitalism requires an as-yet globally unachieved change in human nature (Singh 2005).

---

[4] See Mungekar (2004: 7–13), 'Untouchability and Slavery: A Comparison'.

[5] Juergen Habermas's *Legitimation Crisis* presents the old Frankfurt School position on capitalist systems necessarily suffering perpetual politico-economic crises, such as crises of legitimation. Before too glibly offering the United States as a counter-argument, consider the latest poverty figures there, which now officially stand at 44 million, or one out of every seven Americans (Eckholm 2010) — not to mention the equally horrifying imprisonment data.

After Mungekar brilliantly establishes (2004: 7–13) the distinctive, unprecedented nature of untouchability and graded inequality (that is, Brahmanism), he goes on to say that 'Dr. Ambedkar was equally convinced about the incapacity of Capitalism, as an economic system, to solve India's basic problems of poverty, illiteracy, unemployment, and inequality' (*ibid.*: 13). Dr Ambedkar acknowledged that capitalism may secure economic growth, but he held that the benefits of this growth would necessarily be unequally distributed. Is this necessarily unequal distribution a result of capitalism or of a millennium of graded inequality? Brahmanism led to the Dalit's 'basic problems of poverty, illiteracy, unemployment, and inequality', not capitalism per se. This Mungekar himself implicitly establishes when he contrasts the economic conditions of the Dalits to those of non-Dalits, including the non-Dalit poor. Mungekar examines the condition of the Dalits 'with respect to their access to land, education, employment, and the prevalence of unemployment and poverty amongst them' (*ibid.*: 26). He establishes that in all of these areas, Dalits are worse off than non-Dalits — but it does not follow that the *cause* of this is capitalism. Capitalism *aggravates* the problem, because capitalism everywhere and always exerts its brutal pressures on the most vulnerable, and the Dalits are quite apparently the most vulnerable (Sengupta and Ghose 2010). To be sure, Dalits were oppressed before capitalism; they have been oppressed throughout Indian history as long as Brahmanism has been the theologico-social paradigm — whether the politico-economic system was feudalist, monarchical, colonialist (Ambedkar 1979), capitalist, or even state-socialist (Ilaiah 2009).

The last claim requires support, insofar as many Dalit intellectuals have recently been arguing that current economic liberalization has led to a negation of the socio-economic gains that were made by the Dalit community pre-liberalization (Jogdand 2008). There is too much evidence on the side of these authors for me to deny that steady progress had been made during the state-socialist era, and especially in the 1980s (Kumar 2009). However, Mungekar himself illustrates (2004: 24–37) that the achievements made in post-independence, pre-liberalization India 'have only partially shaken the material base of the caste system, while the social and psychological barriers it has created are far from dead' (*ibid.*: 25). Indeed, the 'annual reports of the Commissioner for the SCs and STs are flooded with statistics showing how [Dalits] are subjected to various types [of] inhuman treatment and all sorts of atrocities' (*ibid.*: 25–26) — torture, murder, arson, looting, rape, etc. Moreover, countless numbers of such acts are carried out with complete impunity. This obviously does not result most proximately from capitalism, but from the graded inequality and untouchability endemic to Brahmanism.

Ambedkar believed that the 'caste system in India embodied in itself an organisation of economic production and a mechanism of distribution giving monopoly of all privileges in the hands of the upper castes and all sufferings to the lower caste Shudras. The conditions of the Untouchables were [the] worst' (Ambedkar 1979: 21). This shows the superimposition of the Marxist critique of capitalism onto the problem of untouchability. This approach ultimately serves to confound the particular (and soluble) theologico-political problem of untouchability with the global (and possibly insoluble) politico-economic problem of extractive capitalism. Interestingly, in many of Sen's own works, caste is also subsumed under issues of access to labour (Sen 1992, 1999).

Part V of Mungekar's work consists of six remedial measures to counterbalance the ill effects that market liberalization does and will continue to exact on the Dalits. These include land reform policies at the state level, a demand to more properly institute the reservation policy, carry-over of reservation to disinvested enterprises, enhanced expenditure by state and central governments on social services and basic human needs, and so on (Mungekar 2004: 58–59). Keeping with the roster of remedial measures that Mungekar forwards, I would go a step further and advocate a *liberalization differential*. For example, there is dire need of labour law reforms, but Marxist parties have been opposing this. Obviously, Dalit intellectuals of the leftist bent would also oppose such reforms, but should they? When the Dalit problem is considered in distinction from the proletarian one, the possibility of an alternative position opens up. That is, the labour regime could be fully liberalized (even *Americanized*, where there is no non-contractual job security, and thus capital is put at an extreme structural advantage over labour, triggering trickle-down economic theory, which all left-leaning parties have hitherto eschewed), *except for reserved slots*, which remain secure as they were in the previous labour law regime. This is what I mean by a liberalization differential. It presupposes that the Dalit movement will pull back from pursuing the idealism of Marxist ideology, and consolidate its concern, seeking above all the advantage of the *Dalit* masses, and tabling — for the time being — the plight of the general masses of poor, exploited labour, the proletariat: in a phrase, global justice.

Conclusion: Deromanticizing Global Justice

The present motto of the international cable news network CNN is *'go beyond borders'*. This phrase appears before and after news reportages (serving to separate the news segments from the advertisements), and strangely is used even when the news headline is about human trafficking or illegal immigration, such as ships laden with impoverished persons headed for Australia only to be ruthlessly turned away by the naval guards at the destination. The cosmopolitan tendency of global justice in the current academic debate (e.g., Tan 2004) smacks of something of the same ironic/romantic elitism of CNN.

In the first place, it is a reasonable conclusion to draw, from the debates on global justice and the fora wherein they take place, that political philosophers profit from the phenomena that urge them into debates on global justice — famine, poverty and the global poor's inequitable access to water, shelter, livelihood — in terms of career advancement, travel opportunities and so on, whereas it is not at all clear if the global poor profit in any determinable way from our debates and publications. That is, academic or scholarly attention on the global poor more transparently benefits academics (we are free — and privileged enough — to change our areas of research and specialization, to 'go beyond borders') than the Dalits or other chronic global poor. We might even put it crudely by stating that we profit off the chronic global poor for the injustices they suffer.

This is not merely rhetoric. The point is, and Peter Singer made it already forty years ago, that despite our academic interests and activities, distant wretched persons are affected only through the traditional mechanisms of our countries' foreign policies and our personal notions of charitable giving (Singer 1972). Romanticized conceptions of the moral arbitrariness and consequent irrelevance of our nationality — and thus the concomitant rejection of the aggressive pursuit of national interest as a legitimate foreign policy axiom — are nothing other than a naïve cosmopolitan appeal for global justice. After all, from the perspective of global justice, how to solve the local (social) justice problem of the Dalits without intervention, either soft or hard?

We do not all agree on the moral arbitrariness of our conditions. Different cultural traditions, in fact, offer competing justifications of privilege, and a large portion of Western political philosophy is devoted to the justification of privilege, such as defence of inheritance and encomia on the so-called rule-of-law. Nevertheless, the deromanticization of this person-centric, moralistic approach to global justice has generally entailed the prioritization of institutions, at least in the Rawlsian tradition. Nagel clearly has had the last word on that cul-de-sac. As Sen has recently attempted to establish, however, alternative ontologies may afford alternative deromanticizations. Thanks to Sen, we political philosophers now have a foothold in our task of deparochializing the global justice discourse. The only problem is that Sen has continued to present his own alternative so romantically.

References

Ambedkar, B. 1979. 'Castes in India: Their Mechanism, Genesis and Development', in *Dr. Babasaheb Ambedkar: Writings and Speeches* (ed. F. W. Pritchett), Education Department, Government of Maharashtra, Mumbai, vol. 1, pp. 3–22.

Bhowmik, S. 1992. 'Caste and Class in India', *Economic and Political Weekly* 27(24–25): 1246–48.

Collier, P. 2007. *The Bottom Billion: Why the Poorest Countries Are Failing and What Can Be Done About It*, Oxford University Press, Oxford.

Eckholm, E. 2010. 'Recession Raises Poverty Rate to a 15-Year High', *New York Times*, 16 September.

Freeman, Samuel. 2010. 'A New Theory of Justice', *New York Review of Books*, 14 October.

Gray, J. 2009. 'Is a Smarter World a Better World?' *Literary Review*, August.

Habermas, J. 1975. *Legitimation Crisis*, Beacon Press, Boston.

Ilaiah, K. 2009. *Post-Hindu India: A Discourse in Dalit-Bahujan, Socio-Spiritual and Scientific Revolution*, Sage, New Delhi.

Jogdand, P. B. 2008. *Globalization and Social Justice: Perspectives, Challenges and Praxis*, Rawat, New Delhi.

Kumar, A. S. 2009. *Global Civil Society 2009 — Poverty and Activism*, Sage, London.

Maffettone, Sebastiano. 2011. 'Sen's Idea of Justice versus Rawls' Theory of Justice', *Indian Journal of Human Development* 5(1).

Marx, K. 1966. *Capital*, Basic Books, New York.

Mungekar, Bhalchandra. 2004. *India's Economic Reforms and the Dalits: An Ambedkarian Perspective*, Dr Ambedkar Institute of Social and Economic Change, Mumbai.

Nagel, Thomas. 2005. 'The Problem of Global Justice', *Philosophy and Public Affairs* 33(2): 113–47 (reprinted in this volume, Chapter 3).

Oakeshott, M. 1975. *On Human Conduct*, Clarendon Press, London.

Pogge, Thomas. 2002. *World Poverty and Human Rights: Cosmopolitan Responsibilities and Reforms*, Polity, Cambridge.

Poole, S. 2009. 'The Idea of Justice by Amartya Sen', *Guardian*, 7 November.

Rawls, John. 1958. 'Justice as Fairness', *The Philosophical Review* 67(2): 164–94.

———. 2001. *Justice as Fairness: A Restatement* (ed. E. Kelly), Harvard University Press, Cambridge, MA.

Romano, C. 2009. 'Amartya Sen Shakes up Justice Theory', *Chronicle*, 14 September.

Sen, Amartya. 1992. *Inequality Reexamined*, Harvard University Press, Cambridge, MA.

———. 1999. *Development as Freedom*, Anchor Books, New York.

———. 2009. *The Idea of Justice*, Harvard University Press, Cambridge, MA.

Sengupta, A., and M. Ghose. 2010. 'Vulnerability in India: A Simple Consumption-Based Approach', *Indian Journal of Human Development*, 4(2).

Singer, Peter. 1972. 'Famine, Affluence and Morality', *Philosophy and Public Affairs* 1(3): 229–43 (reprinted in this volume, Chapter 1).

Singh, Aakash. 2005. *Eros Turannos: Leo Strauss and Alexandre Kojeve Debate on Tyranny*, University Press of America, Lanham, MD.

Strauss, L. 1965. *Spinoza's Critique of Religion*, Schocken Books, New York.

Tan, K. C. 2004. *Justice without Borders*, Cambridge University Press, Cambridge.

8

Post-modern Post-colonial Theory versus Political Liberalism

Avoiding the *Liaison Dangereuse* in Global Justice and IR Theory

Sebastiano Maffettone

The post-colonial view as espoused especially in Indian socio-political theory is usually presented as an anti-Western Enlightenment view. This position is twofold, in the sense that it is partly justified and partly not justified. It is surely justified in terms of historical opposition to a past of Western domination, or when it claims an original path toward secularization and more generally in cases in which religions and society are at stake, or when it finds new patterns of sustainability or women's empowerment in antique local traditions. It is, on the other hand, less justified when spirituality is seen in opposition to science and economic development.

Starting with these general considerations, I would like to discuss the way in which contemporary political theory in India argues within the boundaries of this post-colonial climate. The authors I have in mind when I speak of contemporary Indian political theory are people like Ramachandra Guha, Bhikhu Parekh, Partha Chatterjee, Ashis Nandy, Akeel Bilgrami, Rajeev Bhargava, Neera Chandhoke, Homi Bhabha, Meera Nanda, Gayatri Chakraborty Spivak. Even if they cannot all be ranked within the boundaries of post-colonialism, they have all had to engage post-colonial thought. Moreover, they are all contemporary Indian political thinkers insofar as they have had to take into serious consideration the tradition inaugurated by the intellectual fathers of modern India, such as Gandhi, Tagore and Ambedkar (Singh and Mohapatra 2010). In particular, I wish to discuss the post-colonial political culture addressed by several of these authors and its relationship with the political theory of liberalism. The question is: why, with some exceptions, do they not cross-fertilize? My provisional answer is: because liberalism is timid and post-colonialism is philosophically weak. But, please, read more to know why.

Many political theorists tend to be sceptical about liberalism. In particular, they doubt its motivational appeal. Liberalism appears to them either too thin or extremely cold. It could be right in principle, but without warming our hearts. As Robert Nozick wrote: 'Can it thrill the heart or inspire people to struggle or sacrifice? Would anyone man barricades under its banner? It seems pale and feeble in comparison with, to pick the polar extreme, the hopes and dreams of utopian theorists' (Nozick 1974: 297).[1] This sceptical attitude is widespread and in some way shared by non-liberal and liberal critics of liberalism. Few would deny that liberalism as a source of fundamental rights is a premise for a decent political society. Nevertheless, the price of political liberalism seems to many exceedingly high. The non-comprehensive nature of liberalism causes a perverse division of the self, a quasi-schizoid separation of our deep sentiments from institutional reality. Thus, liberalism cannot fully capture emotional consensus. It appears like a flat consequence of the reality principle, whereas our motivational apparatus is fundamentally attracted by the pleasure principle. Even scholars who frankly endorse political liberalism, like Thomas Nagel, are inclined to admit that, within the frontiers of liberalism, when, confronted with a deep disagreement, we need the 'higher standard of objectivity', we get merely 'a bare confrontation between incompatible personal points of view' (Nagel 1987: 232).

My first aim in this essay is to rescue liberalism from this sceptical attitude. The domain in which my argument operates is that of the global justice debate and international relations (IR) analyzed from the perspective of contemporary cultural politics. By cultural politics I mean a tendency to analyze political global society in terms of cultural conditions rather than merely in terms of legal and economic structures. This 'culturalism' is indeed typical of the post-colonial paradigm, distinguishing it from Marxist and neo-liberal approaches to IR. From this point of view, its origins are clearly extra-Western, and oscillate from Gandhi's Indian

[1] Nozick is speaking here of libertarianism, but he could also analogously address liberalism.

tradition to the Chinese Cultural Revolution, from the work of Islamic agonist culture to the African Cultural Organizations, and (perhaps) also to Liberation Theology in South America and to various indigenous group stances all around the globe. Nevertheless, you can also find Western origins of post-colonialism, from the Frankfurt School to the work of Antonio Gramsci, from French structuralism (Levi-Strauss) to British anthropology and local counter-culture movements (like the Irish).

Within this domain, the way in which I want to rescue liberalism is partially negative. I intend to propose liberalism in IR as an antidote to what I call the *liaison dangereuse* between post-colonialism and post-modernism, in order to open up a new vista for the possibility of global justice in the wake of both liberal as well as post-colonial scepticism. A great part of this article is devoted to discussing the cultural politics of post-colonialism and the nature of its conjunction with post-modernism. This conjunction is — I claim — arguably perverse and its consequences are culturally and politically dangerous. This is a good reason to avoid it. And, avoiding the *liaison dangereuse,* we find the liberal platform in the background, so that we can rescue it. It is superfluous to say that here my conception of liberalism is rather vague and schematic. You can take it as a minimal foundational basis for democratic theory, inspired by contemporary classics such as Juergen Habermas and especially John Rawls.

To put it in a different way, as the Chinese political philosopher Ji Wei-Ci has suggested, one could distinguish, in post-colonial thought, between a first order and a second order argument. By a first order post-colonial argument, I mean here the substantive part through which the main political theoretical thesis is defended. By a second order post-colonial argument, I mean the meta-theoretical perspective through which it is possible to philosophically justify the first order argument. What I am suggesting is that in many post-colonial theses, the substantive part, that is the content of the first order argument, is reasonably sound. On the contrary, what does not work is the second order argument behind it; that is, the meta-theoretical counterpart of the argument. To be more specific, I believe that the post-modernist second order argument — included in many post-colonial theses — does not properly support the main normative or substantive tenets. As a first consequence, it seems that the post-modernist second order argument is too heavy a burden for post-colonialism. As a second consequence, it is possible that the much more convincing liberal second order argument (from Kant to Habermas and Rawls) can offer a surprising support to post-colonialism.

In what follows, my argument goes like this:

1. Indian post-colonial theories present narratives of discontent based on resentment toward colonial exploitation and cultural hegemony;
2. the substance of post-colonial narratives (their first order argument) is sound;
3. post-colonial theories often rely on a post-modern philosophical argumentative structure (their second order argument);
4. the second order argument is not able to support the first order argument;
5. in particular, the nihilist consequences of post-modernism make impossible the construction of a (post-colonial) discourse through which the discontent is transformed into a basis for reasonable political action;
6. the lack of such a discourse is a source of despair and of predisposition toward political fragmentation and violence;
7. within liberalism it is possible to represent post-colonialism as a critical stance; and
8. this reconstructive approach assumes the possibility of a transitional institutional apparatus in IR (thereby paving the way for global justice), even in the absence of a hegemonic liberal-democratic discourse (this is the reason why Rawls works here better than Habermas).

This complex argumentation can prima facie appear the fruit of mere philosophical extravagance, or simply too abstract to be sensible (I should probably discuss some post-colonial authors one by one to be more precise). However, I am really convinced that avoiding the *liaison dangereuse* between post-colonialism and post-modernism can help promote a reasonable discursive path in the global setting. If a narrative based on sound reasons, like post-colonialism, does not find a discursive path, then it will blow up into pieces with destructive consequences, both materially and spiritually. Note that I am not suggesting that post-colonial theories are responsible for this. The real responsibility lies with colonial exploitation and hegemony, not to speak of some liberal blindness unable to see the asymmetry between the theory and the practice of liberal democracy in the global setting, as so well exposed by authors such as Ranajit Guha (2002).

I am quite conscious of the ambitiousness of, and the difficulty connected with, my principal aim here. The deconstruction of part of the theoretical bulk of post-colonialism and the parallel reconstruction of liberalism as political culture in IR are not easy tasks. After all, post-colonialism is vocationally anti-liberal, and liberalism is usually contra-post-colonial. Moreover, my argumentation is surely permeated by some utopian naïveté and several (hidden) assumptions. For example, it would be normal to criticize the assumption that a sophisticated philosophical methodology, like post-modernism, can have immediate practical consequences. Or, it is not difficult to object that my presentation of post-modernism may be too thin, being in other words more a caricature than a fair account.

Eventually, however, my claim is not so bizarre. It is a claim in favour of greater objectivity and universality in approaching cultural politics from a post-colonial point of view. Of course, here the objection from within post-colonialism is that universalism and objectivity are forms of disguised Eurocentric political culture. On the one hand, I am just suggesting that without universalism and objectivity even the right claims implicit in post-colonial political culture cannot be appropriately formulated and communicated. On the other hand, even post-colonial thinkers would admit that liberalism, notwithstanding its European origin, provides a strong foundation from which one can erect critiques of social injustice (Chakrabarty 2000: 4–5). That is why what I am trying to argue is in the end neither too complex nor exceedingly controversial. For, I am saying that post-colonialism should care more about universal discourse, whereas liberals should care more about the effects of the cultural side of political theory. The conclusion of this argument is quite clear: post-colonial scholarship is committed to engaging liberal universalism so as to invoke justice, and liberal scholarship must take into serious consideration post-colonial tenets in significant areas of IR.

As far the economy of this article is concerned, it is divided into four sections: section II discusses some fundamental theses of post-colonialism; section III describes the post-modern arguments usually taken up by post-colonialism and stresses their most evident limits; and section IV presents the liberal approach in terms of a Rawlsian global overlapping consensus.

II

In this section, I sketch some basic tenets of post-colonialism as political culture. Here, I summarize what I have called the first order argument of post-colonialism, that is, the core of its normative and substantive theses. Roughly speaking, I think that there is not too much to object to in this first order argument. In summarizing these arguments, my methodology is voluntarily simplifying, and I do not pretend to completeness in listing the main tenets of post-colonialism. Rather, I have in mind only the general structure of a widespread social-scientific literature such as post-colonialism and the reasons for its main claims. In the following, I will specially draw my theses from an analysis of the Indian tradition, even if I think that my conclusions are potentially more general and could apply to the whole post-colonial literature. My presentation does not intend to be particularly rigorous from a historical point of view. It just aims at providing a minimal framework for the general theoretical purpose of this essay.

Post-colonialism is a political culture continuing the anti-colonial and nationalist trends widespread in the 'third world' after 1945. Its configuration is complex, being a diasporic product in which indigenous and cosmopolitan elements merge (this is particularly evident in post-colonial art [Appiah 1991]). Post-colonialism is basically a mixture of local culture and general political principles. The discourse is diffuse, including the political activism of many movements, ranging from proper political parties to mass migration groups, from sophisticated intellectual elites to suburban activism (Young 2003). From this point of view, there is an inherent ambiguity in post-colonialism, being both a historical trend and a mode of theoretical analysis (Rattansi 1997).

Among the main tenets of post-colonial political culture are the following:

1. explicit anti-colonialism;
2. strong anti-Eurocentrism;
3. emphasis on cultural localism;
4. political priority of marginalized people;
5. return to religion; and
6. counter-history, both as reconstruction of the past from the present point of view and as anti-historicism.

Post-colonialism is a complex and differentiated political culture. The cement of post-colonial political culture is surely the consensus against the legacy of Western colonialism. European expansion in the period 1492–1945 is condemned from a shared moral point of view. In particular, what is in the focus of post-colonialism is the cultural — rather than economic or military — dominance of the West. The political culture of colonial states coincided with an apology for Western modernity, conceived both as the final destination of global civilization and the normative point from which history must be reconsidered. According to the generality of post-colonial thinkers, the trade-off between this (supposed) export of modernity and the costs for the colonized in terms of exploitation, humiliation and suffering have been tragically negative.

This thesis should imply that colonialism must be ethically rejected in universalistic terms from the global (universal) justice point of view. Global (universal) justice in fact cannot approve of systematic exploitation, humiliation and suffering. This straightforward thesis is, however, made impossible by the strong and reasonable anti-Eurocentric background of the post-colonial paradigm. In complex ways, modernity, capitalism and universalism are associated by post-colonial political culture. Modernity implies — in this view — an original form of stability detached from metaphysics and related to the public culture of liberal democracy (as in Rawls). This shift, from metaphysics to public culture, is promoted by capitalism and affirmed by European colonialism. That is why the legacy of European modernity is so controversial from the post-colonial point of view (Chakrabarty 2000: 6). Ranajit Guha presents his post-colonial thesis in opposition to the Hegelian idea of *Weltgeshichte*, or world history, both denouncing the hypocrisy of this 'public' reconciliation of reason and history as Eurocentric, and reclaiming a logical–historical space for Indian subaltern masses. The core of modern public culture, however, is supposed to be universalism. Post-colonial thinkers often see universalism as the other face of Eurocentrism. That is why anti-colonialism, anti-Eurocentrism, anti-modernism, and anti-universalism are — for many post-colonial thinkers — all aspects of the same unacceptable package. This linkage makes difficult the relationship between post-colonial and liberal political culture.

This anti-Eurocentric attitude with its implicit rejection of universalism implies a bias in favour of localism. Localism is the way in which post-colonial thought looks for hetero-spatiality, through which it tries to convert the 'there' of the Eurocentric narrative into a 'here' situated in post-colonial spaces. The scope of this localism can be either terribly wide, like Asia, or much narrower, like the history of Bengal, or even a personal narrative in opposition to a public 'colonial' history. The common core of different forms of localism consists in denouncing the cultural hegemony (*cf.* Gramsci) of the West, proposing on the other hand the richer cultural background of some local cultures (e.g., in Gandhi). There are different degrees of localism, also depending upon the centre–periphery location of the specific culture discussed. Assuming that the core of Eurocentrism is Atlantic, one could distinguish, for example, a Mediterranean peripheral localism from an Oriental one.

Localism has a lot to do with rediscovering marginalization. One of the typical claims of post-colonial political culture consists in the emphasis on neglected populations, in an attempt to rescue their expressivity and role. Here again, the scope of this movement toward the margins can be highly differentiated. Generally speaking, one can imagine three different levels of distinction: Western culture; elite local cultures; and marginal people's local culture. Whereas the moral condemnation of Western culture is ubiquitous, the emphasis on the separation between local elites and marginal people is typically post-colonial. This emphasis could imply several degrees of distinction, ranging from mere separation to explicit condemnation of local elites (for complicity with the West). This aspect permits the disconnection of post-colonialism — which divides elites from marginal people — from anti-colonialist and nationalist trends, which did not. At the same time, the emphasis on marginal people brings post-colonial political culture closer to traditional Marxism (more Sartre than Althusser).

The systematic recovering of religion, however, puts post-colonial political culture largely at odds with classical Marxism (with some exceptions, like Liberation Theology and other religious interpretations of Marxism). What is really extraneous to post-colonial political culture is Marxist economicism. From this point of view, post-colonialism is much more spiritually oriented and community-oriented than Western culture, including Marxism. In this perspective, Marxism and liberalism are both targets of post-colonialism in the measure in which they overemphasize rationality in the motivational set of the individual and in the reconstruction of history. Religions can be rediscovered — within a post-colonial horizon — in different ways, ranging from the most spiritual and apolitical to the more politicized (like often in the Islamic world). It is almost superfluous to say that it is quite impossible to disentangle the religious revival from the localist trend and the traditionalist sympathies of post-colonialism.

Religious revival, localism, but, more than anything else, the revaluation of marginal people, are at the origin of post-colonial counter-history. With counter-history, post-colonialism looks for hetero-temporality, aiming to transform the 'not yet' stage, in which Western narratives locate the Rest, into a 'now'. Counter-history can be presented in at least two different ways. First, it may be viewed as exploiting unusual reconstructive paths in the reinterpretation of the past. With time, the marginalized colonial subject begins to be separated from the bourgeois nationalists, the post-colonial story being told from the perspective of the first rather than that of the second. This trend implies a re-politicization of subaltern masses seen as the real victims of exploitation and hegemony. Indian historians representing this trend, led by Guha, try to locate revolutionary agency and the force of change in the hands of 'subalterns'. In this way, the theory of culture intersects with the theory of change. The attempt is of course to make this new subaltern point of view hegemonic in an original way. Cognitive failure is consequently denounced when the counter-historical interpretation is confronted with traditional historiography. Finally, the narrative of the subaltern, alienated consciousness is written to substitute the elite reconstruction of the past.

Second, post-colonial thought often presents itself as frankly 'anti-historicist' (e.g., Chakrabarty 2000). Here, the counter-historical point lies in a critique of the historicist argument, according to which the history of the East is a primitive phase of world history (which culminated in the Western apotheosis). This thesis is typically Hegelian–Marxist, but can also be liberal (John Stuart Mill is quoted by Chakrabarty in this respect). The liberal recommendation for the colonized here is to wait. From which one can derive a vision of history based on the 'not yet' (not modern enough), to which the nationalist colonized opposes his/her 'now' (*ibid.*: 9). The opposition here is to the idea that the colonial world is in some way pre-political (Guha 1999).

III

In this section, I recapitulate some elements taken from what I called the second order argument for post-colonialism, that is, its meta-theoretical apparatus insofar as it is based on post-modernist thought. As I suggested earlier, on this point my view is critical. Of course, it would be preposterous if not absurd to present post-modernism in a few lines. This is the reason why here I try only to sketch some guidelines with respect to a sub-set of post-modernist visions, to see how it influences the post-colonial movement. By post-modernism I mean a philosophical climate characterized by the rejection of Western modern philosophy from Descartes to Kant, along with their contemporary descendants, like analytical philosophy with all its political consequences. This philosophical climate includes a sceptical attitude toward modern epistemology and metaphysics and their claim to knowledge. In some ways, this trend is antique, tracing its origins to the 'Young Hegelian' disempowering of philosophy, and to Nietzsche. Philosophical post-modernism presents itself in conjunction with similar cultural patterns in aesthetics and political theory. In political theory, which concerns us more here, post-modernism (e.g., Lyotard, Jameson, Rorty) is usually associated with the condemnation of great meta-narratives, from Marx to Rawls.

On the one hand, to the rationalist outlook that characterizes philosophical methodology in the tradition from Descartes to Kant, post-modern thinkers generally oppose the contingency and the conventionality of the 'normative'. Against the rigour of logical argument, post-moderns make a plea for the force of rhetorics and the metaphorical significance implicit in artistic works. In this way, they contrast modernist universalism with the absolute specificity of particular life-worlds and forms of knowledge. The main consequence of this contrast is a rejection of philosophical foundationalism. In opposition to foundationalism, post-modern authors privilege heterogeneity, fragmentation, particularity, contingency, localism.

On the other hand, post-modernism presents itself as a dramatic revision of modern subjectivity, around which the tradition from Descartes to Kant was centred. Against the universalistic, noumenal and mentalist self, post-moderns invoke an embodied subject whose partition is revealed by the relevance of the (Freudian) unconscious. Against the rational subject of modernity, post-moderns launch their claim for the economy of desire and the power of the irrational. Against the unencumbered individual of the Kantian legacy, post-moderns emphasize the social character of the person. The negative discourse about the subject, inaugurated by Levi-Strauss, becomes — especially in Foucault and Derrida — the starting-point of a radical critique of modernity.

I rely here on that particular segment of the post-modernist trend that is often called 'French Theory', which label can be taken as an American popularization of some post-structuralist French argumentative patterns and styles of thought. Following the interpretations of Heidegger and Nietzsche, already in the period between the two world wars of the 20th century, some French intellectuals began to nourish anti-Western sentiments in matters concerning metaphysics and politics. In this unusual way, they often became anti-colonial before the time of post-modernism. Frantz Fanon and Jean-Paul Sartre represent, in different moods, this anti-colonial attitude, and can be considered among the forerunners of the Western influence on post-colonialism. For several reasons, however, they cannot be properly ranked among the authors of French thought, such as Foucault, Derrida, Deleuze, Lyotard, Lacan, Bourdieu, Baudrillard. My thesis is that this post-modern (French thought) background — notwithstanding its oppositionist contribution to the Western discourse of the Enlightenment — makes impossible the potentially objective and universal rights claims of post-colonialism, usually directed to rescuing the worst off from exploitation and hegemony.

French thought intersects with post-colonialism in different ways, including radical constructivism in IR and the social sciences, literary criticism, legal hermeneutics, women's studies, and psychology. Here I will mention just two post-modern options influencing post-colonial political–theoretical literature: (*a*) the Foucauldian option; and (*b*) the deconstructionist option.

The work of Foucault constitutes a basic inspiration for post-colonial studies not only in India (e.g., the work of Partha Chatterjee [1986, 1993, 2004]). Authors like Edward Said (see his *Orientalism* [1979]) and Valentin Mudimbe (see *The Invention of Africa* [1988]) rely strictly on Foucault, when they formulate their central tenet connecting colonial power with science and knowledge.

Foucault's work is silent about colonialism. From this point of view, his work remains strictly Eurocentric. His main theses, however, present a significant and radical criticism of the Western theoretical tradition. That is why some of his theoretical tools can be used and have been used for the sake of post-colonial argumentation. In particular, I have in mind three of these patterns:

1. the idea of bio-political power;
2. the relation between truth and power; and
3. the local character of the critical point of view.

The idea of biopolitics, and of a biopolitical power, dates to the last part of Foucault's career. In some ways, it derives from the Nietzschean origins of his thought and from the post-modern emphasis on the economy of desire (Deleuze–Guattari). In contrast to the traditional *Lebensphilosophie* (Dilthey), Foucault sees power as the real, transcendental space from which a historical approach is supposed to begin. The significance of biopolitics is linked to the disciplinary power of the state and totalitarian institutions (prisons, mental illness clinics, etc.). For Foucault, politics moves progressively from the manipulation of life and death to the care of bodies. The biopolitical stance reveals the centrality of the body and the complexity of the self in its relationships with social practices. The idea of the centrality of the body is invoked by many post-colonial authors as an instrument against the rationalistic and scientific dominance of the West.

The emphasis on the relationship between truth and power is formulated by (the younger) Foucault in his *Archaeology of Knowledge*, and basically re-presented by Said (and used by Chatterjee). It depends on conceiving any discourse with truth claims as part of dominium. In this sense, truth and power are not two different things. On the contrary, truth claims are part of the legitimatory apparatus power physiologically needs to be stable. This intersection does not operate at the conscious level of the researcher; rather, it represents a hidden premise of any inquiry aiming at truth. Power, in this view, does not work in a uniform way, but rather through a series of micro-practices. In the concept of practice, Foucault sees the moment of coercion. All forms of social control are included in the range of practices, from police measures to legal devices, from pedagogical disciplines to clinical instructions. The unmasking of these forms of social control as potential forms of exclusion (as in the case of clinics) should make evident the intrinsic relation between discourse and power. Foucault's central argument, from this point of view, goes from (pure) knowledge to the *savoirs*, from the *savoirs* to discursive practices, and finally from discursive practices to truth-seeking norms. From this perspective, power is never fully pervasive, to avoid a performative contradiction that would completely close the logical space for any possible critique.

The local character of the critical point of view takes radical historicity seriously. What the deconstruction of metaphysics is for Heidegger and Derrida, is for Foucault the deconstruction of historicity. It has a double meaning, one being cultural, the other political. In the cultural sense, Foucault's method of historical deconstruction presents an invitation to doubt totalizing paradigms and, in general, any form of structural coherence. For Foucault, only limited and marginal forms of knowledge are seriously revelatory. In the political sense, there is a claim for the point of view of subalternity, of the unspoken and of the repressed. Within the complex Foucauldian notion of genealogy, the fusion of local memories and of rare and erudite forms of knowledge are one face of the moon, the other being the rescue of the 'underdogs' and the forgotten. In this manner, this radical historicist point of view challenges liberal pluralism in the name of emancipation from marginalization. Against epistemic objectivism, taken as the background of Western thought and political liberalism, Foucault defends an anti-scientific and particularistic vision strongly oriented toward emancipation.

Derrida was an internal–external (that is, a Jewish-Algerian, philosophically French) radical critic of Western metaphysics, following in the tracks of Heidegger. Conceiving of himself as a 'Marrano' (a converted Jew), he saw himself as a subaltern subject. His work can be put under the label of 'post-structuralism' (since his readings of Saussure and Levi-Strauss are integral to his philosophy). In structuralism, Derrida always saw a powerful form of Western ethnocentrism. Against this background, he threshed out his theory of 'deconstruction', which is a philosophy and a strategy whose main aim is to shake the whole basis of Western thought.

Deconstruction is directed toward fighting the ontological violence that sustains Western metaphysics and that is revealed in the structure of the language. Its effects concern history, politics, ethics, and language. Derrida's main contributions to post-colonialism include the following:

1. Margins: This concept, coming from the core of the critique of metaphysics, meets with the need to redefine subaltern positions that is typical of the post-colonial enterprise (e.g., in Gayatri Spivak and Partha Chatterjee). The post-colonial subject is obliged to inhabit the cultural space of the colonizer, and deconstruction offers an alternative logical niche from which to create a derivative discourse. In this sense, Derrida radicalizes the work of Levi-Strauss, whose first merit was to dispute the cultural difference between civilized and primitive. Related concepts, developed by Derrida, are diaspora and difference (note the distinction in French between 'difference-differance'), both of which can be naturally extended from the original meta-theoretical intention to being reformulated in the light of the experience of subaltern groups.
2. Otherness: The centrality of the other — following Levinas — is an essential element of Derridean philosophy. The deconstruction of Western metaphysics and the very idea of 'differance' presuppose the linguistically other (here the derivation is from Jacques Lacan). In this way, Derridean deconstruction becomes an element of radical multiculturalism. This fact explains why his international success is in some way linked to the expectations of the American multicultural community. Post-colonial thinkers adopted Derrida's idea of otherness to formulate basic concepts such as hybridism, métissage and creolization, used to give an account of the inextricable nexus that is the basis of every culture (European included). It is also possible to use this Derridean idea to distinguish Western subalterns from 'third-world' subalterns, comparatively defending the latter (Spivak 1999).

Even admitting that my account of post-modern contributions to post-colonialism is cursory and exceedingly simplistic, I think one can derive from it some weaknesses of the combined paradigm (i.e., what I have characterized as the *liaison dangereuse*):

1. *Lack of objectivism*: This is a standard critical stance toward post-modernism. Post-modernism relies strongly on a sort of normative criticism of normativity. Major institutions, starting with capitalism and the state, are considered able to impose their own patterns through a series of practices in a falsely neutralized way. This kind of pattern is present both in Foucault and Derrida. It is, however, difficult to find in their theses any argument for such a critical point of view. The post-modern radical normativity represents a *contradictio in adjecto*. To be clear: it seems that the Archimedean perspective that such a radical criticism of objectivity (the post-modern one) presupposes is a privileged point of view. In other words, it needs more and not less objectivity, which is impossible by definition within the post-modernist framework (Dworkin 1996).
2. Lack of objectivism is connected with *anti-scientism and anti-rationalism*. It has been noted that the relativistic stance, implicit in the post-modern trend, implies a kind of epistemic populism (Nanda 2004). Hegel wrote in his *Phenomenology* of a permanent 'struggle between Enlightenment and superstition'. The Hegelian account is apologetic toward the West. We must admit, however, that too often, through the legacy of post-modernism, post-colonial thinkers have been on the side of 'superstition'. Often, it would have been more sensible and simple to state that colonial power was deeply unjust and irrational. Even sophisticated intellectuals like Ashis Nandy, Ranajit Guha, Gayatri Spivak, Partha Chatterjee, and Homi Bhabha run the risk of considering antique Indian astrology and the classic religious texts (like the Vedas) on par with modern science. This attitude, shared in different contexts by Islamic fundamentalists (*cf*. Gilles Kepel) and — outside the realm of post-colonialism — by the inglorious 'Soviet biology' of the past, puts at risk not only Western modernity but any possible vision of modernity. It can also be seen as a premise for a false progressivism and a substantial traditionalism. From this point of view, false progressivism and real conservatism — connected with anti-scientism — could be accused even of favouring the caste system (as Ambedkar himself hinted).
3. Anti-objectivism and anti-scientism imply *the impossibility of universalism*. For post-modernism, universalism can be considered as a kind of false consciousness. For post-colonialism, it is strictly

linked with that *entelechia* of reason which is considered essential to the Eurocentric narrative. The impossibility of universalism has two pernicious consequences. On the one hand, post-modernist anti-universalisms rely on a perverse trust in spontaneity and naïveté (as seen in Spivak [1999: *passim*]). Contrary to the Marxist legacy, in which the hegemonic claim of the oppressed is defended through a universalistic apparatus of revolt, here the voice of the subaltern is supposed to be immediately able to rescue itself from a history of domination. It is highly debatable, however, whether the localism of community and religion can support a radical revolutionary claim like the post-colonial one. On the other hand, and for the same reasons, the post-modern attitude of post-colonialists localizes the conflict by, so to speak, 'depoliticizing' it. In such a way, it deprives the political stances of the subalterns of vision, condemning them either to being confined within the aesthetic realm (as would happen with Habermas) or to being confronted in a series of particularistic negotiations (as in Zizek). This condemnation is connected with the impossibility — from a post-modern point of view — of raising the bar up to the level of universality, the preclusion of which makes it impossible to reclaim the humanistic (in the Kantian sense) basis of the post-colonial claim against exploitation and hegemony. Thus, post-modern anti-universalism precludes the appeal to dignity and human rights, with all the emancipatory options these notions provide. Otherness, within a post-modern outlook, is always confined in the singularity of an experience (African, Indian, Islamic, even of a village, etc.) or even to the privatization of the emotions against public history, and never offers the possibility of an emancipatory *Aufhebung* through the universal mediation of reason.

4. *Anti-modernism*: Post-colonial thought is often ambiguous about its relation with political modernity. It is characterized by the coexistence of two logics. One logic derives from the experience of subalternity and protest, and is clearly anti-historicist and anti-modernist in the sense previously defined. A second logic derives from the liberal constitutional legacy and the universalist philosophy of European origin. I think that both these logics are necessary parts of the post-colonial argument and that the *liaison* with post-modernism makes it impossible to rely on the second logic.

To conclude, it seems of general interest to salvage a post-colonial political thought that can embrace the pursuit of reason in the name of social and global justice. To do this, post-colonial political thought has to find ways to associate its preoccupation with hetero-spatiality and hetero-temporality with notions such as reason and justice. It has to abandon the view of the (original) ethnographer and the historicist, to sensibly transform the 'there' into the 'here' and the 'not yet' into the 'now' (Chakrabarty 2000). But this aim seems better served by the admission of a path-independent of universalism, modernity and objectivity rather than by their post-modernist nullification. In other words, from a post-colonial point of view, modern pluralism — there are many relevant 'nows' and 'heres' — works better than nihilism.

IV

In this final section, my intention is to see whether the first order argument for post-colonialism can be combined with a different (and unusual) second order argument. To put this more explicitly, I will try to show how a post-colonial substantive and normative outlook — based on the tenets I listed previously — can be wedded to a liberal-democratic meta-theory. My premise is that post-colonialism can combine with the Rawlsian model better than with the Habermasian model. This is so because Rawls is, generally speaking, more well disposed toward pluralism and contextualism than Habermas. In fact, Rawls does not base his political model on a whole philosophy (of the Enlightenment) like Habermas. Even when Habermas insists that his position is post-metaphysical, it is because in discussing religion, for instance, from a post-metaphysical point of view, he is convinced that reason in the public sphere can erode every form of religious radicality. Dialogue, for Habermas, can change identities and help the rational cleaning of prejudices and non-rational belief.

I conclude by arguing that post-modernism, in its conjunction with post-colonialism, implies a significant privatization and depoliticization of post-colonial claims. Perhaps post-modernism even makes post-colonial claims meaningless, insofar as it obliges post-colonialism to maintain a critical cultural stance while separating it from its *universalizing* political force and its objective meaning. This effect is not new, and — as I indicated earlier — is connected with the nihilistic substance of the post-modern attack on modernity. From Nietzsche and Heidegger to contemporary French thought, post-colonial thinkers, if influenced by post-modernism, can retain the flavour of a radical, anti-Western philosophical attitude, but certainly not the emancipatory force of a progressive post-colonial political argument (which is the substance of their first order normative argument).

From the beginning of this essay, I have aimed to show how liberalism can supplement post-colonial claims, once the divorce between post-colonialism and post-modernism has taken place (so that the *liaison dangereuse* is interrupted). It is obviously a difficult task, if not for other reasons, then at least because the contemporary liberal argument seems to fully embody the Enlightenment project opposed by the post-colonial mentality. For this reason, we do not follow the path laid out by Habermas, where a neo-modernist, rationalistic outlook would be at odds with post-colonial intellectual interests. Instead, my idea is that the pluralistic and not-comprehensive Rawlsian account of political liberalism would permit a more plausible fusion of horizons (than Habermas's framework).

And this is all the more plausible because, in Rawls, the first order normative argument and the second order meta-theoretical argument can be much more easily split than in Habermas. As a consequence, Rawlsian pluralistic liberalism allows some integration of the hetero-temporality and hetero-spatiality which the post-colonial argument requires in the effort to transform the 'not yet' into the 'now', and the 'there' into the 'here'. Thus, I argue, post-colonialism could accept the tenets of Rawlsian pluralistic liberalism. This argument is pursued here through two progressive steps. First, I present the idea of a global (Rawlsian) overlapping consensus. Second, I try to anchor its plausibility in the (Rawlsian) idea of 'basic structure'.

Standard overlapping consensus presupposes pluralism: there is only one and the same institutional reality that we can approach starting from different moral, religious and metaphysical premises. Within this institutional reality, it is plausible to assume that different comprehensive doctrines face each other reciprocally in a regime of reasonable pluralism and toleration. This overlapping consensus model is clearly linked historically to the fact of the nation-state. In this case, it is reasonable to think that the majority of intellectual conflicts are partial (or 'reasonable', to use the standard term); in other words, it is reasonable to assume that everybody can accept, keeping out his/her profound comprehensive view, the institutional framework within which these conflicts take place. The same strategy could not seem prima facie applicable to the international domain and to transcultural problems. Here, there is no such thing as a common institutional framework to uphold (as Nagel argued; see Nagel, this volume).

This way of reasoning — which forbids a global overlapping consensus — can be made dependent on Rawls's basic structure argument. The group of major institutions is the 'basic structure', being the main subject of a theory of justice.[2] Rawls's theory of justice as fairness addresses only those who belong to the same basic structure. In *A Theory of Justice* (Rawls 1971), membership in a (institutional) community is fundamental to being entitled to a justification of inequality and, therefore, to being an outright subject within the context of the distributive paradigm.

A straightforward application of the basic structure argument to global justice runs roughly like this:

1. justice requires the existence of the basic structure as a precondition;
2. the basic structure applies only to national societies;
3. thus, there is no justice beyond national societies.

This reading seems to exclude global overlapping consensus. There are, however, different possible readings of this argument. The basic structure is conceived as the way in which the major social institutions work together to assign rights and duties that arise from social cooperation. The political constitution, legal property, the organization of the economy, the nature of family, all belong to the basic structure (Rawls 1996: 258, 2001: 10). If Rawls's goal in *A Theory of Justice* is to find first principles that can provide reasonable guidelines for the problem of social justice, then it is clear that these principles are not independent of the social practices that the basic structure frames: 'There is no attempt to formulate first principles that apply equally to all subjects' (Rawls 1996: 258).

This thesis implies that historically existing practices are relevant in formulating a conception of justice. This relevance does not concern

[2] As Rawls writes in the initial pages of *A Theory of Justice*: 'For us the primary subject of justice is the basic structure of society, or more exactly, the way in which the major social institutions distribute fundamental rights and duties and determine the division of advantages from social cooperation' (Rawls 1971: 7).

only the implementation of a conception of justice. It concerns, also, its fundamental justification. If we accept a basic structure argument *à la* Rawls, then the justification of the first principles of justice depends on the institutional practices it is meant to regulate. Principles of justice like Rawls's do not appeal — unlike Habermas's — to independent and primitive moral considerations, but rather to the specific kind of political setting they refer to. From this point of view, the basic structure establishes through its network of institutions — which represents, in the case of Rawls, an interpretation of liberal democracy — a set of political relationships that shape the reasons for and against specific principles of justice.

With this in view, we can ask whether a limitation of justice to the nation-state is still acceptable in the light of all that has changed at the global level. There are two main reasons why we tend to resist such a limitation today:

1. The first reason is empirical. Global interdependence, both in socio-economic terms and in terms of the creation of international institutions, is now so relevant that states can no longer be considered the only subjects of international relations. As a consequence, our rights and duties, our opportunities and life chances, no longer depend on the state alone, but also on the international community. To use David Held's famous expression, we are now all members of the same 'overlapping community of fate'.
2. The second reason is normative. Many ethical and legal structures, starting from human rights, are now implicit in the shared bases of global politics.

These facts permit a wider interpretation of the basic structure argument. If we adopt a wider interpretation, we can reconcile a 'relational' framework — one in which membership is important, *à la* Rawls — with the demands of global justice. Starting from these conceptual premises, one can attack the traditional impossibility theorem on global justice. If we assume — as it seems customary to do — that human rights are not only a set of moral imperatives but also a set of institutional requisites, then we can maintain that this set of legal norms constitutes a formidable background for a wider basic structure.

Assuming that a global overlapping consensus is plausible, given the wider reading of the basic structure argument, we next have to show why this option makes the second order liberal argument generally compatible with the first order post-colonial argument. Now, the philosophical idea that underlies overlapping consensus envisages dual levels of belonging and loyalty on the part of each person. At an ethical and metaphysical level, each person maintains her own traditional cultural and religious perspective but, at the same time, at a political level, she chooses a vision that is convergent with that of the other members of the international community through the progressive affirmation of a sort of cross-cultural 'overlapping consensus'. According to the overlapping consensus thesis applied to human rights, human rights are shared elements, of an institutional nature, that are consistent with various moral, religious and metaphysical foundations. Hence, this thesis presupposes the existence of a critical potential inherent in all cultures that, eventually, will cause them to converge partially in the direction desired by the advocates of human rights.

This vision permits us to reconcile two contrasting views concerning this issue. According to the first view, cultural sensitivity to local traditions is supposed to override the universality of human rights. In contrast, according to the second view, it is the universality of human rights that is supposed to override local traditions. The thesis based on pluralist integration and overlapping consensus via a tolerant interpretation of the basic structure seeks to reconcile these two theses on a higher level.

Given this background, the Rawlsian second order argument can work as a complementary part of a post-colonial first order argument: through the separation between levels, it permits saving traditions, localisms and religions. It also allows the operation of that function of hetero-spatiality and hetero-temporality that is necessary to the post-colonial first order argument. The basic structure is a historical concept. Principles of justice depend on the basic structure. If we accept this option, then principles of justice are practice-dependent. This does not mean that they merely depend on the culturally different practices to which they apply. Rather, they depend on the way in which shared institutions shape and give sense to these already existing practices. Institutions form a network of relationships by providing background conditions that influence the way in which participants interact. 'And these institutionally mediated relationships, in turn, shape the reasons we might have for endorsing (or rejecting) a given set of principles' (Sangiovanni 2008).

One of the main themes in post-colonialism consists in criticizing a specific temporal and spatial conception of culture. This conception of culture is seen as dependent on colonization. It is supposed to distort our understanding of the forces that shape our present condition. It presupposes a world made up of cultural stages, such as pre-modern and modern, with the modern being considered normatively better. Within the same conception, the modern tends to coincide with the West. Post-colonialism refutes this hierarchy. The post-modern contribution to this critical thesis consists mainly in stating that cultural knowledge cannot be separated from the political conditions in which it is produced. Therefore, reflection upon the political context is needed from an epistemological point of view. As I have tried to show, the price we pay for this post-modern contribution to post-colonialism is too high, and liberalism offers a more sober solution. Habermas's comprehensive liberalism, however, cannot meet this challenge because it links dialogue with some necessary epistemological premises. Political liberalism *à la* Rawls, on the other hand, disconnects political theory from truth. Moreover, the historical nature of the basic structure permits us to disentangle the political argument from its epistemological and ethical bases and to adapt it to the historical reality.

To put it as succinctly as possible, I believe that the division, implicit in the idea of overlapping consensus, between two spheres, the epistemic and the political, presupposes a separation between a first order normative argument and a second order meta-theoretical argument. From this perspective, it seems plausible to accept a first order argument inspired by post-colonialism with a second order argument based on liberal meta-theory. Post-colonialism requires us to be aware of the cultural subalternity of the colonized. This passive status can be considered unjust from a liberal political–theoretical point of view, thus opening a new vista for a fully inclusive, post-colonial account of global justice.

V

In a famous article, Bhikhu Parekh insisted on what he called the 'poverty' of Indian political theory. He meant contemporary political theory, that is, political theory in post-independence India (Singh and Mohapatra 2010). His argument about the poverty of Indian political theory is based on its incapacity to discuss the most relevant topics of the country, like social justice, secularism, the specificity of the Indian state, legitimacy, or political obligation. According to Parekh, this incapacity is connected with the lack of attempts to engage seriously with contemporary Western thought. In particular, Parekh maintains that liberal Western political thought — beginning from the works of Rawls and Nozick — is largely ignored in Indian political theory. Instead of proceeding in this direction, Indian political theory is nationalist and relativist, intentioned toward showing the ethnocentric nature of Western thought. I would suggest that in some ways this so-called poverty is also connected with the post-colonial trend I have discussed in this article — the perverse connection between post-colonialism and post-modernism.

References

Appiah, K. A. 1991. 'Is the Post- in Postmodernism the Post- in Postcolonial?' *Critical Inquiry* 17(2): 336–57.

Chakrabarty, Dipesh. 2000. *Provincializing Europe: Postcolonial Thought and Historical Difference*, Princeton University Press, Princeton.

Chatterjee, Partha. 1986. *Nationalist Thought and the Colonial World: A Derivative Discourse?* Zed Books, London.

———. 1993. *The Nation and Its Fragments: Colonial and Postcolonial Histories*, Princeton University Press, Princeton.

———. 2004. *The Politics of the Governed: Reflections on Popular Politics in Most of the World*, Columbia University Press, New York.

Dworkin, R. 1996. 'Objectivity and Truth: You'd Better Believe It', *Philosophy and Public Affairs* 25(2): 87–139.

Guha, Ranajit. 1999. *Elementary Aspects of Peasant Insurgency*, Duke University Press, Durham, NC.

———. 2002. *History at the Limit of World History*, Columbia University Press, New York.

Mudimbe, Valentin. 1988. *The Invention of Africa*, Indiana University Press, Indianapolis.

Nagel, Thomas. 1987. 'Moral Conflict and Political Legitimacy', *Philosophy and Public Affairs* 16(3): 215–40.

Nanda, Meera. 2004. *Prophets Facing Backward: Postmodern Critiques of Science and Hindu Nationalism in India*, Rutgers University Press, New Brunswick.

Nozick, Robert. 1974. *Anarchy, State, Utopia*, Basic Books, New York.

Rattansi, A. 1997. 'Post-colonialism and Its Discontents', *Economy and Society* 26(4): 480–500.

Rawls, John. 1971. *A Theory of Justice*, Harvard University Press, Cambridge, MA.

———. 1996. *Political Liberalism*, Columbia University Press, New York.

———. 1999. *The Law of Peoples*, Harvard University Press, Cambridge, MA.

———. 2001. *Justice as Fairness: A Restatement*, Harvard University Press, Cambridge, MA.

Said, Edward. 1979. *Orientalism*, Vintage, New York.

Sangiovanni, A. 2008. 'Justice and the Priority of Politics to Morality', *Journal of Political Philosophy* 16(2): 137–64.

Singh, Aakash, and S. Mohapatra. 2010. *Indian Political Thought: A Reader*, Routledge, London and New York.

Spivak, Gayatri Chakraborty. 1999. *A Critique of Postcolonial Reason*, Harvard University Press, Cambridge, MA.

Young, R. 2003. *Postcolonialism: A Very Short Introduction*, Oxford University Press, New York.

About the Editors

Sebastiano Maffettone is Dean of the Faculty of Political Science and Professor of Political Philosophy at Luiss University, Rome, and Director of the Centre for Ethics and Global Politics there. He has been Visiting Professor at Harvard University, Tufts, Boston College, University of Pennsylvania, and Sciences Po in Paris. He is author of the recently released *Rawls, An Introduction* (2010), as well as nearly a dozen books in Italian.

Aakash Singh Rathore is Research Fellow at the Centre for Ethics and Global Politics, Luiss University, Rome, and Visiting Fellow at the Centre for the Study of Developing Societies, Delhi. He is author/editor of several books, including a French edition/translation of Maulana Azad's *India Wins Freedom* (2006); *Reading Hegel: The Introductions* (2008, co-edited); *Indian Political Thought* (2010, co-edited) and B. R. Ambedkar's *The Buddha and His Dhamma: A Critical Edition.*

Notes on Contributors

Neera Chandhoke is Professor of Political Science at the University of Delhi, and Director of the Developing Countries Research Centre, University of Delhi. Her main teaching and research interests are political theory, comparative politics, and the politics of developing societies, with a special focus on India. She is the author of *The Conceits of Civil Society* (2003), *Beyond Secularism: The Rights of Religious Minorities* (1999), and *State and Civil Society: Explorations in Political Theory* (1995). Her normative study of 'secession' is forthcoming.

Thomas Nagel is University Professor, Professor of Philosophy, and Professor of Law at New York University. He specializes in political philosophy, ethics, epistemology, and philosophy of mind. He is the author of *The Possibility of Altruism* (1970, reprinted 1978), *Mortal Questions* (1979), *The View from Nowhere* (1986), *What Does It All Mean?* (1987), *Equality and Partiality* (1991), *Other Minds* (1995), *The Last Word* (1997), *The Myth of Ownership: Taxes and Justice* (with Liam Murphy; 2002), *Concealment and Exposure* (2002), and *Secular Philosophy and the Religious Temperament* (2010).

Gianfranco Pellegrino is Assistant Professor of Political Philosophy at Luiss Guido Carli University, Rome. His main interests are the global justice debate, utilitarianism, climate change and environmental ethics. He has written a book on Jeremy Bentham's liberal utilitarianism — *La fabbrica della felicità* (2010) — and essays on global justice, climate justice and future generations.

Thomas W. Pogge is Director of the Global Justice Programme and Leitner Professor of Philosophy and International Affairs at Yale University. Among numerous other works, he is the author of *Politics as Usual: What Lies behind the Pro-poor Rhetoric* (2010), *The Health Impact Fund: Making New Medicines Accessible for All* (with Aidan Hollis; 2008), *World Poverty and Human Rights: Cosmopolitan Responsibilities and Reforms* (2008), and *Realizing Rawls* (1989).

Amartya Sen is Thomas W. Lamont University Professor, and Professor of Economics and Philosophy, at Harvard University and was until recently the Master of Trinity College, Cambridge. Sen's books include: *On Economic Inequality* (1973, 1997), *Poverty and Famines* (1981), *Choice, Welfare and Measurement* (1982), *Resources, Values and Development* (1984), *On Ethics and Economics* (1987), *The Standard of Living* (1987), *Inequality Reexamined* (1992), *Development as Freedom* (1999), *Rationality and Freedom* (2002), *The Argumentative Indian* (2005), *Identity and Violence: The Illusion of Destiny* (2006), and *The Idea of Justice* (2009).

Peter Singer is the Ira W. DeCamp Professor of Bioethics at Princeton University and Laureate Professor at the Centre for Applied Philosophy and Public Ethics at the University of Melbourne. A prolific writer, some of his numerous books include: *Animal Liberation: A New Ethics for Our Treatment of Animals* (1975), *Democracy and Disobedience* (1973), *Animal Rights and Human Obligations: An Anthology* (co-edited with Thomas Regan; 1976), *Practical Ethics* (1979), *Marx* (1980), *Animal Factories* (with James Mason; 1980), *The Expanding Circle: Ethics and Sociobiology* (1981), and *Hegel* (1997).

Index